The Politics of Women's Rights in Iran

The Politics of
Women's Rights in Iran

Arzoo Osanloo

PRINCETON UNIVERSITY PRESS

PRINCETON AND OXFORD

Library of Congress Cataloging-in-Publication Data

Osanloo, Arzoo, 1968–
  The politics of women's rights in Iran / Arzoo Osanloo.
    p. cm.
  Includes bibliographical references and index.
  ISBN 978-0-691-13546-5 (hardcover : alk. paper) — ISBN 978-0-691-13547-2
(pbk. : alk. paper) 1. Women's rights—Iran. 2. Islamic modernism. 3. Khatami,
Muhammad. I. Title.
  HQ1236.5.I7O83 2009
  305.420955—dc22   2008030923

British Library Cataloging-in-Publication Data is available

To my parents

Contents

Preface

> I would like to propose, in the name of the Islamic Republic of
> Iran, that the United Nations, as a first step, designate the
> year 2001 as the "Year of Dialogue among Civilizations."
> —President Khatami, addressing the United Nations
> General Assembly, September 21, 1998

IN HIS SPEECH before the United Nations in 1998, President Khatami announced his initiative to institute a Dialogue among Civilizations. The newly elected president's initiative was meant as a response to Huntington's "clash of civilizations" (1996), aimed at fostering cooperation and averting the ultimate clash. The UN endorsed this call by declaring 2001 the "Year of the Dialogue among Civilizations."

That year, Muslim extremists, mostly of Saudi Arabian descent, attacked the United States by hijacking planes and rerouting them into the World Trade Center and the Pentagon. In view of this tragedy, Iran's president and other heads of Muslim-majority nation-states expressed condolences to the United States and condemned the attacks. But the opportunity for dialogue was lost in the U.S. administration's renewed conviction to remake the Middle East. At the onset of the U.S. war on terror, lame-duck President Khatami expressed an entirely different approach to the United States on the twenty-sixth anniversary of the Iranian Revolution. Speaking before tens of thousands, Khatami responded to U.S. Secretary of State Condoleezza Rice's threats to use force in Iran:

> Will this nation allow the feet of an aggressor to touch this land? If, God forbid,
> it happens, Iran will turn into a scorching hell for the aggressors. . . . The Iranian nation is not looking for war, violence and confrontation. . . . But the
> world should know that the Iranian nation won't tolerate any aggression and
> will stand united against aggression despite differences. (Associated Press, February 11, 2005)

In some ways, these two statements serve as bookends to this project, tracing a trajectory of hope as it increasingly shifts to despair. While many critics of the Iranian system of government have decried Khatami's "reform period" (1997–2005) as a failure, as having accomplished nothing, this period allowed Iranians and Iran observers to better understand how the postrevolutionary state operates: that it not only presents possibilities but is constantly changing. Khatami's presidential campaigns, moreover, raised political awareness among women, who had overwhelmingly voted for him. This book explores some of the lasting effects of his administration's attention to the rule of law and the discourse of Islamic modernity through a focus on women's discourses of rights.

WRITING "RIGHTS-CULTURE"

> The difficulties become most acute when culture shifts from something to be described, interpreted, even perhaps explained, and is treated instead as a source of explanation in itself.
> —Adam Kuper, *Culture:*
> *The Anthropologist's Account,* 1999

Tehran, Iran, February 1999. In the moonlit sky, I could make out the shape of the outlying mountains that encompass and gather in the giant sprawling city like a child outgrowing its mother's lap. The taxi driver proudly reminded me that Tehran is not a "Third World" city but is "modern" and "civilized." Peering out on the urban cityscape, I got a feeling that the dilapidated nature of the city was less like a beautiful woman whose looks fade as she ages; it was rather more like an old man whose life has fallen into disarray once his caretaker wife has passed.

Iran's population has more than doubled in the years since the revolution, to just over seventy million. Since the 1960s, land reform and industrialization have pushed many villagers into the capital, now home to one-fifth of the country's population. Thus Tehran, the country's largest city and its capital, faces the problems of many large cities: overpopulation, traffic congestion, pollution, urban sprawl, and scarce affordable housing. Although Iran's population growth slowed from over 2.3 percent per year in the 1980s to approximately 1.7 percent, the country has a very youthful population, with over one-third under the age of fourteen. Consequently, well over half the population has little or no memory of the revolution or the prerevolutionary government.

In early 1999 I moved to Tehran to begin research for a project on women's rights. I lived in the city for a year and have returned for follow-up trips each year since. This book represents the culmination of this project in which I sought to understand the meaning that some urban Iranian women give to "rights." It is not intended to be an exhaustive account of women's rights, but an exploration of women's practices of rights in postrevolutionary Iran, given the contingencies of local and international discourses about rights.

This project actually commenced much earlier, in the early 1990s, when I was a law student, and grew out of concerns I had about concepts of rights, especially human rights and women's rights, even as I became a practicing human rights lawyer. My colleagues in human rights practice sought to engage law in domestic and international venues in order to remedy numerous hardships of people all over the world. The tools we used to seek remedies were legal documents, including international treaties and local laws. The rights that these laws provided were intended to guarantee individuals, who were often but not always citizens of various countries, some protection from state actors or actors that states were unable or unwilling to control. As human rights lawyers and activists, our focus was on the law, violations, and finally, remedies. It was about putting human rights documents, which up to very recently had been just "soft power" approaches, into actionable legal force. Law and human rights, it seemed, were the neutral, universal forces that could literally reach into the frontiers of the nation-state and override the customary principle of nonintervention, enshrined in law as article 2(7) of the United Nations Charter. And I was all for it until we started talking about the women, particularly those in the Middle East and in Muslim societies, who needed our help. My good-intentioned classmates vociferously defended women from oppressive cultural practices that kept them out of the workforce, denied them an education, the right to vote, and the right to choose whom they wanted to marry, and forced them to cover their bodies against their will.

My colleagues' concerns with human rights were overriding: cultural values that often led to women being oppressed could be remedied with the spread and implementation of human rights laws. Although inspired, I was also troubled for a few reasons. First, in this vision, human rights, or just "rights," were completely neutral; they were altogether depoliticized and seemed to transcend culture. As I was becoming aware of the deeper, far more complex politics surrounding human rights violations around the world, I also grew to question how human rights issues emerged. What, in fact, counted as an actionable human rights concern? Which of those were actually acted on? For instance, while we studied the 1972 failure of the United Nations to act on Idi Amin's expulsion of South Asians from Uganda, we never thought about the broader global and historical process that led people from the Asian subcontinent to Africa in the first place: colonialism. Second, I was curious about the use of culture. Culture, it seemed, was the object and sometimes perpetrator, to be confronted by human rights. This set up an oppositional discourse about rights and culture that I found troubling. Rights, in this equation, had no culture, while culture was often devoid of rights. They were in direct opposition to one another: one (culture) stood in the way of the other (rights). What I found troubling was not just that culture was approached as bounded and static, something anthropologists had been arguing against for decades, but also that culture was not seen as something to try to understand or make sense of, but rather something that was discernible from the outside and whose distinctiveness was often assumed and exoticized.

In the context of women's status in the Middle East, I became curious about how my peers attributed a poor record on women's status or human rights to abstract "cultural" values, devoid of attention to global geopolitics. It seemed that to blame something on "culture" was an easy deflection of more complex issues and even empirical research. When I looked to the women in my own family, a working-class Iranian family, I saw lawyers, doctors, and teachers, working both before and after the revolution. My own mother taught high school in Tehran while my father attended medical school. She did not feel oppressed by her "culture." Nor did the stereotypes about women in Iran match the experiences of my relatives, most of whom still live there. And although up to that point I had lived in Iran for only a short time, I knew that the idea of "rights" had become a much politicized discourse during the 1979 revolution, with agitators for rights being branded Western puppets by revolutionary forces. Thus, in a revolution that was ostensibly anti-Western, some supporters of the revolution reified rights talk as an unwelcome intrusion into reinvigorated cultural values. It seemed that numerous actors deployed the concept of culture, some to claim a privileged position from which to speak, others as an obstacle to achieving full respect for humanity. In short, culture became a response to a potential outside intervention on human rights grounds. Some said that respect for human rights would emerge from within culture, but others saw this as an apology for a relativism of values or tacit endorsement of an "anything goes" policy with regard to how state institutions treat their polity, a dangerous course that could lead to another holocaust.

Yet something else was also happening: those who claimed to assert cultural values as a response to the threat of intervention, imperialism, or neocolonialism were now responding to rights talk *in kind*. These actors were coming up with their own statements about indigenous forms of human rights. Even during my first years in Iran, I saw this as an interesting *production* of culture. Culture, from this vantage point, was always in motion, in seeming dialogue with contemporary global issues. And human rights, although universal in rhetoric, were placed in historical and political context. Importantly, this new yet revitalized and localized notion of human rights was, in Persian, *hooqooq-e bashar* (a literal translation of the English term). Thus the term curiously retained its anglicized significations, despite its local appropriations.

That human rights were rooted in European philosophical traditions was increasingly seen as a reaction to pre-Enlightenment dogmatism that gave way to the theory of divine right of kings, state-led religion, and the classificatory sciences that divided people into racialized bodies, which at their apex led to the ethnic cleansing of Jewish people in Germany. As a result, ideas about the inherent value and dignity of humankind and the *collective* obligation of nation-states to protect individuals from the otherwise unbridled powers of the nation-state became central to theories of human rights. Of course, understood this way, human rights also placed greater emphasis on the concept of the nation-state, which is the entity charged with protecting minority rights. The institutions of the nation-state not only make human rights possible but indeed make the object of "human" possible, through their powers to assign value to human life—by giving official recognition to members of the polity, whether as citizens, nationals, exiles, expatriates, students, employees, convicts, or refugees.

But when non-Western peoples started to use "human rights" or "women's rights" as part of a local lexicon of entitlements and claims that members of the polity can make, there was also transference of certain values, perhaps even cultural values, that signaled an acceptance of the forms of governance, such as the nation-state and its institutions. So there was not simply a process of reaching into the depths of local culture to produce and justify human rights; indeed, human rights, as cultural signifiers of Western liberal societies, were also *reproducing* cultures.

And yet what did we, human rights lawyers, actually know about culture? It was not simply the study of other cultures that led me to anthropology. Instead, I was interested in how we understand "culture"—what the tools for understanding how other people make sense of their lives are, and who can lay claim to knowing "culture." In short, what were the politics of studying culture, or in this case, the culture of rights?

The Politics of Studying "Women's Rights"

Writing a book on women's rights in Iran is tricky business and a highly controversial endeavor. The aim of this book, however, is not to evaluate whether women in Iran have rights or to make a judgment about the state of their rights. The primary thesis is that in order to understand the notion of women's rights in Iran, it is important to understand how such discourses are politicized, specifically in the past thirty years. Obviously, "women's rights" have been politicized for much longer, but in this book I study the effects of the politicization of women's rights in the contemporary period, since the 1979 Iranian Revolution. I seek to understand the reemergence of rights discourses in the postrevolutionary period, not because I see them as "real" or "positive" effects of the Islamic republic, but because I am interested in understanding the meaning that such discourses carry in Iran's postrevolutionary society, at least among the populations I studied.

With regard to Iran, it is perhaps easy to observe the Western media's stereotypical approaches to human rights, making the argument for saving the Muslim women, but once we are plunged into Iranian debates about human rights, we are forced to rethink what human rights mean. In doing so, we discover the multiplicity, diversity, and openness of human rights. Reflections in Iran offer an ethnographic example, showing interactions between nongovernmental organizations (NGOs) and Iranians as they debate these questions. New ideas can emerge from such encounters and make possible and facilitate new ways of thinking about these issues, and possibly new actions.

Exploring rights through women's perceptions is not arbitrary, it is the fitting choice to tackle and study the process of (re)invention to which I have alluded. Women in these cases are key actors in the process and are reinventing Islam, the past, Iran, and rights. In this work, I show the capacity for lay people (nonexperts), especially women, for challenging the monopoly held by state actors and elites in defining "culture" and "rights." But what follows is not a study of women's resistance; instead, it is a study of how rights operate within the innovative Islamic republican state. Moreover, this study is not a causal analysis of Iranian women's rights. I am, to the contrary, seeking to open up and explore the gaps in understandings of women's rights in Iran. To do so, I employ an approach that allows me to excavate the fissures that causal analyses leave untouched because they reify the very categories that should instead serve as the analytical agents of the study: the women themselves.

In this work, moreover, I show some women accessing the laws and making use of them. Drawing from the statements of respect for the rule of law by government officials, some women have attempted to put into operation statist discourses of rights. Of course as in any society, not all the members of the polity can access the legal infrastructure; here I am referring to some of the women who have attempted to do so. I do not make a claim for the correctness or legitimacy of the system but show how some actors, women among them, have put aspects of the legal system into operation and have pressed the government on its stated aims of seeking to improve the conditions of women's lives. Such women have also pressed the parameters of the new state form, the Islamic republic.

By shedding light on some of the legal practices that pertain to women's rights and human rights in Iran, I also wish to give a perspective on the marginalized voices in these debates that are often neglected, dismissed, or discounted because of politicized rhetoric on the Islamic republic, its system of governance, and the fear that any work analyzing the system stands to legitimize it. Denying the existence of such voices, however, serves to reinforce the stereotype that women in Iran, and perhaps the greater Middle East and North Africa (MENA) region, are passive victims in need of saving. It not only privileges the perspectives of outside and elite actors, but also produces the women in these regions as outside of social and (geo)political relations, and it suggests that such women are without opinions, needs, and desires specific to their unique experiences. By exploring the emergence of women's rights discourses through their social and political relations, especially the postrevolutionary Islamic republic, I seek to add a layer of specificity to these women's experiences. This research can also help human rights advocates tailor their activism in the most precise manner to improve the status of women in Iran and all over the world.

Acknowledgments

THIS PROJECT, which is the culmination of almost two decades of thinking about human rights, has many inspirations. My first debt of gratitude is to the Iranian people who gave me their time, brought me into their homes, and shared with me the details of their lives. While in Iran, I had the opportunity to learn from amazing lawyers, professors, students, and literally hundreds of people. They offered me their stories, experiences, ideas and opinions generously, warmly, and hospitably; I can never justly recognize them by mere acknowledgment. This book is for them and would have been impossible without them. While I could never exhaust the list of people to whom I owe deep appreciation, I would like to thank my closest Iranian friends and advisors throughout this journey, Golnar Ebrahimi, Roshan Jaberi, Shahnaz Massoudi, S. Mowlaverdi, Reza Ansari-Rad, and Parvaneh Assadi. This list extends to my relatives who encouraged and supported my research, including my amazing grand-mother, Nayereh Assadi, whose incomparable storytelling my words barely capture.

At the outset, my ideas about women's rights in Iran were shaped by the dynamic law professors at Washington College of Law, American University, especially Joan Williams and Jamie Boyle, who first introduced me to the critical conceptual issues in legal theory. Tom Farer introduced me to the complex legal issues in international human rights law and advocacy. All encouraged further critical inquiry into the fields of human rights production. Richard J. Wilson, as the founding director of WCL's International Human Rights Law Clinic, paved the way for my legal prac-tice as he trained us with the intense passion for human rights that he brought into every meeting, to every case. Integrity and professional ethics are crucial in human rights practice; I deeply admire human rights lawyers Christine Brigagliano and Marc Van Der Hout for their zealous advocacy of the human rights of immigrants and refugees. They are as ethical in real life as in the courtroom. I thank them for their inspiration, guidance, and friendship, not just for having given me the opportunity to work with them.

At Stanford University, I had the gift of a vibrant intellectual commu-nity, which began with a graduate cohort that has developed into a last-ing intellectual community of transcontinental colleagues, especially Ara-dhana Sharma, Kathleen Coll, Monica DeHart, and Mei Zhan. My apprenticeship at Stanford was fortified through the guidance of Carol

Delaney, Sylvia Yanagisako, Paulla Ebron, and Joel Beinin. My advisor, Carol Delaney, was especially instrumental in encouraging this project in Iran when it seemed almost impossible to pull off. During 2001–02 I was a Geballe Dissertation Fellow at the Stanford Humanities Center. There I began to develop the raw data from my fieldwork. Under the stewardship of Thomas Bender, the SHC community was especially supportive during a troubling post-9/11 year for all.

At the University of Washington, I had a supportive intellectual community with colleagues in anthropology, including Celia Lowe, Ann Anagnost, Lorna Rhodes, Janelle Taylor, Laada Bilaniuk, Danny Hoffman, Mimi Kahn, and Charles Keyes. Colleagues in the Law, Societies and Justice Program created a scholarly community with a weekly workshare group that benefited my thinking enormously and included Michael W. McCann, Steve Herbert, Angelina Godoy, Jamie Mayerfeld, Katherine Beckett, Rachel Cichowski, Gad Barzalai, and George Lovell. Other colleagues at UW, including Donald Gilbert-Santamaria, Cabeiri deBergh Robinson, and Jonathan Brown, provided intellectual, practical, and diversionary sustenance. I thank my research assistant, Cade Cannon, for finding those elusive citations. I especially thank Mona Atia for deep critical engagement with the overall project and the finite details of the argument.

In 2005–6 I was a Fellow at New York University's International Center for Advanced Studies, where I completed the first draft of this book. There I was fortunate enough to meet scholars I had long admired—especially Timothy Mitchell, Nivedita Menon, Alexei Yurchak, and Michel Callon—and met wonderful scholars such as Leshu Torchin, Valdimar Hafstein, Tavia Nyong'o, Ilana Feldman, Munir Fakher Eldin, Forrest Hylton, and Jangam Chinnaiah, who brought sustained, invaluable engagement.

Along the way, I have had the opportunity to gain insights from an array of scholars, including Sally Merry, Lila Abu-Lughod, Michael Fischer, Nikki Keddie, Mary Hegland, Ahmad Dallal, and Richard Roberts, all of whom have offered advice, critique, and encouragement. Their work has influenced my own.

Due to U.S. government sanctions against Iran since 1996, funding for this research has been scarce and limited. I am grateful to Stanford University's Department of Social and Cultural Anthropology for funding the initial twelve months of research in 1999–2000 through a Mellon Doctoral Research Grant, and to the Institute for International Studies for its O'bie Shultz Fellowship. This research was also supported by the Stanford Humanities Center, the International Center for Advanced Studies at New York University, and the Law, Societies and Justice Program at the University of Washington.

I wish to extend my gratitude to Fred Appel at Princeton University Press for believing in this project and seeing it through. His knowledge, patience, and editorial oversight have brought this book to fruition. Two anonymous reviewers gave this book detailed critical comment; their suggestions much improved the manuscript.

This book would have been impossible to write without the ever-present support of my family and friends, especially my father, Enayat, whose experiences and narratives of Iran so vastly differed from what we hear in the mainstream news and who encouraged me to find out the story from the people themselves; my mother, Parvin, whose spirit of courage and strength is embodied in this book's stories; and my sisters, Azadeh and Azita, who cheered me on and always heard me out. Finally, Anne Kearns, Andrew Mergenthaler, Wendy Schuller, Connie Wellnitz, and Laurie Schulwolf offered the counsel of friendship throughout the writing process.

An earlier version of chapter 4 appeared in *American Ethnologist* as "Islamico-Civil 'Rights Talk': Women, Subjectivity, and Law in Iranian Family Court" 33 (2) (May 2006): 191–209.

The Politics of Women's Rights in Iran

Human Rights and Cultural Practice

GIVEN THE NATURE of the Islamic state, Iran's claim to a 2,500-year-old civilization, the effects of prerevolutionary "Western"-style modernity, and the influences of globalization, one of my central questions when I began this study was whether women in this "Islamic society" envision their rights solely through the lens of Islam, especially Islam as handed down by state agents. As a complement to this question, I also wondered if the women who referred to their "rights" (*haqq* in Persian) or their "human rights" indeed referred to a Western or international vision of rights. In my research, I sought to explore how the women I came to know made sense of their status and "rights," and I aimed to do this by observing their daily practices in different aspects of Iranian society.

By exploring "women's rights" in the context of postrevolutionary Iranian society, I sought to move scholarship on women's rights in non-Western societies away from a premise based on a simplistic dichotomy of liberal and universal "rights" versus insular and local "culture" and instead account for the people I encountered as multifaceted, dynamic, and contingent subjects (McRobbie 1996) who are shaped through layers of discourse that we all inhabit, including human rights.

Many human rights studies that look beyond "Western" cultural practices suggest that there is an antagonism between the ideal of a universal system of human rights and the notion that human rights are relative to discrete cultural values (Donnelly 1984; Mayer 1991). Relativism understood in this way is characterized as a limit concept that prohibits any judgment or critique by outside observers regarding local cultural practices. In such a case, cultural relativism appears to oppose the notion that human rights as universal principles form the bottom line of values to which all societies in the community of nations must adhere. The contention that universalism and relativism are in opposition to one another, however, implies that both culture and rights are static rather than ever-changing concepts (Merry 2001). By placing rights outside of culture, this assertion fails to recognize that "rights" in general, and rights talk in particular, are themselves cultural practices emerging from a specific Euro-American historical and political trajectory that encompasses colonialism and thus are shaped by global power relations (Cowan, Dembour, and Wilson 2001; Preis 1996).

The universal language of rights, which privileges individual autonomy, has inhered throughout much of the world, especially since the creation of the United Nations in 1945. The notion of the universality of rights is itself a category constructed in an ever-increasing world of global traffic and dialogue. After World War II, the victors decided to create a document based on standards agreed upon by numerous state parties and thus entitled "universal" standards. This process, as documented in studies of the "making" of the Universal Declaration of Human Rights, points to "universal human rights" as constructed through social, political, and economic relations with specific geographical significance (Glendon 2000). Thus, while human rights standards and practices are localized, they are also constructed within global economic and geopolitical practices. Although human rights are put into practice locally, this is a particular discourse of rights that carries with it cultural values associated with Euro-American liberalism. In this sense, human rights, even as they are translated into a vernacular, carry with them distinctly Western cultural markers (Merry 2006).

Finally, this false opposition conflates rights, the object of our study, with the challenge posed by how to study rights in non-Western societies. Said differently, what methodological approach will allow us to contextualize rights, which are rooted in Western legal and philosophical traditions, in other contexts? In this way of looking at it, relativism is not meant as a concept that implies limiting judgment, but rather, in the anthropological context, relativism references a need for historical, political, and local specificity in order to better make sense of distant practices. Thus it highlights the need for *an approach* to studying cultures outside of our own. The ethnographic method in sociocultural anthropology provides a systematic approach for conducting studies that are situated in both local systems of meaning and global relations of power.[1] In the anthropological sense, then, relativism suggests that in order to understand the meaning that humans give to certain practices, here human rights, we must better understand the contexts through which they attribute meaning and give significance to such practices.[2]

"RIGHTS TALK" IN POSTREVOLUTIONARY IRAN

On International Women's Day, March 8, 1979, thousands of women in Iran marched to protest state officials' interference with what they considered to be unsanctionable spaces: their hard-fought civil and personal liberties. Women took to the streets to rally against newly imposed restrictions on their dress, the suspension of the 1967 Family Protection Law, which had given them some rights in marriage dissolution, and their possible disenfranchisement. Ayatollah Ruhollah Khomeini, a high-ranking religious leader who had spent the previous fifteen years outside the country in exile, had returned to Iran only a month earlier, while the shah, Mohammad Reza Pahlavi, had tearfully departed just two weeks before.

On March 8, and for three days after, women's marches went on at different locations within Tehran and throughout the country. Iranian newspapers reported that at the height of the demonstrations, some twenty thousand women marched from Tehran University to Freedom Square carrying banners that demanded "freedom in the choice of clothes," "equal rights with men," "the abolition of laws discriminating against women," and "free speech and association" (Paidar 1995). Revolutionary guards stood by as counterdemonstrators armed with knives, bottles, and clubs attacked the protestors and caused numerous injuries. Angry supporters of the new government dubbed the protesting women "Barbie dolls," "Western puppets," and Western-struck (*gharbzadeh*), a term also denoting that they were diseased by the West.[3] The women were primarily urban, working class, middle class, and upper-middle class, many of whom were educated, and thought of themselves as modern precisely because of the way they dressed, their mobility, and their self-perceptions as bearers of rights.

Just after the revolution and until recently, various state forces of the Islamic Republic of Iran denied the legitimacy of a language of rights as these women used it, that is, in this individuated liberal sense. At the time, proponents of the new government condemned the women's outcry for civil and personal rights as the tools of Western imperialist forces who sought to undermine Iran's commitment to Islam.

• • •

Jumping ahead twenty years to April 1999, Azam Taleghani, a supporter of the revolution and then head of her own NGO, the Association of the Islamic Revolution's Women, told a local newspaper, "Throughout history, women have won certain rights but unfortunately were never officially entitled to them. . . .The laws of the country have to be modified to enable women to truly exercise their legitimate rights" (*Iran Daily*, April 29, 1999). She directed Iranian women to familiarize themselves with their rights and added that as long as women were not fully aware of the governing laws, they could not stand up for their rights. Taleghani called on women to "avail themselves of all the relevant information pertaining to the rights of women and get more effectively involved in social and political activities." Another newspaper quoted Iran's judicial chief, Ayatollah Yazdi, a hard-line religious leader, reaffirming "equality of people before the law" (*Tehran Times,* April 6, 1999). In 1998 Ashraf Geramizadegan, a newspaper editor who previously edited the monthly *Zan-e Ruz* (Woman of Today), started a monthly magazine, *Hooqooq-e Zan* (Women's Legal Rights) to teach women about their legal rights.[4]

While conducting fieldwork in early 1999, I heard many views that echoed these accounts. One of the attorneys I came to know told me that "nowadays women are much more aware of their rights than ever before. They seek information about their legal rights before they marry." A receptionist in another law office conveyed a similar sentiment: "Today it is much easier for these girls than when I got divorced [in the early 1980s]. They are more aware of the system and are not afraid to go to court and say 'this is my right.'" Clients in those offices repeatedly told me that they were going after their "rights." In fact, I observed newspapers, magazines, and other media and educational outlets replete with similar messages to women. Likewise, discussions about rights were ongoing in the streets, in parks, in taxis, on buses, in people's homes, and at public meetings. Well-known supporters of Iran's 1979 revolution spoke publicly in support of women's civil and political rights, and many openly declared women equal to men. Calls for women to learn about their rights, to participate in government, and to vote in elections were also common both in the press and in everyday conversation. Appeals like Ms. Taleghani's and others I mentioned provide examples of how women were again appropriating a discourse of rights cut partly from the cloth of liberalism, the very ideological tenets that the women protestors of 1979 were attacked for mobilizing. At stake in these references to "women's rights" was precisely the ideological location of the concept of rights in postrevolutionary Iran. But now, these new liberal calls for attention to women's rights, deployed in numerous spaces, are sanctioned by Islamic values and appear to be acceptable even to hard-line officials and state agencies as legitimate expressions of entitlements and claims. Today, this renewed emphasis on a language of rights marks an ideological shift in the meaning of rights—one that emerges through the confluence of Islamic principles and republicanism.

In Iran, the debate between "Islamic republic" and "Islamic government" has simmered since the early days of the formation of the Islamic Republic of Iran. Given the number of groups that participated in the shah's overthrow and those that were vying for control of Iran's postrevolutionary state apparatus, the resulting government was a mixed constitutional design incorporating theocratic, republican, and even direct democracy components. The once taboo language of individuated rights has taken on new meaning in Iran's Islamic republic and is employed copiously by members of Iran's polity, including women and national leaders, in spite of their internal fractiousness. This book about "women's rights" discourse begins with the premise that this discourse is highly charged precisely because it has been defined since the revolution through these and other contemporary debates about the status of women, the role of Islamic values, and the centralization of authority in Middle Eastern countries in general. In the international community, moreover, "women's rights" has become a measure of "progress," "modernity," and "democracy." I consider how such debates contribute to the way women's rights are practiced by myriad groups, including state officials, nonstate legal experts (i.e., lawyers), as well as nonexperts who engage with the legal system. Postrevolutionary state institutions came into being through debates of this kind and have contributed to a complex and often unpredictable hybrid legal order and discourse about rights. This book seeks to locate and trace some of the small actions by women on behalf of their rights. These are the actions that animate the conditions of possibility presented by the state formation and its hybridized institutions. In broader terms, this book reveals the incomplete and dynamic nature of the state form that is made legible when women and others act on its bodies and set into motion a range of effects that further give shape to the novel enterprise of the Islamic Republic of Iran. The importance of rights talk in Iran, moreover, has pushed the international human rights agenda more broadly, effectively challenging and even transforming the parameters of human rights claims in Europe and North America.[5]

SPEAKING OF RIGHTS

While talking about rights may appear as a natural way to express one's sense of entitlements in society—a self-evident or ahistorical term of common parlance— the way women in Iran talk about their rights today emerges from a specific post–World War II historical trajectory in which some rights, while guaranteed by the state, are deemed actually to precede the state, in that they are inherent in all human beings (Arendt 1951).[6] Speaking in terms of rights has become the primary way for people around the world to make claims, both domestically and internationally, about grievances and entitlements (Chanock 2000; Glendon 1991; Henkin 1990; Ignatieff 2000).[7] Since World War II, rights talk has spread throughout the world through international accords, especially the Universal Declaration of Human Rights, and rests on the notion of individual autonomy and free will in society, tied to property ownership, labor, and the market economy.

More specifically, rights talk, as I refer to it, references the language of legality expressed by individuals through claims of positive rights or negative freedoms that are guaranteed by state institutions or actors and are founded on the fact of some legally recognized personal status. Rights-based claims made by individuals are founded on specific relationships that they have with the state on which they are making their claims—citizenship or some other legally recognized category of individual, such as legal resident. The human rights movement shifts the idea of lawful protection beyond the state-based relationship to one that recognizes legal protections simply or merely because an individual is human, and nothing more. That is, it is not *supposed to be* based on the relationship the individual has with the state. The troubling dilemma of human rights protections remains, however—that in a state-based world system it is difficult, if not impossible, to guarantee stateless individuals those protections that are afforded uniquely by nation-states. Thus, despite novel thinking and transnational institutions that recognize human rights, state recognition still appears to precede human rights protections in practice.

Rights talk is an essential concept for understanding how various groups use legal institutions to address social grievances (Engel and Munger 2003; Gilliom 2001; Lazarus-Black 2001; McCann 1994). While most claims are made through the mobilization of rights-based claims, rights talk problematically privileges the individual with disregard for social or communal responsibilities in larger social relations (Glendon 1991). Premised on the inherent dignity of the human who is endowed with certain inalienable (nondelegable) rights, rights talk presents possibilities for democratic pluralism (Ignatieff 2000). And the global human rights movement has built upon the essential quality of human dignity for approaching grievances worldwide (Henkin 1990). The international human rights movement has made the concept of rights, as a way of stating grievances, an everyday part of life in a broad range of environments. Through the spread of an international legal framework and the networks they generate, transnational actors have been adept at finding connections through human rights language and the legal system generated by the post–World War II order (Keck and Sikkink 1998). Thus, human rights principles can become normative in local contexts through the transnational mobilization of human rights–type pressures on national government practices (Risse, Ropp, and Sikkink 1999). In local contexts, however, international human rights talk takes on a vernacular language, mindful of indigenous values, consisting of a layering of social concerns (Merry 2006).

But exclusionary practices also premised in liberal individualism have spread alongside of the universalizing discourses of rights.[8] Liberalism simultaneously allows for the "lawful" exploitation of peoples yet makes claims to universal human rights. The contradictory logic of human rights, drawn from liberalism, uses the same logic that underlies colonization (Wallerstein 1995). First, in the colonial era, liberal sentimentality justified "civilizing missions," and second, in the postcolonial context, liberal state-formations depended on recognized legal categories and identities, such as citizen, while excluding others who did not fit into those categories (Comaroff 1995). Even though human rights discourse was said to be universal, the necessary element in protecting human rights, the state, was in fact the arbiter of the propertied classes. And liberal categories produced particular legal subjectivities, borne of Locke's "possessive individual."

The relationship between rights talk and subjectivity suggests that a consciousness about rights emerges in tandem with exposure to courts and civil process (Lazarus-Black 2001; Merry 2003). Exposure to civil process illuminates the deep connection between liberal legal institutions and subject formation (Fitzpatrick 1992). The civil legal administration of the modern liberal state produces individuated subjects—subjects both *with* and *of* rights. Indeed, a nation-state's legitimacy depends on managing populations through legal regulation (Foucault 2003). The quandary that rights talk presents, however, is that while the people have certain claims on the state, simply because they are human, they need to be a part of a state and recognized in some way by the state to be able to make those claims. Rights, then, come to be part of the circular logic of sovereignty where individuals legitimize a power over themselves and believe in their ability to rein in that power through a rights-based discourse (Buck-Morss 2000), while the state's laws simultaneously come to give state actors a monopoly on "legitimate" violence (Benjamin 1978).

The difficulty with *supranational* human rights ideals is made visible when observed from the perspective of those humans without a state, for whom human rights protections are intended (Arendt 1951; Agamben 1998, 2000). The problem with the logic of rights is that they depend upon state recognition of the humanity of an individual; only those who are already endowed with citizenship can actually make claims to rights.

Rights talk, generally, can refer to myriad kinds of claims, in numerous contexts. Indeed, I have written elsewhere about the shifting meanings of rights when the local comes into contact with the international human rights movements (Osanloo 2006b). But rights talk is also heavily laden with political implications, especially outside of Europe and North America, where it is perceived to be "Western" and often carries with it the weight of ethnocentrism. Thus the issue with which I am concerned is not rights in general, but the resurgence of the Euro-American rights talk initially proscribed by Iranian revolutionaries who considered it to be an attack on revolutionary values, specifically for its emphasis on individuality over the needs of the community. In Iran today, women and their advocates are at the forefront of these increased public discussions of rights (Najmabadi 1998a). The main questions that I consider, then, are what conditions have allowed for the discussion of rights to materialize in a language that was unacceptable just after the revolution, and what possibilities it presents today.

Thus, I explore the relationship between the postrevolutionary state form and its institutions and the ways that some women come to make rights-based claims on the state. In doing so, I seek to bring into dialogue two seemingly distinct but closely related areas of scholarship on Iran: that is, analyses of the postrevolutionary state (Abrahamian 1993; Arjomand 1988; Zubaida 1989) and scholarly work on Iranian women's rights (Afshar 1998; Mir-Hosseini 1993, 1999; Najmabadi 1991; Paidar 1995; Tohidi 1991, 1994). The former include extensive writings about the hybrid nature of the state and its formation as a republic alongside its conformity with principles of Shi'i Islam. The latter concentrate on women's rights and status since the revolution. In bringing these works together, I explore the productive relationship between the hybrid state and conceptualizations of women's rights, recognizing that rights talk is a politically and historically laden discursive practice. Understanding how some Iranian women are talking about and envisioning their rights also depends on understanding the complex historical processes of Iranian state formation and its relationship to subject-making.

The postrevolutionary formation of an Islamic republic has been fashioned through a dynamic and modern notion of Islam alongside of newly developed and redeveloped political and legal institutions. Herein unfolds a story of modernity that is neither a blind acceptance nor a wholesale rejection of "Western values," a common trope for modernity, but rather a hybrid discourse that locates a distinctive form of modernity at the juncture of Islamic revivalism and Western political and legal institutions.

My central concern is to understand how this new rights discourse presents a form of modernity arising out of Khomeini's message of a return to "pure" Islam. What conditions resulting from this new modernity have allowed for the emergence of sites for dialogue and debate? By modernity, I refer to a post-Enlightenment idea of liberalism, premised on Locke's notion of the sovereign individual, which I will elaborate on shortly. By a *new* modernity, I refer to the effects of the merging of republicanism, born of liberalism, with the concerns and values of Iranian Shi'i Islam, which came about upon the Iranian Revolution and continues through today.[9] The Islamic republic was founded at the crossroads of these discourses of modernity even while some of its founders claimed to be reaching into modernity's other: tradition. Some readers may sense that these legal and political institutions are not new; Iran had a constitutional revolution over one hundred years ago. In this context, however, I highlight the sanctioned linking of "secular" institutions with the appeals for the creation of a true Islamic society.

NOTES ON METHOD: STUDYING RIGHTS AS DISCURSIVE PRACTICE

One of the biggest methodological challenges I faced was to determine how to collect data that would illuminate the shifting meanings of women's rights over time in Iran. These shifts reflect ideological changes brought on by a larger cultural revolution. In order to learn how women I met perceived their rights, I first had to explore the contingent histories of rights that served as a backdrop for my informants' perceptions of their rights.

Discussions of rights often draw on liberal Enlightenment values, including the autonomous individual endowed with free will, but Iran's revolutionaries made explicit their intent to purge this "Western" individuated subject from the values of the new Islamic state. Yet the postrevolutionary Iranian state was modeled on a republic, a state form that produces autonomous subjects with and of rights. I sought to develop a research design that would capture the expression of rights in the new political and ideological climate of postrevolutionary Iran and reveal how women's contemporary rights talk is produced through this contradictory dialogic. For this reason, rights talk, as a discursive practice, is a starting point for this book.

My knowledge of the political history of "women's rights" in Iran led me to choose Tehran as research location and to concentrate on a demographically specific group of women whose status and rights were affected in particular ways by the 1979 revolution. Fieldwork in an urban setting presented the challenge of specificity that research within a small village, by virtue of demographic limits, may not. In my case, the realization that women's status was politically and socially reconfigured by an ideological rupture in the meaning of the term "rights" just after the revolution was a defining constraint of my research design. This constraint helped me locate specific sites in which I could observe women's discussions about and perceptions of their rights.

I also sought to collect data that would account for the historical and ideological ruptures that impact women's perceptions of rights and then resurrect the political dimensions of these shifts through ethnographic fieldwork. At the same time, I had to determine how to handle the contingent definitional authority of research terms—"women's rights" in my case, a term densely packed with political implications.

When I embarked for Tehran in January 1999 to conduct the initial twelve months of fieldwork, I was already aware of the connections between the ideological reconfiguration of political and social discourses in Iran some twenty years earlier, and the situation in which women find themselves today. Women's rights were caught in the fold of a historic project: the new government's proclaimed turn to Islam. The government was determined to rewrite the national laws and, in turn, the nation's identity to reflect the renewed embrace of Islam. Women were placed in central focus and perhaps were even the objects of the materialization of this ideological shift, ostensibly, away from liberal Western values to "pure" Shi'i jurisprudence.

As I set out for fieldwork, I envisioned my data to emanate from the institutionalized legal arena, such as courts. It did not take me long to realize that such a methodologically rigid locus concealed the complex politics of rights and restricted the issue that I wanted to explore, which was how women themselves perceived their rights. Rights are not born in a vacuum, nor are they mere abstractions, but are framed by their specific political and historical contexts and thus manifest differently in peoples' lives. It became increasingly apparent in the course of my fieldwork that the locus of rights existed throughout the society, in the minutiae of everyday life. Now I had to face the methodological challenge of capturing the complex and dynamic social flows that, taken together, offer not just a picture, but a diorama of the genealogical history of rights in Iran. I set out to collect data that would bring women's rights to life.

"Sites" of Rights

To gain a better understanding of how universal ideals of human rights play out in local Iranian contexts, I consider how actors mobilize human rights and women's rights in dialogue with both global and local politics. Herein lies an intense production of new problems and solutions, and instead of offering a view of Iran as a blocked or closed society, this approach offers a view that there are a lot of forces moving, issues arising, and solutions imagined; thus it is a view of disseminated openness. That is to say, when I asked questions without preprogrammed answers, I was met with openness—the process of reinterpretation and reconfiguration. What is the best way to show the process? In addition to exploring sites through scales, I move from well-structured settings to more loosely framed sites—from women's scriptural reading groups to the Islamic Human Rights Commission. Both are sites where rights are debated and produced. Thus I break apart the barriers between individuals, the community, and the state by showing the interaction between individuals, groups, and state actors and then weaving together these interactive processes on multiple social and political scales.

Beginning with Iran's newly formed republic and the apparent acceptance and mobilization of a discourse of rights by the state actors and my women interlocutors, I sought to understand how it is that a liberal rights talk was once again becoming the primary mode of referring to the promises made by agents of the state. Through the combination of Islamic principles and the republican state formation, new and renewed "sites" for public discourse and debate have emerged, but the nuances that have made these sites possible are not captured by Habermas's concept of public sphere alone (1989, 1992). I seek to move beyond the homogeneous and monolithic public sphere, laden with an inside-outside binary, by exploring the public "sites" constituted by the issues I consider, thus allowing for a cartography of public sites. The point is not to investigate all such sites; that is not possible, as it is not possible to conduct an exhaustive survey of sites of rights. The aim, rather, is to visit some sites that I found important for illustrating how some women are developing interpretations of rights within the possibilities of the Islamic republic.

Intent upon tracing the political changeability of rights through time and in different contexts in everyday life, I located those sites where women talked about their rights, where they expressed concerns, showed understanding, and questioned rights. I began attending scriptural reading groups, visiting newspaper and magazine offices and NGOs, and observing women at their places of work, in their homes, and in schools. When I observed that distinctions in women's rights emerged as women's activities changed, I started to travel throughout the city from home to work and to other sites as my informants went about their day. My insights, and consequently my methodologies and my data, emerged organically as my research plan unfolded during the early months of my project (Osanloo 2004). Following Tsing's (1993) admonition to find out what issues women really care about, I had to learn how my informants' shifting identities—arising from various economic, religious, social, and political histories—informed their perceptions of rights. For this reason, and also because it influenced their perceptions of me as a researcher, I paid close attention to the personal locations of my informants.

The term "rights," moreover, carried different meanings for women as their settings changed. Such changes included temporal, life-altering ones, such as the revolution, the war with Iraq, marriage, or divorce, and spatial and quotidian ones, such as going from home to the workplace. I sought to record how the women I came to know thought about, talked about, and put into practice their notions of rights in various contexts. To show how this happened in everyday practices, I found I needed to locate the "sites" where the women I encountered spoke in terms of rights.

To show the distinctiveness of the rights discourse in Iran, I explore how these sites are effects of the bringing together of seemingly liberal values with Islamic values. I do this in multiple venues by locating "sites," like nodes within a network where I found women's ideas of their rights and roles come to be shaped. Drawing from Bakhtin (1981), I refer to these as "dialogical sites" that the women themselves are, in part, creating in urban centers today. These sites afford women a place in which to voice and shape their opinions on topics previously out of their domain—topics that, nonetheless, shape their lives and guide their roles as women in Iranian society.

Dialogical Sites

Often discourses appear to be and even sometimes act as self-evident objects reified through constant employment and repetition. In this case, I seek to identify and open up the discursive formation of rights talk to find out what kinds of assumptions are associated with it when the Iranian women I encountered mobilized the term rights. As such, I seek to investigate how that object (rights) is being considered—what kind of work that object performs, and what uninvestigated assumptions are associated with it that I can lay bare. In doing so, I seek to undo the sedimented nature of the rights discourses by investigating in context what the discursive object, women's rights or human rights, might mean to the multiple players shaping the term through their use of it. What meaning is being carried with the utterances "women's rights" or "human rights," and what other meanings are associated with them in the particular contexts in which I observe these ideas being discussed? Dialogical understanding of rights, then, would mean jettisoning the idea that rights come from a finite or "monologic" source, (i.e., the state or Islam).

Discourses and practices of rights are not limited to certain sites and people but are more widespread. Thus my approach suggests itself in multiple sites. Exploring these as dialogical sites, moreover, I can discern the heterogeneity of groups that are developing interpretations of rights. As I do, I also point to new actors in unlikely places and consider the institutions that constrain, define, and delimit sites of rights production. Each site is an exploration and a sample of sites where women are engaging in interpretation, discussion, and, sometimes, action with other groups. I am not seeking to present an exhaustive or representative picture of all women or rights but explore some of the sites of rights production I encountered and through which I explored the effects of the multiple layering of history and politics on women's discursive rights practices. While my entry point is law and these are all sites in which the law is being discussed, I follow the discussions of law as a heuristic device that can help explain the connection between governance and rights, between state institutions and rights talk. Exploring Iranian women's rights talk through dialogical sites, then, allows us to see and hear how this knowledge about rights in Iran is dynamic, collectively engaged, and relational.

From an analytical point of view, it is not easy to delimit the sites of rights production, since questions about rights are raised in multiple environs: "What do rights mean in this context?" This points to the circuits or networks of configurations of sites, and a dispersed notion of sites thus emerges. For this, I focus on the possibility of productivity and performativity of these conversations about rights. Said differently, I consider the capacity in those sites for the discussions to perform and shape some categories and entities, such as relations between Iran and other nations, sovereignty, justice, human rights. In this way, we can understand that all the sites in my book are related, all perform the social reality of Iran. But this is not just a question of adaptation, enforcement, or relations between individual and institutions—not as Wallerstein (1995) says, about relations between imperialism, but a coproduction of categories that are transformed, in which a new type of Iranian woman is invented, not a "Western" woman, not the monolithic "Muslim" woman.

The site-based dialogical analysis shows that rights are redefined, reconstituted, and reshaped in every day practice. I am not just envisioning an adaptation and accommodation but rather am observing the ongoing process of the elaboration of new categories, inventions of a new reality. Certainly state and nongovernment actors mobilize around women's rights or human rights, as we see in the news or mainstream press, but smaller actors exist, too. This book explores some of the smaller groups, nonstate actors who, on their face, appear to have less power than statist actors yet are able to mobilize the law and legal processes to forge new interpretations of rights. As a result, the diversity of actors involved in this process makes possible the reconstruction and performance of new realities and fresh alliances.

Thus, the sites I explore are those spaces where the reshuffling of ideas and reformulation of law are happening. I open up the existence of a diversity of voices and perceive the sites as *moving alliances*, even though the organization of the book is site-specific, organized to show the diversity of views more within each site than across them. The book is organized on the basis of scale, shifting from an exploration of individual enactment and perception to a larger scale of a broader community—law firms and courts, and concluding in the international, or perhaps even transnational, and geopolitical arenas.

To open up the "sites" and "scales" of rights discourse and practice, I begin by exploring several sites in which "rights talk" emerges as a common activity or practice and highlight the ways in which women I spoke with thought about and put into operation "rights talk." The book is divided into three substantive sections that inform one another. In chapters 2 and 3, I explore discussions about rights, first from the historical and scholarly record, interlaced with interviews I conducted, and then in women's Qur'anic meetings.

Chapter 2 is a portrait of some of the events that have shaped the recent popular awareness of, if not contempt for, the institutions of the state. The goal is to provide some sense of the landscape through which women's rights activists must navigate. I briefly describe the political events that led to the creation of the Islamic republic and set the stage for the kinds of contests that are now emerging in Iran. I also show how the private and public sites are connected to one another.

Chapter 3 introduces Qur'anic meetings as one such site. Through these women-only scriptural reading groups, I show how nonexpert women interrogate and shape their rights through dialogue, not just through religious exegesis, but through articulations of their own and shared experiences of life as well. There, women strategize about their roles and rights. Qur'anic meetings, loosely organized to meet the psychic needs of participants, are informal social and informative gatherings designed to bring together women with an interest in exploring spiritual questions in light of present-day concerns. While the women participants use the same scriptural sources as theological scholars, they assert the validity of their own interpretations of the Qur'an over those of the religious community (*'ulama*), to which state actors defer. Qur'anic meetings are sites of social production where new concepts and ideas can emerge, and in which women carve out conceptual sites of agency in other aspects of their lives.

In chapters 4 and 5 I move on to the arena of the courts and lawyers. First, an analysis of Tehran's family court, an official state context, stands in contrast with the Qur'anic meetings. Legal sites—courts and law offices—are spaces that inform women's perceptions of their rights. Seemingly a fixed institution of the statist discourse on rights, the court, I argue, is anything but a place where agents of the state pronounce dogmatic doctrine. Law offices permit productive exchanges of ideas about rights and place new legal formulations that lawyers and activists have carved out of the Islamico-civil institutions into the public spaces. In these chapters, I consider the specific conditions that constitute the plurality of laws in Iran today and show that this plurality is shaped by historical and political conditions, which in turn produce the specific discursive rights practices we see in the courts. The lively contests in the courts over women's rights are a set of practices distinct from the kinds of contests that occur outside of the courts, which do not necessarily entertain the infrastructure of modern republicanism in the same way. The domain of law has its own cultural productions, the effects of which are distinct and uneven in different settings.

Finally, in chapter 6, I move beyond the legal setting of courts and law offices and explore the sites in which human rights discourse circulates. This chapter is a more fluid, less regimented search for sites given the openness of the discourse of human rights. To do this, I explore the formation of a quasi-nongovernmental organization, the Islamic Human Rights Commission, and another organization, formed in the executive branch of the Islamic republic, the Center for Women's Participation. Through the creation of these organizations and Iran's uncertain participation in the transnational human rights framework, I explore how state officials assert a local human rights discourse to lay claim to the fruits of modernity: nation-state legitimacy and sovereignty.

Through the creation of an Islamic state, Iranian state officials have strived to construct the "state" as a legitimate independent nation. Women's rights in Iran are very much constructed through transnational legal discourses and emerge through Iran's claims of ideological opposition to the "West." In doing so, however, the local discourses of rights become manifestations of broader global processes, demonstrating that Iran is already working within the international rights framework, even if unwittingly.

Which Women?

Given my contention that the ideological field of rights had shifted, how I chose to set the limits of my field site became increasingly important, since I wanted my data to reflect what I saw as a rupture, crystallized when *Iran Daily* printed an interview with Azam Taleghani, a major figure in the women's rights movement in Iran since the revolution. Taleghani's statements were comparable to those of the women protesters in 1979 who were attacked and discredited when they made similar demands twenty years earlier. I wanted to understand how women could now make the same kinds of statements publicly without violent reproach. For this reason, I chose to focus my data collection on women whose demographic characteristics were similar to those in the 1979 protests: urban middle class; most with high school education or more, and willing to express an opinion about religion.[10] Many of them also work outside of the home, some in professional capacities and some in nonprofessional roles. In this work, I try to understand how rights talk shapes legal and other social practices by trying to understand the experiences of the women themselves, and not women as the object of policy or discourse. In doing so, I see these women as nonexperts who are actively shaping a practice about and around women's rights, but whose contributions are often neglected by scholarship on Iran.

Due to the major demographic shifts in Iran since the revolution, data collection from this group had other implications for research as well. Even before the revolution, industrial development had led to the rapid increase of urban populations. Currently, roughly two-thirds of Iran's approximately seventy million inhabitants live in urban areas (*Iran Statistical Yearbook*, 1379 [2000]). About 37 percent of the over two hundred women in my study had moved from a rural area to the city. That percentage doubled when I considered the parents' origin. Only about 25 percent of the women said that both parents were born in Tehran. Class is an increasingly difficult category to employ as a data-gathering variable, particularly in developing countries, given that class analyses derived from the Marxist tradition presuppose an industrial labor market. I found it best to allow my informants to self-identify. Based on my assessment of literacy and standard of living, and on self-identification, most of my informants belonged to the middle class.

I limited my study to a particular group of women whose urban middle-class characteristics matched those of the women protestors of 1979 for several reasons. First, I began this project with a question about how women perceive their rights since the revolution, given the particularities of everyday life in the Islamic republic. I thus situate the project in a historical trajectory that began with women protestors of 1979, whose use of a liberal discourse of rights brought them much criticism at a time when the postrevolutionary state was still in its nascent form. Now, some thirty years later, the language of rights seems to have a legitimate place in the discussion about women's status in Iran. I sought to discuss with women of comparable backgrounds their experiences of rights from the revolution through to the present.

Second, it is the lives of these women that were most drastically altered by the revolution. The effects of the reinvigoration of Islam in the Iranian state disparately affected women living in urban areas, who were also among the shahs' (both Reza Shah and Mohammad Reza Shah) primary targets during the modernization schemes of their times. Such measures included unveiling and modern education. After the revolution, the new government also placed particular emphasis on "the woman question" and targeted urban, educated women to serve as primary symbols of change in Iranian society. Middle-class urban women felt disproportionate changes in their everyday lives in comparison to the upper and lower classes for a number of reasons. For instance, upper-class women had the means to insulate themselves from many of the effects of the revolution, while lower-class women did not experience the effects of the social regulations to the extent that middle-class women did. For lower-class women, the everyday minutiae of their lives was based on material concerns that kept them closer to home than middle-class women, who were more likely to venture outside the home for work or school and thus fell within the newly introduced regulations. This is not to suggest that the categories of class are in any way static. Many of the women whom I interviewed came from rural or lower-middle-class families who had moved to urban hubs in search of higher education or nonagricultural work.

The focus on middle-class women also emerges from a disciplinary concern for parity or greater breadth in choices of interlocutors. Much research on women in Muslim societies portrays women from small villages as representative, or worse, as somehow more authentic, which tends to support the prevailing views of women in Muslim societies as underdeveloped and undereducated. In Iran, noting that fully one-fifth of the country's population lives in Tehran, not to mention the four or five other urban centers, it is all the more crucial to highlight urban women's lives.[11] Some of the most popular studies of women in Muslim contexts locate their study group in small, rural villages, making it difficult for Western audiences to appreciate the breadth and variety of social positions in a given society.[12] By providing a sampling of the urban women in these classes, I seek to add to a literature that has an abundance of scholarship representing voices of rural women.

One of the effects of the revolution was the reinvigoration of Islam in political and social life. Even in talking about rights, it was important to understand how women integrate their faith into their lives, and particularly into their roles in society. Islam appeared to be more in evidence in the everyday lives of my women informants after the revolution, though I am not suggesting that prior to the revolution faith or spirituality was absent. Finding out how the visible and seemingly austere permeation of Islamic values in the Islamic republic affected women daily was not a problem; most women readily expressed an opinion about religion. Ninety-nine percent of the women I interviewed referred to themselves as Muslim. Rarely did I meet a woman who said that she did not give spirituality an important place in her life, even if it was not always within institutionalized religion. Less than one percent told me that they did not believe in God.

In collecting data that captured the fluid nature of rights, I was careful to obtain generational diversity. Older women in Iran have lived through periods that profoundly affected their rights. For instance, in 1935 women were prohibited from wearing the veil; now they are required to wear it. Women in mid-adulthood today may well have marched through the city streets some three decades ago in protest of the abrogation of their rights—indeed, some of my informants had done so. About 65 percent of Iran's population is below the age of thirty. The youth in Iran represent an important section of the population not just because of their numbers. Because they are products of this government, their demands for reform cannot credibly be labeled as *gharbzadeh*. Age, then, became an important factor in helping to demonstrate women's fluid perceptions of rights in the course of the history of rights discourses in Iran.

When the "Field" Is Not Quite Home

Tehran, February 1999. I arrived at Tehran's Mehrabad Airport and filed in line for the passport and customs inspections. When my turn came, I perilously entered the gate that, with a buzz from the customs inspector, unlocked to let me in. Out of a desire to cooperate and even convey my solidarity to the young customs official, I casually pulled my black headscarf forward, hoping the action might appear as modesty on my part. Frankly, I had no idea what the officer might say to me and wasn't about to risk being sent home for inappropriate attire. Although only a glass window separated us, I felt as if we were still worlds apart, for I had not yet entered the world of the Islamic Republic of Iran. The inspector could not have been more than twenty-five years old. His mustache and full beard were short and to the point. He wore the official uniform of the airport customs officials, a light green uniform shirt with black pants. I didn't dare look him in the eye as I silently slid my newly acquired Iranian nonresident passport under the slot. I was conscious of following what I had heard were the rules of public comportment; men and women who do not know each other should not look into one another's eyes. The customs inspector took my newly obtained Iranian passport and swiftly paged through the unmarked booklet. His large brown eyes, seemingly alive at three a.m., glanced up at me—not avoiding eye contact. Then he glanced down again . . . and up again, and finally looked me straight in the eyes and exclaimed, "You haven't been here for twenty-nine years?" I couldn't help but crack a small smile. I nodded and quietly spoke the polite word for yes, "balleh." He took his stamp and triumphantly branded my unmarked passport, and I was in. I sailed out of the baggage claim and into the vast crowd of people awaiting loved ones from overseas. I quickly found mine and we scurried off in a taxi.

When a researcher is thought to be returning "home," the question of what it means to be a native anthropologist arises (Abu-Lughod 1986, 1993; Narayan 1995). My own background became a curiosity for friends and informants who saw me as Iranian, but not quite so. I had lived in the United States for all but the first two years of my life and in 1999 was returning to Iran for the first time in almost thirty years. I spoke fluent Persian, but with an American accent. Unlike many Iranian expatriates who had left after the revolution, my family had left Iran a decade earlier and had remained in the United States for no apparently political reasons. For this reason, government officials and religious groups regarded me with less suspicion than they did people who had left Iran just after the revolution. Since I was born in Iran, authorities in the more reformist administration of that time more readily gave me permission to conduct fieldwork in governmental offices, which, they sometimes told me, they saw as an educational opportunity for me to learn about Iran, "my fatherland."

Several government officials remarked that I was in a better position to explain women's rights in Iran to Americans than they were and briefed me on the ways the new government had improved the quality of women's lives. But there was also no shortage of suspicion toward me. Perhaps I was a spy for agents of the Islamic republic, who might be checking on their government employees, or maybe I was working for the U.S. government. I was not blind to the fact that people were telling me things based on their perceptions of my bias. I had many conversations that started out with "What are you looking for?" and in many cases I was presented with a seemingly ready script of commentary—about the head-scarf, divorce and inheritance laws, how badly women were treated under the previous system, or how women's rights were not respected in the United States either, all ending with the assertion that the postrevolution-ary government had ultimate respect for "woman" and the integrity of her character.

Of course I found none too many detractors, most of whom did not occupy government positions, who sought me out after my interviews with government officials, asked me what I had learned, proceeded to debrief me on how I had been lied to, and armed me with questions to ask the government official the next time I spoke with him or her. I also had more nuanced conversations with both government officials and non-government personnel about the status of women, what forms the im-provements took, what still needed to be done, and who they helped.

CHAPTER ONE

A Genealogy of "Women's Rights" in Iran

THE CONCERN WITH "women's rights" in Iran, as elsewhere in the Muslim Middle East, has been a persistent trope of modernity. This genealogical exploration of women's rights attempts to situate the research question in broader historical processes that consider the power relations inherent in the approach to research or interpretation (Foucault 1977). The aim is not simply to address biases we bring to our subject matter, but also to consider how research questions and terms are shaped through contingent political and historical formations. To make sense of such terms, it is important to consider their significance in ever-changing contexts. The following discussion is not intended to be an exhaustive account of the scholarly literature on women's rights in the Iran but offers a glimpse of how rights talk in this context emerges through a dialogical engagement, through political and scholarly efforts.

WOMEN'S RIGHTS: TROPE AND CONSEQUENCE

Nashat (2004) categorized the approaches to women's rights in Iran as either Western secular feminist, Islamic apologist, or a third kind of approach in which Islam is seen as not opposed to women's rights and equality. I seek a different approach: I consider how rights are discourses embedded in and in dialogue with multiple ideologies while at the same time they are also hegemonic. This approach not only considers how notions of rights are constructed but indeed contemplates how and why concerns with "women's rights" emerge locally and transnationally as legitimating tropes of modern law and state institutions derived from liberal and Muslim values.

I do not search for the origin of the women's rights movements, but rather trace rights formations through an analysis that considers the shifting tensions underlying hegemonic forces through which claims to rights manifest. Women's rights talk is always changing insofar as it is intertextual—it cannot be understood out of the historical, political, and social contexts, and it occurs as a dialogue among multiple voices, that is, it is dialogical. Understanding rights in this way, it becomes apparent that the scholarship on women's rights in Iran is part of broader discussions about rights throughout the world.

In Iran, as elsewhere in the Muslim MENA region, the role and status of women have been subjects of much scholarly research and debate, particularly since the early 1970s.[1] Such studies have illuminated women's varying positions in different sectors of society (Beck and Keddie 1978), adding the oft-forgotten component of gender to early historiographic records written by scholars who did not have access to women, and clarifying or rebuking stereotypes of women's status in the Middle East. Historians explored formulations of women's roles according to sacred sources (Ahmed 1992; Mernissi 1991); the role of patriarchy in producing historical records and in studies of gender in the region (Keddie and Baron 1991; Nashat and Tucker 1999); and women's status before the rise of Islam in the region (Spellberg 1994; Stowasser 1994). Women's legal histories added an analysis of gender to the law, legal records, and legal practices both before the period of state building and after, especially in the Ottoman region (Peirce 2003; Thompson 2000; Tucker 1998). In addition to historically grounded research, anthropological monographs gave ethnographic detail in contexts where little or no previous research existed, due in part to the lack of access by male scholars to these sectors of the societies (Abu-Lughod 1986; Delaney 1991; Fernea 1965; Friedl 1989).

The interventions of Said's *Orientalism* (1978) and Mohanty's *Under Western Eyes* (1991) exposed the latent biases in research methodologies and showed how research methods are already colored by a set of assumptions about the subject of study. It is not only the researcher who brings bias to her field of study but often the categories of study that we take for granted or as self-evident are in fact shaped through historical and political contingencies. For instance, women's roles were redefined in the context of nation-building after World War II and the fall of the Ottoman Empire (Kandiyoti 1991a; Moghadam 1993) and during wars for independence (Cherifati-Merabtine 1991; Peteet 1991), and in defining the postindependence state (Brand 1998; Joseph 2000). After independence, women's roles continued to be reshaped in connection with modernization (Moghadam 1994a, 1994b, 2005), development (Elyachar 2005), and human rights (Afkhami 1995). As a trope of nation-building, gender constitutes legal categories, such as citizenship, while nation-states, in turn, shape gender systems (Kaplan, Alarcón, and Moallem 1999; Joseph 2000; Joseph and Slyomovics 2001). In this vein, Charrad (2001) studies the gendered effects of the intersection between national legal codes and kin-based paradigms of social control. Postcolonial studies of nationalism reveal how women's status and the sacred role of domesticity are related to and in conversation with imperialist calls to "save women" from their male kin (Chatterjee 1993; Spivak 1987, 1988). Their insights have allowed for increased attention to global and transnational influences, including secularism, feminism, human rights, and neoliberal economic policies (Abu-Lughod 1998, 2002; Elyachar 2005; Hatem 1998; Hoodfar 1997; Moallem 1999). These later clarifications situate understandings of terms, whether "citizenship" or "freedom," by placing them in historical and political context (Altorki 2000; Mahmood 2005; Osanloo 2006a). The post-9/11 flurry of attention to the Middle East, North Africa, and Central Asia brought with it explorations of women's roles in international and political contexts, especially with regard to Islamic piety and modernity (Deeb 2006), geopolitics (Hirschkind and Mahmood 2002), and globalization (Nouraie-Simone 2005), with a renewed focus on global discourses on women's rights movements (Anwar 2005; Barlas 2005; Hatem 2006). A seemingly new area of research within this field emerges as scholars begin to study the relationship between the global war on terror and women in Muslim societies, adding a much-needed gender component (Ferguson 2007; Hunt and Rygiel 2006; Salime 2007). In what follows presently, I situate the specific literature pertaining to women in Iran. To give this literature more material context, I weave in ethnographic accounts.

• • •

Negar

> Reza Shah came one day. I was about ten years old. My father brought home a hat and coat. It was the "constitution celebration" (*jashn-e mashrutiat*). Then Reza Shah went into parliament and said that women have no right to wear the chador and if they do it will be pulled off them. I saw it happen with my own eyes. They ripped scarves off women's heads, even in Tehran. When [his son] Mohammed Reza Shah came, we were still without, but we could do as we liked.

Negar[2] lives in a comfortable house on a street along the well-manicured lawns of Tehran's Exhibition Hall. Her house is also near the large Shahid Beheshti University and a short walk to the infamous Evin prison. Her husband of almost sixty years had died in an accident about five months earlier, and she is now left in her four-bedroom house with her youngest son, his wife, and their six-year-old daughter. Almost eighty at the time of our interview in 2000, she lives off of her husband's retirement pension.

Negar was born in a small village to the north of Tehran, Taleghan. When she was fourteen, a visitor from out of town, the treasurer of his village, came to her house on business. When he saw her, with two long braids down each shoulder, he decided that he wanted to marry her. She liked how he looked, and her parents approved. It happened very fast. After they married, he took her to his home, where she learned that he had another wife. She did not like this and decided that she could not stay, so she left and returned home to Taleghan.

"Was that difficult?" I asked.

"No, it was not difficult," Negar answered. "I told my mother he had another wife. We didn't know this when I married, so I returned home."

On the day of our interview, Negar invited me over to lunch, where we ate chicken kebabs grilled outdoors and picked ripened cherries from their last surviving tree. We began the interview just before lunch at the kitchen table. After lunch, we resumed the interview, but Negar hastily finished it—she was getting tired. She had an endearingly abrupt way about her. She spoke her mind and laughed at herself and others openly.

A few years after her first marriage ended, Negar met and married another man, Firouz. Just before the war, she and Firouz went to Tehran together, where they began their lives. Firouz was a construction foreman and was able to provide a decent living for his wife and their six children, some of whom live in Tehran, while others live abroad, in Europe and the United States. Now the house seemed empty without Firouz, though I had never seen it with him there.

> We worked very hard to make our home in Tehran. Making money was not easy in those days. First there was the war and the English were here fighting with the Russians. It was very expensive in those days. I had six children, one after the other. I kept telling Firouz to save. We have this house because of me. He never saved. Then he died and all I have left is this house.

Left with only the house to be divided between herself and her children, Negar lamented her situation. In spite of this, she was left with a monthly pension, savings interest, and a house, in which she had partial ownership, and which her children agreed not to sell as long as she wanted to live in it. The fact of her economic status was not what bothered her, however. She clarified this for me in specific terms:

> I worked all my life. I raised these children. Why does this house automatically belong to them? Where is my portion? Do you know I am due only one-eighth the value of the house, not the [more valuable] property it sits on?

I interject, drawing from the legal rationale that others had given me for the gendered inequities in property division: "Isn't this because your sons are legally bound to support you financially?"

> Supposed to, perhaps, but I am not anyone's burden. I worked all my life. Why should I be dependent on my sons to take care of me? My children grew up;

each found a way, a life for him/herself. Now I am here, alone except for my one son. I taught my daughters to know their rights—and to go after them, so they do not end up disadvantaged like me. This is the most important issue facing women in Iran today.

• • •

WOMEN BETWEEN REVOLUTIONS, 1906–1979

Detailing the significance of historical changes in the region gives depth to otherwise reified topics, such as the veil (Hoodfar 1997; Yeganeh and Keddie 1986; Nashat and Beck 2003), gender roles and sexuality (Najmabadi 2005), education and domesticity (Najmabadi 1998b), and the inadequacy of the private/public dichotomy as an analytical concept (Friedl 1991; Hegland 1991).

With the 1979 Iranian Revolution, a shift in scholarship, not limited to Iranian studies, focused on the effects of the politicization of Islam and the relationship between Islamic values and the formation of modern nation-states. Although the concerns with the status of women can be traced to nineteenth-century reformists who favored the creation of a strong centralized state (Algar 1973; Amin 2002), the use of the liberal language of "women's rights" to express demands on state institutions for attention to women's concerns can be traced to the 1906–1911 constitutional revolution and the creation of a modern nation-state.

Constitutional Revolution, 1906–1911

In early 1905, an economic crisis was followed by a series of public protests led by merchants, shopkeepers, and lenders in alliance with some members of the 'ulama. The protests movements converged around the imperialist policies of the Qajar rulers (1794–1925) and eventually ended in a constitutional revolution. The strategic coalition called for limiting the powers of the dynastic rulers with the formation of a representative national assembly and a house of justice. Coming in the early days of the twentieth century, Iran's constitutional revolution raised many questions about the relationship between the centralized state and the practices of the 'ulama, especially as they pertained to women, including the degree to which they should participate in the operations of a new centralized state (Bayat-Philipp 1978; Cole and Keddie 1986).

There is some dispute over the effects of the constitutional revolution on the status of women—whether it did not do much for the status of women at that time (Mahdavi 2003) or was a moment in which important contributions for women arose because of the attention given the "woman question" (*masaleyeh-zan*) (Afary 1996). Women participated in nationalist struggles against imperialist encroachment as well as on the side of constitutionalists hoping to abolish the monarchy. Their later agitation, based solely on women's issues, independent of the broader revolutionary goals, was rebuffed by state authorities (Bahar 1983). The establishment of a constitutional system, however, eventually laid the groundwork for formal claims to be made on state institutions for women's legal and political rights. More significantly, in this period, the formation of women's political councils (*anjoman*) increased. Although such councils were not particularly new, the public acknowledgment of such groups and their improved organization led to more structured agendas for women's activism. These groups also legitimated public discussions about women as a sector of society and raised women's political position as a question for debate. The councils began publications, magazines, and newspapers focused solely on women's concerns, with special emphasis on their education and literacy. Although circulation of publications was limited, the transmission of ideas made women's rights and status important markers for the growth of a modern civil society. It was also at this time that schools for girls first opened.

Pahlavi Period, 1925–1979

Women's roles were of considerable importance for the modernizing reforms of Reza Shah (1921–1941) and later his son, Mohammad Reza Pahlavi (1941–1979), especially in the realms of education, literacy, employment, and legal rights. Major contributions during this time included the formation of the judiciary, despite the fact that the constitutional movement had laid the groundwork for this much earlier. Legal developments included the formal codification of laws for the first time. Personal status laws, including laws on marriage, divorce, custody, guardianship, and inheritance, were integrated into the civil legal system and codified in increments during this period (Paidar 1995). Modernization practices were complex and uneven, and affected women's lives on a practical level differently from the level of the ideal. For instance, much has been written about Reza Shah's decree to ban women from wearing the veil in 1936, but this decree, often related as an emancipatory measure, primarily addressed elite women's dress practices and specifically focused on the removal of face covers (*picheh*) and the chador, the long, tentlike body covers,[3] rather than head covers (Rostam-Kolayi 2003). Such policies hindered some women's status and decreased mobility when they or their families felt discomfort or even shame in permitting women to leave the house "naked" (Hoodfar 1997). The prohibition on veiling was a factor in the decline of Reza Shah's popular appeal (H. E. Chehabi 2003).

This period was perhaps the single disruption of the Shi'i 'ulama's monopoly over women's status since the Safavids declared Shi'ism the state religion in 1501 (Mahdavi 2003). Reza Shah advocated and adopted policies intended to "modernize" Iran and used the question of women's status as a marker for this modernization. Such policies, while often hailed as achievements by some, primarily affected those whose families were in a position, both ideologically and economically, to benefit from literacy, education, and nondomestic work programs. For instance, the educational measures in the end applied to only about 1 percent of Iran's population (Mathee 2003). Despite declarations of progress and modernization, many were ensconced in new difficulties engendered by these policies: uneven development and poor distribution of resources.

Reza Shah's practices, however, did benefit a certain class of women and witnessed the emergence of public discussions about women's rights in the new centralized but autocratic system. This period again saw the production of women-centered publications (Amin 2002), increased attention to education (Najmabadi 1998b), and more public discussion about issues concerning women. Indeed, education was made a legal right for women (Bahar 1983). Such discussions led to changes in popular consciousness about women's social roles, including expanding the scope of appropriate professions for women (Rostam-Kolayi 2003). While Reza Shah's modernizing policies led to questions about the role that women could play in society and even in governance, limits were also reached in the point of view of families who were considering these changes in the context of the appropriate upbringing of their daughters.

Reza Shah's aggressive modernizing policies were hindered both by internal conflicts, including his own liberal opponents (Martin 2003), and by outside events. During the Second World War, Iran was divided and occupied by Allied forces, which feared possible sympathies with Germany. The Allies needed Iran to provide a ground route between Russian and Western European fronts to deliver provisions, and they made use of Iran's petroleum resources in order to win the war. With the Allied victory, Reza Shah was sent into exile in Johannesburg and replaced with his young son.

Mohammad Reza Shah was only twenty-two years old when he was anointed shah of Iran in 1941. Despite being considered weak and malleable by the Euro-American forces that put him into power, he continued to focus on modernization and again used women's status as a marker for it. Although some have great nostalgia for this period of marked change in women's status, the focus was mostly on urban, educated women. The uneven forms of modernization affected the lives of urbanized elites but also brought about concern with social mores and were often associated with women.

In this period, however, women gained certain legal and political rights as part of the shah's wider industrialization and modernization program, dubbed "The White Revolution." In 1963 the parliament (Majlis) enacted a number of legal changes, some of which were first inspired by Reza Shah. While historians have traced the roots of the women's movement to over fifty years before this period, Mohammad Reza Shah's inclusion of women's status as an important component of broader reforms seemed to give the appearance of such gains emerging independent of a half century of women's activism. These changes included the right to vote and the right to serve as a member of parliament. In 1967, Majlis passed the Family Planning Act (revised in 1975), that gave women rights in dissolving marriage, and circumscribed the unilateral right of men to dissolve marriage.

• • •

Marjan

Marjan was in her early thirties when I met her at a women's exercise club in northern Tehran. She worked at the gym in various contexts, from trainer to food server. Divorced from her husband, she lived with her two children and ailing mother in a small apartment. Her family, originally from the city of Kashan, had relocated to the vast capital just before the revolution so her father, an engineer, could find work. Her father had died years earlier and left her and her other siblings to care for their mother. Her two sisters and a younger brother, all married, lived nearby, while two other brothers lived outside Tehran. When I first met with Marjan, my initial query focused on her experience of the 1979 revolution.

> I was about twelve years old at the time of the revolution. I remember that there was a lot of noise. We thought, "What is going on?" And they said that the *kharab kara*, trouble-makers, are demonstrating in the streets.

"Who are the *kharab kara*?" I asked.

> They are the people against the shah's government. Then, little by little, the demonstrations (*tazahorat*) grew and we heard a lot that the shah was bad and steals and gives the country's money away to Europe and the "West." Slowly we became provoked (*tahrick*). I was a child and just understood that he was bad. And my mother just understood that the country's, the people's, portion from oil goes abroad and that the shah must leave, and if he does and Khomeini comes, we will not even have one person who is poor. We heard that we would not have to pay for water and electricity. And the older people heard this and believed it. The people were convinced by what the others said and did not want them to think they did not understand. They would see the demonstrations, and

however they spoke, we spoke louder and clearer and better, and I did the same and sang the songs like "'Eh shah-e khaen!" [O traitorous shah!]

They [the demonstrators] said, "Look at Behesht e Zahra [a well-known cemetery], all the young people who were killed by the shah are buried there." One time, some friends came and said, "Let's go to the cemetery and see." My mother said, "Let's go." It was so crowded. From a distance I could see. The people were so stupid. There was a small child who had been killed with a gunshot wound. A man stood on another man and held the child in his arms like this [she holds up her arms in front of her face as if ready to hold a bundle]. I saw a child with gunshot wounds lying limp, with blood all over him. Everyone could see from a distance. I could see that the shah had killed. I saw them coming towards me and I screamed and cried, and my mother took me home. But that vision stayed in my mind. From then on, whenever I would hear these demonstrations, the boy came before me, and one time I saw the boy's face and I screamed, "Marg bar shah!" [Death to shah!].

"How did your life change as a result of the revolution?"

Our friends would go to demonstrations—maybe ten out of the two thousand even knew what the revolution was about and what it meant. We did not know. But if we didn't go, they would say that we didn't agree.

As we were doing this, we saw that one day they said that the shah left. Then they were happy and so were we. We saw that instead of a new shah, an *akhund* [member of the 'ulama] came in his place, and we thought, how rich he is that he is going to pay our water and electricity!

As I got a little older they said to us that we need to wear a headscarf. This was really hard for my age; I was around fourteen at the time. And these were the people who were going to pay our electricity, and now, not only are we not rich, but also there is some other stuff that is making life a bit harder.

• • •

KHOMEINI AND THE 1979 REVOLUTION

A theocracy is a state governed by immediate divine guidance or by officials regarded as divinely guided. In 1979 the Islamic Republic of Iran formed the interesting mélange of a theocracy and a republic and created a power structure that is at once divinely guided and yet democratically representative. While readapting Iran's laws to Islamic guidelines (*shari'a*), the leadership of the Islamic republic also re-effected a parliamentary system to take into consideration the interests of a voting populace.[4]

From the outset, Khomeini came to power in the name of the dispossessed (*mostazafin*), especially those who were the most dispossessed of the nation's recent wealth from oil.[5] Khomeini advanced Islam as providing the solution to the socioeconomic grievances of a certain cross-section of society. Khomeini and other members of the scholarly Shi'i community used their authority to interpret scriptural texts to address, validate, and offer redress for the concerns of the dispossessed. At the same time, the 'ulama borrowed the term *gharbzadeghi* from Jalal Al-e Ahmad, a former member of Iran's Communist party, a devout Muslim, but also a nationalist.[6] Ayatollah Khomeini, endowed with the authority of the supreme leader, essentially became the final human authority with respect to the interpretation of Islamic law. The revolution, Khomeini argued, would pave the way for an Islamic republic, which in time would lead to what he considered a true Islamic society,[7] one that adheres to the codes for life set out for Muslims in the Qur'an and *sunna*:[8]

> I ask the government that, fearing neither East nor West and cultivating an independent outlook and will, it purge all remnants of the tyrannical regime, which left deep traces upon all the affairs of our country. It should transform our educational and judicial systems, as well as all the ministries and government of Western models, and make them compatible to Islam, thus demonstrating to the world true social justice and true cultural, economic, and political independence. (Khomeini, April 1, 1979)[9]

The newly formed Islamic republic was the product of a coalition of groups supporting the shah's ouster. Some in that group called for an Islamic revolution (*enghelab-e Islami*), even as they formed and participated in the nation-state system and created a constitutional republic.[10] The Constitution of the Islamic Republic of Iran, written in 1979 and revised in 1989, employs much discussion of equality and rights, promising all citizens many social guarantees such as pensions, social security, unemployment and disability benefits, medical services, and free primary and secondary school education.

While the constitution is replete with references to Islam, the structure of the republic is modeled on that of De Gaulle's Cinquième République. Borrowing from Montesquieu's concept of separation of powers, the state is divided into an executive, a judiciary, and the nationally elected parliament, the Majlis-e Shura-ye Islami (literally, Islamic Consultative Assembly) and extends universal suffrage to followers of Christianity, Judaism, and Zoroastrianism, in addition to Islam. A departure from the French constitutional structure, which attempts to balance power by dividing authority among three separate branches of government, is the mandate of the Guardianship of the Jurist (Velayat-e Faqih), the highest authority on Islam in the country, and in effect, the guardian of Islamic values. The 'ulama, who managed to monopolize control over most government institutions, were able to justify the modification by arguing that the concept the Velayat-e Faqih implicitly involved a social contract between the religious judges and the people (Abrahamian 1993).[11] The Iranian revolution is best characterized as populist, and the nature of the state and its civil structures are modern:

> In insisting on a strict Islamisation of society and government (and it should be emphasised that it is never very clear what this actually means in institutional detail), the modern fundamentalists represent a departure rather than a continuity with Islamic political traditions or precepts. This break is accentuated by the fact that modern Islamic groups are operating ideologically and politically within the context of the modern nation-state and the political concepts related to it. (Zubaida 1989: 3)

Paradoxically, in establishing the Islamic republic, one of the ways in which the leaders consolidated power and legitimized their rule was through the manipulation of "East"–"West" binaries that rendered liberal constructions of rights and equality not only ineffectual but traitorous, as these leaders claimed to rid themselves of Western influence. They did this, however, through a reconstitution of political and legal institutions that draw from and foster the very European-inspired liberalism that the government had condemned, setting into motion, therefore, potential for conflict over the unfolding of the form of the governing institutions. This apparent contradiction, however, is a new kind of modernity, one that is "outside of the geography of the West" and yet still of it (Mitchell 2000). The consequences of this apparent inconsistency are increasingly evident today and play out in volatile public spaces that are also products of this seeming contradiction.

The 1979 Iranian Revolution transformed a dictatorial monarchy into the first-ever Islamic republic, founded on principles of republican democracy and Shi'i Islam. The curious manifestation of the state as an Islamic republic was drawn intentionally from the form of the state that arose after France's popular revolution. At the time, disparate revolutionary groups who had come together to overthrow the shah and the monarchy disagreed on the composition of the new polity. Different factions, including Islamic reformists and secularists, envisioned a power-sharing arrangement with the 'ulama (Arjomand 1988). Nationalists and intellectuals who had joined forces with the 'ulama to overthrow the shah now argued for a democratic republic with multiple parties, as did Islamic reformists such as Mehdi Bazargan, the prime minister of the provisional government.[12] Khomeini and his supporters, however, wished to form an Islamic state, even rejecting the word "democracy" in its title (Arjomand 1988: 137).

When an Islamist student group took over the American Embassy on November 4, 1979, the dual power arrangement fell apart because Khomeini was able to consolidate his power through the rampant anti-American sentiment. After the fall of the liberal reformists, Khomeini secured ratification of several articles in the constitution that granted extensive governmental powers to the leader, including the Velayat-e Faqih, which the previous provisional government had failed to approve. For this reason, the November 1979 takeover of the U.S. Embassy is sometimes referred to as a second revolution.

Islamic governance and republicanism in Iran are not necessarily at odds but come together in particular instances and in the everyday lives of the polity. It would not be accurate to say that there are two separate systems at work. Rather, the judicial system builds directly upon the scriptural texts and the shari'a, while the process through which the text is construed and interpreted is contained within a civil legal framework, neither of which is static. Islam, of course, represents a worldview, but that worldview increasingly engenders republican-style promises, such as equality before the law and the protection of fundamental rights, language that is inherent in the way many Iranians I interviewed spoke about state actions and promises. The description of the governing bodies also lays the foundation for my argument that the way the institutions of the Islamic republic come together in public life permit the creation of new sites that allow Iranians to explore multiple avenues for understanding their rights before the state.

"WOMEN'S RIGHTS" AND REVOLUTIONARY DISCOURSE AGAINST "WESTERN" INDIVIDUALISM

Outside Iran, perhaps especially in the United States and Europe, popular images of Iran evoke the 1979 revolution and, perhaps, the U.S. hostage crisis. In images of the revolution, women were prominently shown in chadors, seemingly put on display by revolutionary forces and, in many instances, on their own initiative as revolutionary actors. Their change in attire was to serve as an indication to the world of the refounding of a cultural essence that had been repudiated by the previous government. Indeed, a prominent member of the 'ulama at the time, Ayatollah Taleghani, called on women to take up the chador because "we want to show that there has been a revolution, a profound change" (1982: 107). Taleghani's statement evidenced the very political nature of the aims of reveiling women.

In connection with these political goals, the officials presiding over the fragile new government questioned, recalled, and reconsidered women's roles. This reconditioning of women's status was part of an agenda by the Islamico-nationalist coalition aiming to distinguish postrevolutionary Iran from the previous government's excesses and its perceived capitula-

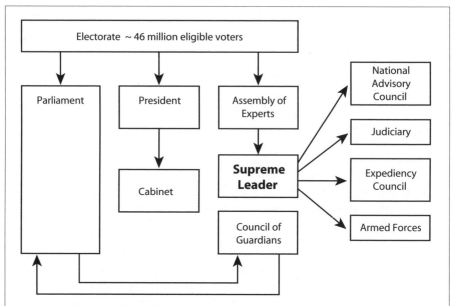

Fig. 1.1. Diagram of formal government structure of the Islamic Republic of Iran.

In addition to the three branches of government and the Council of Guardians, Iran's republic has an overriding authority in the leader (*rahbar*). The president, who is the head of the executive branch, and the members of parliament come to power through direct popular elections. The supreme leader, who is deemed to be the highest authority on Islamic jurisprudence, is endowed with the Velayat-e Faqih, or Guardianship of the Jurist.

The Velayat-e Faqih is an innovation in the republican state's structure theorized, though not originated, by Khomeini in the 1960s while he was in exile in Najaf, Iraq, and began thinking about an alternative to Iran's monarchy. He delivered a series of lectures on this theory in 1970 and published the work in the same year. The Guardianship of the Jurist requires that the governance and administration of the state conform to the sacred laws of Islam as interpreted by a select group of religious scholars. Khomeini's theory is controversial in Shi'i Islam because it rejects the separation of political life from the religious and delegates the authority of leadership of the state solely to qualified Islamic jurists.

The person in this position, currently occupied by Ali Khamenei'ee (since 1989), has the final word on all questions that concern the administration of the state, and particularly whether economic, social, legal, or political initiatives conform to Islam and to the goals of the Islamic revolution. In this way, the rahbar can make a statement or issue a legal opinion (*fatva*) that enters into the numerous domains of everyday life. The rahbar acts in concert with other branches of government, which are set up to advise him. The most powerful among those groups is the Expediency Council. The Expediency Council is a later development in

(continued)

Iran's republican state; it is an arbitrating body that determines the outcome of disputes between the Council of Guardians and Majlis. Since 2007, Iran's former president, Ali Akbar Hashemi Rafsanjani, has been its chairman.

As the person who presides over the Guardianship of the Jurist, the leader controls the military, selects the highest-ranking members of Iran's judiciary, and controls what airs on the radio and television, though not the print media.

The leader and the members of the Expediency Council come to power through appointment by an elected body, the Assembly of Experts, a group of Islamic theologians who are elected every eight years. In September 2007 Ali Akbar Hashemi Rafsanjani was also elected chairman of the Assembly of Experts.

As with the ministers and candidates for elections, all laws passed by Majlis are also held in check by the Council of Guardians, a nonelected group of senior religious and legal scholars who determine whether the laws and actions of government officials conform to Islamic law. Half of the twelve members of the council are scholars of Islamic jurisprudence and are appointed directly by the rahbar. The other half are experts in constitutional matters and are recommended by the judiciary, but Majlis must approve their appointments as well.

The president has a cabinet of ministries for which he appoints the ministers. Iran's parliament must approve his candidates, but only after they have been vetted for government service by the Council of Guardians.

The theory of the Guardianship of the Jurist had mass approval when Khomeini was in the position, but gaining the 'ulama's approval proved more difficult. When it was first put into practice, none of the highest-ranking members of the 'ulama completely agreed with the theorization. Khomeini's leadership among the oppressed masses brought legitimacy to his position. Knowing this, as he grew older, Khomeini grew concerned that the Islamic republic, in the terms that he had developed, would not survive his death. For this reason, he was intent on politically normalizing the position he occupied so that the aims of the revolution would endure.

---

tion to the United States and Europe. For many, this apparent betrayal was embodied in women's appearance and behavior. As a result, one of the goals of revolutionary policies was to remedy Iranian society from within, at its core. This core was recognized in the body of Iranian women. Women, as mothers and wives, and thus the foundation of the family (*kian-e khanevadeh*), had to be rehabilitated in order to rehabilitate the family, a microcosm of society.

At the time of the revolution, the provisional government, revolutionary forces, and private sympathizers denied women and other activists the legitimacy of a language of positive rights or rights talk, calling them the tools of "Western" imperialist forces seeking to undermine Iran's commitment to Islam. Some characterized these events as trivial and saw the activists as taking advantage of the situation to raise petty concerns. Hamid Algar (1981) noted that it was significant that the women protestors were dressed in the latest fashions and had dyed their hair. Algar contended that the thousands of protestors were from the upper echelons of society who had benefited under the shah's government and were led in their thinking by a U.S. feminist, Kate Millet. He suggested that the women protestors who were raising rights concerns did not represent the sentiments of the majority of the people. Indeed working-class families were reaping benefits of a wide class struggle that was also under way at that time. Many middle-class women were dismissed from decision-making positions and replaced in the labor force by women from lower-middle-class families (Arjomand 1988; Poya 1999).[13]

Something else was also happening, and it had greater effects and implications for Iranian society than the bourgeois concerns that Algar intimated. By denying women the language of rights, discrediting those who used it as "West"-obsessed, the supporters of the new Iranian government were acting against what they saw as problematic outside influences, especially ones that advocated individual autonomy over the interests of the community. Thus many of the founders of the new Islamic republic claimed that in accordance with their Islamic values, the new system would give priority to the rights of society over those of the individual.

The aim of this distinction between the rights of the society and those of the individual was to emphasize a division between the sphere of the "social" and that of the "family." To its proponents, the creation of a republic would permit the development of a civil society, which is governed by "man-made" laws, albeit laws checked by Islamic guidance. The sphere of the family, however, would be governed by the laws of nature that accorded predetermined rights and responsibilities to men and women founded, in their view, on a God-given biological essence. The proponents of this kind of thinking were not limited to Islamists or the 'ulama. Some secular leftists also shared the beliefs that women and men had inherent biological qualities, and that women were better suited to domestic affairs, such as child-rearing and housekeeping (Moghissi 1993: 162). These officials often based their beliefs on the teachings of Ayatollah Morteza Mutahhari, an important scholar associated with the new government, who was Khomeini's close associate and the chairman of the Revolutionary Council.

Mutahhari rejected a concept of equality that did not recognize the biological differences between men and women, differences that he considered to be fundamental to the proper functioning of society. In his writings, which had appeared in women's journals, Mutahhari criticized Euro-American individual autonomy. Although he found that Islam, indeed, approved of gender equality, it did not "agree with identicalness, uniformity and exact similarity" (Mutahhari 1981: 135). He also opposed the Universal Declaration of Human Rights as the measure of women's status because it and documents like it were based on the idea of individualism irrespective of gender difference and obligations to family and society. Mutahhari believed that Islam gave priority to societies, communities, and families over individuals. For society to function optimally, human beings must subordinate individual will to the greater good, and their roles, best exemplified through the texts of Islam, should be in harmony with their biological and psychological essences (Mutahhari 1981). Accordingly, Mutahhari found that a woman's most important duty is motherhood, so her "natural" activities occupy her with family. In 1979 Mutahhari's writings served largely as the basis for the gendered social divisions that were being emphasized by many of the officials in the new government.

In the years soon after the revolution, women in Iran feared being forced back into the home and denied their civil and political rights (Azari 1983; Nashat 1983; Sanasarian 1982; Tabari and Yeganeh 1982). But the early predictions did not correspond with the highly public roles played by many women. Even just after the revolution and due to the war, women in the new government seemed quite visible, and their roles emerged within what appeared as a modern reading of Islam (Esfandiari 1994; Ramazani 1993). Given the wide-ranging effect of Islam in societies like Iran, women's rights and roles would be unlikely to emerge independent of it (Afkhami 1995; Moghadam 1993).

Locating women's agency within Islamic principles sometimes appeared to reinforce static and oppositional notions of East versus West, or religious life versus secular. Proponents who located women's agency through a renewed discussion of Islam failed to capture the multiple and indeed converging sources that inflected women's subjectivities and produced agency. This work adds a new perspective on the sources of women's rights by questioning the validity of the problematic binaries sometimes supported by these readings. I argue that a new source of agency emerges in Iran at the points in which Islamic governance comes together with a republican state form and allows for new expressions of individuated rights, expressions that were discredited by the leaders of the revolution almost three decades ago.

This new source of agency became much more visible after the 1997 election of Mohammad Khatami as president by an overwhelming and surprising mandate. About 80 percent of all eligible voters went to the polls, and he received about 78 percent of the vote. The sheer volume of votes cast was important as well: Iranians were acting within the political and legal institutions that have come into existence since 1979—forms of republican governance such as direct representation—to press their political, social, and economic agendas. Significantly, what came into greater perceptible view to many was that the system of governance that was emerging in postrevolutionary Iran was a form of government built on the foundations of a republic.

. . .

Farideh

When I first met Farideh, she was living near one of my relatives. I met her while visiting them in central Tehran. After we became acquainted, she dropped by sometimes when I was in the neighborhood, and I learned a great deal about life and politics from this married mother of two. One hot summer day in 1999 she invited me over. We sat in her small, two-bedroom apartment and discussed the nature of the state while her children napped.

> Most people outside of Iran do not understand that this government is a republic, an Islamic republic (*jomhuri-e islami*). In fact, I think most of us Iranians are just learning what this means, too.

"So what does it mean to you to live in an Islamic republic?" I queried.

"*Jomhuri*," Farideh carefully enunciated, "means the people govern; that we do not have a king, as before. *Islami*," she added,

> means along with the principles of Islam. Some may take issue, saying Islam is more about believing in the Prophet and the oneness of God and practicing the commands He gives. But believing in humanity is also a religion in itself. This may be in the person's personal life and public life and political life and foreign affairs. People here accept that there is an Islamic government over our heads, but in my mind, it does not have to be a religious organization, just something that the people all accept and agree to. I think that the government should deliver to the people what the people want and vote for.

"How does that affect your rights as a woman in this society?"

> I have rights in many contexts, not simply as a woman. I have rights as a member of society, as a wife, a mother, and a woman. Any rights that you have, you have due to some identity. If you are asking me about my rights as a woman in an Islamic country, I must be able to have the right to live comfortably and must have a right to work and have a place to work that I know is safe and secure. It is my right to have a job that is sound, to be able to care for my children. This is my right to have work that I can do, to have safety and education for my children.

"In your opinion, what does it mean to have a right?"

Rights come from the idea of the individual—the person gets rights through family, society, and the people with whom one interacts; they determine how these rights manifest. I feel that I have the right to do what is best for my future; I have the right to live for myself. The personal right of the individual is better. That is, perhaps it is the society or government that gives a person a right, but that government cannot be in my mind and think what is best for me.

The personal right of an individual belongs to that individual. You must be able to think and it is better to think for yourself and to determine what is right for you. There are rights that do not have a place for debate; they are things that are personal and private, such as who you will marry or what your spiritual beliefs are. Those you must be allowed to determine for yourself. There are some rights that the government gives you; these are different from personal rights and private rights. For instance, I have a right to get married; the government cannot prohibit this. I also have a right to speak and think freely. This is something that is getting better now in our society. People speak out; they read the paper. Then there are a series of questions that are personal, that depend on the family and you have to determine whether you have access to those rights or not. The meanings of rights depend on the issue.

"Do you feel you know what your rights are and that you can obtain them?"

It is, first of all, the subject of debate throughout our society. Most women I know seek equal rights in society. I have the right as a woman, whether or not I am married, to live well, with solitude and peace. There is no reason that I should not have the right to live alone comfortably.

"What are some of the issues that most concern you these days?"

I am most concerned with the economic situation. There has been terrible inflation and prices continue to rise. People have to work very hard to make a decent living. I want to give my children a good life, get them a good education, and support them and look after the rest of my family, too, their health, safety, and things like this. I do not think I am different from mothers all over the world in this respect.

"What issues about equal rights concern you today?"

As I said, rights depend on your family, husband, you know, immediate relations, even your place of work, your supervisor, and so on. I have a good husband and supportive family, but if I did not, if I had problems with my husband, for instance, I would have difficulty getting help. This is not only a problem with the laws. We have many laws. We are not sure how to use them, and some women are even afraid that it will bring shame to the family. This is a larger problem of our society. The views need to be changed. They say if a woman is going to court, getting her rights, she is damaging the family or dishonoring it, but this slowly changing as women learn to use the system and people grow accustomed to it.

There is still some problem with the way people think. Rights do exist, but some people do not let women reach them; there are still many patriarchal views in thinking about women's rights and equality.

• • •

AN ISLAMIC "REPUBLIC"

Although Islamic values have been a part of the Iranian cultural imaginary in varying degrees for almost fourteen hundred years, in 1979 a government in the form of a republic was something new.[14] And while the stress on Islamic values was one of the unifying agents of the revolution, popular support for overthrowing a dictator was another. During the Khatami years, renewed attention to the foundations of republican governance highlighted the importance of this latter factor.

A number of circumstances have come together to produce the conditions in which many Iranians are once again couching their claims in a legalistic discourse of rights and making calls on state institutions for civil liberties and equal protection of the laws. One important circumstance is the vivid memory of a grisly eight-year war with Iraq. Another issue revolves around the fact that two-thirds of Iran's nearly seventy million people are below the age of thirty, and universal suffrage begins at sixteen (Population Reference Bureau 2005). The power of this contingent does not come from numbers alone. Many of these young people were not alive at the time of the revolution, and for that reason they have a degree of credibility when they assert claims as "rights" that the women protestors in 1979 did not have. That is, the hard-line 'ulama in government have more difficulty discrediting the rights talk of these young people when they make claims on their government based on constitutional promises legitimized by the religious authorities themselves. Most important, however, it is the election of Mohammad Khatami, which ushered in the changes in attitude and made state practices more legible to the population.

The features of this curious state system began to come into view more clearly after the 1997 election of Khatami to Iran's presidency because they not only showed both possibilities and limits but, more important, revealed the unfixed and changeable nature of the new governing institutions of the Islamic republic. This book, which was researched in large part during the Khatami period (1997–2005), shows how debates about the status of women and women's rights in Iran take shape through the religio-political tensions concerning the kind of governance, forms of institutions, and role of Islamic values that were going on at the time. This confluence of Islamic guidelines and republican forms allowed for new formations and articulations of, among other issues, the position of women, women's rights, and human rights. I show how new possibilities and new alliances are made available at the conjuncture of Islamic values and republican institutions, and how it is this space that permits some Iranian people, women among them, to recast their arguments for rights in those same apparently liberal terms when just after the revolution they could not. I do not imply that the process is a smooth one; rather, since the Khatami years, it has become more evident that the disputes about rights must be understood through the conflicts engendered in the larger debates about the style of government and the place of Islamic guidelines in governing the population. Since it was state actors who deployed women's status as a trope to advance the cause of the revolution, the status of women's rights later became a real recourse by women to make claims on state officials and institutions.

"WOMEN'S RIGHTS" IN THE ISLAMIC REPUBLIC

The Islamic republic challenged contemporary notions of rights steeped in Western ideals with political and social entitlement vested in Lockean possessive individualism. The 'ulama appeared to base their conception of rights on their interpretations of the shari'a, calling for clearly defined gender roles amid clearly delineated divisions between public (read social) and private (read familial) arenas of life, claiming these were the foundations for building a "true" Islamic society. Ostensibly, the 'ulama defined rights in gendered harmony with obligations given by God through revelations to the Prophet (Qur'an) and the sunna, the Prophet's words and deeds. Thus the rapidity with which Khomeini's government instituted controls over women's conduct, appearance, and mobility outside of the home and nullified legislation that it said pertained to family matters because they were sufficiently addressed by Islam cannot be overlooked in an analysis of women's rights in the Islamic republic.

This sudden rupture in the discourse and practices of women's rights brought with it serious material consequences and led to considerable debates about women's status in postrevolutionary Iran, about which much has been written and continues at present. The effects of the revolution on the lives of women, including middle- and working-class women as well as poor urban women and rural villagers, came into view (Afkhami and Friedl 1994; Azari 1983; Nashat 1983a). The reinvigoration of a discourse on Islamic values appeared to justify women's redefined social and familial roles (Friedl 1985; Nashat 1983b) and a patriarchal understanding of Shi'i values (Azari 1983; Ferdows 1985; Ferdows and Ferdows 1983; Rahman 1983). While numerous and varied women participated in the movement to overthrow the shah, many urban, educated, and middle- or working-class women were surprised by the renewed emphasis on their roles as mothers and wives. Women from rural backgrounds had less involvement in nondomestic activity outside of the home and did not expect that their participation in the revolution would create new public roles for them, but they viewed their participation in the revolution as part of their broader commitments to Islam (Hegland 1983). Women's networks, especially those that were religiously or politically based, were potent channels for disseminating information about the revolution to poor urban women (Bauer 1983).

Early studies just after the revolution engendered somewhat contradictory, even binary, conclusions about women's status in postrevolutionary Iran: were women liberated from the yoke of Western imperialist values that objectified them, or were women now relegated to domestic roles that kept them oppressed and in the home? Historical analyses of Iranian women's movements showed consistency in the turbulence surrounding women's movements since the last Qajar period (Sansarian 1982). That is, women's rights movements in Iran, like elsewhere, have historically been subsumed by bigger questions of governance, often concerning imperialist or autocratic threats (Bahar 1983; Sansarian 1985).

Women were effective in the Iranian political process (Beck and Nashat 2004; Esfandiari 1994). Soon after the revolution and the consolidation of power by the 'ulama, policies toward women were aimed at destroying the corruption left behind by the shah's Westernizing programs, with control and purification of women as a central theme.

Through authoritative interpretations of Islamic texts, Iran's Shi'i 'ulama placed a great burden on women to be the spiritual saviors of the society. They presented the idea of a "traditional" and "Muslim" Iranian woman in opposition to that of the Western woman, exploiting monolithic dualisms. The moral virtue of the polity was a major concern of the religio-political restructuring of civic and family life, which initially led to a reduction in the legal forms of redress available to women. The state's hybrid apparatus, however, began to allow for new questions about the nature of citizenship (Hoodfar 2000) and women's legal standing in the Islamic republic.

In all, these debates offered insights into the way the language of women's rights in Iran has, for well over a century, been an important measure of modernization both inside and outside the country and has simultaneously been grounded in discourses of Islamic and liberal rights talk. As a result, women's legal status and rights became the subject of renewed interest not only among the 'ulama, but also among lay persons, accompanied by new attention to the fields of Islamic law and jurisprudence. From this point questions emerge about the relationship between the practices of governance and discourses of rights: what is the relationship between the Shi'i 'ulama and the system of governance today, and how does it effect women's rights? From what sources do the contemporary discourses of women's rights emerge? How are discourses of rights in Iran practiced within the system of governance?

CHAPTER TWO

Producing States: Women's Participation and the Dialogics of Rights

CITY COUNCIL ELECTIONS, FEBRUARY 1999

"So tell me about the candidates in Tehran," Narges asked as she soaked what looked like a gallon of rice in cold water. I was upstairs at the home of my neighbor and landlord as she was preparing a midday feast. Every Friday, Narges prepared a bigger lunch to accommodate her family and friends who came to visit, and she always included me in these holiday gatherings, giving me an opportunity to meet an array of people. I had met Narges through a rental agency in which she advertised her apartment—only to foreigners—so she could earn funds for her son's impending departure for Canada. She also wanted her twenty-one-year-old daughter, Hoda, to be exposed to foreign visitors and have someone with whom to practice her flailing English. It seemed I met these criteria, despite having been born in Tehran. Narges, like many I would meet, appreciated my status as "native" Tehrani and yet foreign.

On this particular Friday, Narges was talking to me about the candidates of the first-ever city council elections, held in February 1999. The elections were mandated by the Constitution of the Islamic Republic of Iran, which had provided for the transfer of some administrative authority to city councils across the nation and was part of an overall plan for decentralization after the creation of the Islamic republic. It was not until the mid-1990s that the various government institutions began attempting to transfer centralized authority to local councils. When Khatami became president in 1997, he promised reform in this "bottom-up" vision. So on February 26, 1999, some 53,000 voting stations around the country stayed open until nine o'clock at night so that people could cast their votes as almost 300,000 candidates competed for 197,000 posts throughout the nation.[1] In Tehran alone, almost 4,000 candidates ran for the fifteen coveted city council seats. For weeks before the elections, candidates had plastered designated areas of the city streets with election posters, and newspapers reported that a small but significant number of women were also running for city council seats.[2] Voters in over 700 cities and 40,000 villages across the country elected about 20,000 local council members, including over 500 women.

"Why do you want to know? You don't care. You never vote," Hoda said, barely rising from her seat as she spoke.

"No, this time I am going to go. It's a local election. I can go and it might make some difference."

At that, Hoda turned to me and said, "Do you see how my mother is? She says she doesn't believe in this government, but now she says she can make a difference." She then turned and spoke louder so that her mother, despite her one deaf ear, would hear: "I think my mother just wants to show you, so you will write that women in Iran vote and that means they have rights."

"What? What are you saying, Hoda?" her mother replied. "I don't believe in this government. No, I don't like these akhunds, but I saw some candidates I liked. I saw some people I like. One man was pictured in a tie; that looks good to me. The women are all like this—." She dramatically swept her hands over her head and around her face with an imaginary headscarf in her hands. "I don't like them. You can vote for them."

Hoda feigned anger. "I don't like all of them, but I do have to vote. I am different from my mother. She dreams of this other time, but I don't know it. All I know is this government. My mother doesn't even go out of the house. She refuses to see what it's like. But this is my country, I am Iranian, and I would never leave," she loudly proclaimed. And she added, "This is the only way we can do something, by voting for the candidates we like. Even though I didn't vote for Khatami, look what big changes he has brought."

Indeed, Hoda was one of the only young people I had ever met who did not vote for the reformist underdog of 1997. Instead, casting her first ever vote in that presidential election, she had voted for the conservative candidate who, as she saw it, promised to do more for the economy; this was Narges's and Hoda's primary concern in this election as well. More than once Hoda had said to me that foreigners who come to Iran are preoccupied with the way women dress. "They think that it's our only problem. Maybe it bothers some people, like my mother, who doesn't like to go out because of it, but I don't care. It's just like a uniform. Of course if they said we didn't have to wear it, I would take it off, but I have bigger concerns than this."

Reluctant supporters of the reformist logic and agenda, Narges and Hoda were caught up in the momentum of hope and possibility that this period offered, but their participation in elections was also important in producing the issues relevant to the reform agenda. In this chapter, I consider how the women I was speaking with at this time started to believe that their participation mattered, even though some of them were skeptical of reformists and the entire governmental system. Through their increased participation, such women began to make claims on state institutions and officials. Not only did they become better informed about the system, but their claims helped determine and reveal the possibilities and limitations for reform. By raising new questions and claims, they were also participants in producing the system of governance, the Islamic republic. Thus this chapter illuminates two important issues with respect to women's rights practices in Iran today: the limits of the Islamic republic as a model for rights formation, and the importance of popular participation for testing those limits.

Narges and Hoda lived in the lush, hilly northern section of Tehran, Shemroon, part of the city that was actually considered to be outside of it and thus dubbed "north of the city" (*shomal-e shahr*), by most. Within Shemroon, Niavaran was known as an upscale hamlet that housed old wealth. The shah's summer palace had been there (just up the road from his primary residences), and former royalists, even members of his cabinet, had once lived there. When I first moved in, Narges took me outside and pointed to a gaudy, mustard-colored home that jutted out from the hills overhead. "See that yellow house? That's where Hoveyda used to live," she remarked, referring to the executed former prime minister. "But they confiscated it and divided it up and now ten different families live there; they're all hardliners," she said with disdain. Narges, like many wealthy, Westernized elites, had seen the reversal of fortunes first-hand when the revolution came. She boasted of being born in Tehran, unlike many of the city's postrevolutionary inhabitants, and hailed from a landowning family of four sisters and two brothers, all of whom were in Tehran, and who, from what I could tell, dropped by quite often. She had married well for her time, to a ranking member of the military's noncombat unit. Her husband, now a rather demure college professor, had barely escaped persecution, and they had not fared as well economically as, for instance, Narges's sister Nahid, whose husband was a civil engineer. His concrete and mortar business had grown in Tehran's postrevolutionary population boom into one of the city's wealthiest and best-known construction firms. Thus, Narges's foray into the business of renting the apartments, which she had ostensibly hoped to one day present to her children, was a major source of income for the family.

Niavaran, however, was much more complicated, even as a quiet hamlet. It was also a religious hub, where high-ranking officials of the new government now resided as well. But the real claim to fame of Niavaran was the Jamaroon section, where Khomeini had lived and where his wife was still living. Khomeini's residence was now something of a tourist sight, where on holidays, busloads of people were brought into the neighborhood to view the residence—a few rooms where Khomeini stayed, a mosque, and Khomeini's *hosseinieh*, the adjoining room from which he delivered sermons. Khomeini's house was just a five-minute walk through narrow alleyways from where I was staying. The alley-by-alley (*koocheh-pas-koocheh*) style had been conserved in this elite neighborhood and gave it an air of a very old or poor section of town, but it was neither.

For Narges, who had an extreme asthma condition, Niavaran offered a cool, quiet escape from the noise, heat, and pollution of the city's center. Before the revolution, Narges had bought the piece of property with the inheritance she received after her father's death and had built a three-story building. Her family lived in the second-floor apartment, and she rented out the floors above and below her. All three of the apartments were modest, single-floor units. For six months I resided there, living in the ground-floor apartment that looked out onto a small enclosed yard with a concrete deck and a tiny but inviting pool. In the summer we often hung out by the pool in swimsuits, shorts, and dresses, barely aware of the restricted dress codes just beyond the doorsteps.

Narges's family belonged to the landed wealthy of Tehran. Many of her friends had left for Europe or the United States, but most of her relatives remained, and for that reason, so did she. Like many of the wealthy elites of Iran, Narges avoided the effects of the government. She stopped working at her government post after the revolution ("After they told me I had to wear a headscarf, I left") and mostly entertained and socialized within her own group of family and friends. Parties, celebrations, or mourning all took place in private homes. She considered herself Muslim but did not agree with the interpretations of Islam by the ruling 'ulama. And while she did not pray regularly, Narges sometimes went to the mosque to meditate and to find inspiration and solace. Although she often complained about the city's new urban populations—formerly rural poor and wealthy religious classes—she frequently dropped money into the alms boxes located all over the city. When her husband's father passed away, she asked their friends and family to pay respects by donating to a state-run (and thus religious) orphanage rather than giving flowers. Narges often told me that she just wanted "them" to leave her alone. The "them" she referred to was the country's religious leadership and their supporters, with whom she felt she had nothing in common. It was for these and other reasons that Narges's decision to vote was such a surprise to her daughter. Narges felt that a time for change had arrived, and she was not alone.

In 1999 discussions of the possibilities for change through elections were common. Serious talk on important social and economic issues could be seen and heard throughout the city, for it was well known that twenty million people had elected Khatami, and it was because of this, many people told me, that changes were coming about. But limits were soon to be revealed as well. It was significant, however, that women's participation was an important contribution to the revolution, to the foundation of the state, and even to the election of the winsome Khatami;

it was rumored that his good looks garnered none too few of the women's votes. But the women with whom I spoke made plain their feeling that their votes counted for something, and because of it they could now get things in return. They recognized that by voting, they were further legitimizing the Islamic republic as a system of governance—for better or worse. The point was not that women made Iran into a democracy, or even that Iran was or is a democracy. The conversations point, rather, to a growing perception among the women I spoke with that their participation mattered and that government officials were responsive to them. What was indeed interesting, and perhaps a bit different, was that some women recognized that not only were their votes making a difference, but in order to get their votes, the candidates had to consider their demands.

The questions of rights were emerging from a perception among these women that they were autonomous individuals endowed with rights. This perspective was quite different from the communitarian view of rights articulated by some members of the 'ulama, like Mutahhari, in which rights (*haqq*) were coeval with obligations (*takleef*) and were based on social position. Instead, in Narges's case, expectations of rights emerged from a long-standing commitment to the women's rights movement in Iran, dating back well before the revolution. For Hoda, however, appeals to women's rights emerged from her postrevolutionary education and understandings of rights and equality. While she was undoubtedly affected by the experiences of her mother and other friends and relatives, her own encounters with the Islamico-republican system engendered certain expectations of rights that did not also require her to reject the legitimacy of the government or its sponsorship of a discourse on women's rights.

In contrast to Narges's and Hoda's wealthy family in northern Tehran, Pardis, a distant relative who had taken me on like a school project, had modest means but fared well in her marriage to a dental assistant. Pardis lived with her husband, their six-year-old son, and her mother-in-law in a small but adequate three-room apartment in central Tehran. She was trained as an aesthetician, but since giving birth to her first child she had stayed away from the raucous beauty salon at which she had worked. Her mother-in-law, Jamileh, a round-faced woman in her seventies, often sat at the kitchen table and read the small, wiry print of the local daily. A few days before the election, I was speaking with Pardis and her family about it. *Neshat*, a reformist paper, had listed the candidates for the upcoming city council elections.

"I already know who I am voting for," said Jamileh, skimming the list of candidates through thick bifocals. As she spoke, her forty-year-old son walked into the kitchen and served himself tea from a samovar on the stovetop that had been steeping the fine, aromatic leaves for the last hour.

Ali teased his mother about her preparedness. "Does it really matter to you?" he said with a smile.

Jamileh replied dismissively, without acknowledging her son's playfulness, "Yes, it matters a lot to me. This is the first time we are having city council elections, and I must express my opinion. I must vote. I have voted in every election since the revolution. Why, didn't you hear Khatami on the television? This is your duty. It is the duty of every Muslim to vote."

"You should listen to your mother, Ali," joked Pardis. "They have been talking about this on the news." Then, turning to me, she explained, "This is supposed to be a shift toward the power of the people. They keep saying that more power will go to the people because of the low-level elections like these."

Reformers viewed the councils as essential components of the growing civil society, as they were thought to provide a check on the power of elites (Tajbakhsh 2000). That afternoon, the television news continued to air its footage of the president, the leader, and other state officials casting their ballots in their neighborhood polling stations. On the television, Khatami, true to form, stressed the democratic ends of the elections: "The people's rule over their own destiny is a manifestation of one of the revolution's biggest ideals."[3] Khatami highlighted the goal of decentralization: "The elections will trust the administration of cities and villages to public hands. The government is honored to transfer parts of its authority to the people." He also reminded the people that he had made good on one of his promises during his presidential campaigns.[4] Although constitutionally mandated since 1979, city council elections had not taken place prior to this point for several reasons: the turmoil of the eight-year war with Iraq prevented such a transfer of power to local authority; some of Iran's leaders feared that city councils would only fuel the ethnic strife that was taking place in some provinces and lead to calls for separatism; and some government officials felt that the central government was too weak to begin the process of handing over governance to local sectors.

Although Khatami's initiation of city council elections suggested newfound confidence within the central governing bodies of the nation and was part of the reformist agenda to ensure some check on the unelected bodies of government, the advent of city councils had an earlier history in Iranian politics and governance. Popular political associations were influential in shoring up support for the 1906–1911 constitutional revolution (Tajbakhsh 2000), and consultative councils (*showra*) have a distinct signification, in this case referring to the requirement of consultation in Islamic law. So while a planned decentralization exemplified the populist strategies of democratic reformists, these policies were in line with the parameters of older local forms of dispersed governance as well.

I asked Jamileh and Pardis what they hoped would come about as a result of the elections. Jamileh spoke first: "Nothing, just some people to make sure that we have clean streets and that if something happens, like a problem with sewage, then the city will come and clean it up."

Pardis added, "If we have a problem in our city, or if we need something, like a new school, then a group of us writes a letter or, if we know one of the city councilors, goes and tells that person that we need something to be done. I think it's good because we are regular people and don't have the ability to talk to members of parliament or the president, but we should be able to reach the city council members. I think that was the point of the city council. Of course, we have never had this in Iran, so I don't know what will happen, but this is what I have learned so far from newspapers and friends."

Then Jamileh said, with a laugh, "Tehran is such a big city. I don't think I could even find the city councilors." After a moment's reflection she added, "But, I think, if I had a problem that had to do with the city, I would send my son or his wife to go and talk to someone and tell them."

Curious about Pardis's preceding comments, I pushed the women further on the impetus for their participation. I asked, "What made you decide to vote? I mean, you had to learn about the candidates and decide who to support."

Jamileh looked at me in with a strange expression on her face, as if she didn't understand the question. I looked at Pardis for clarification. "Oh, I am not sure I understand what you mean. Do you mean why did I vote?"

Jamileh then interjected, "Nobody told us to vote. Don't you vote in America? It's the same thing here. It's the same all over the world, England, France, except in places like Saudi Arabia and Kuwait where they have tribes and a *shahanshahi*.[5] But [our] revolution got rid of that."

I tried to clarify my question. I wanted to get at the impetus for their involvement in local and national politics, including voting. During the shah's government, there were also elections, but participation was extremely low. I rephrased my question: "Since when did voting become important to you, and what do you think will come of your vote?"

Pardis nodded as if to convey understanding. "Sometimes my sister and I go to the mosque by her house for the meetings there. About two weeks ago the woman leading the prayer said something to us about the elections. She said that we could make a difference."

"So," I said, "you found out about it at your mosque meeting?"

"No," replied Pardis, "I was going to vote anyway. I read the newspapers and learned about the candidates. I discussed it with my husband, and we debated who is going to be better for our future. I was always going to vote, but hearing the women talk about it at the mosque was also good; they are instructing the women that it is their [Islamic] duty to vote."

The realization of the city councils in Iran evidenced a strengthening of local spaces of action and activism in which women were also participating, as voters and candidates. Women's participation in these processes is all the more significant given their ostensible return to the domestic realm after the revolution. Even more striking, given this discussion, was that the realms of private and public were revealed as both connected and co-implicating. The spaces of the indoors or private spheres, it seemed, were not accurate ways of characterizing the spaces in which women participated and moved.

In the early days of my fieldwork in Iran, I noted the active participation of the women I was meeting, at least at the level of discourse, in everyday local and national affairs. I was impressed by the readership of newspapers, the attention to news and radio, and the discussion about society and politics that women, in their everyday situations, like Pardis and Jamileh, making lunch in the kitchen, would take up. As such, I began to note the permeability of the notion of the public sphere. What about discussing local politics in the kitchen or in the mosque was *public*? The answer is that the women saw themselves as public actors, or at least as people having some ability to affect public spaces, and in turn recognized that this space of politics or civil society can and will touch their lives. And they can participate in it in meaningful ways.

Feminist scholars, of course, have critiqued the division of public and private spaces (Benhabib 1992; Fraser 1992; Landes 1988). What should be noted, nonetheless, is that in Iran the hegemonic discourse of the gendered division of space does exist (Khatib-Chahidi 1993). Women, however, mediate the formal segregation of space through their participation in civil and political spaces, such as elections, but also by forming and utilizing spaces for consciousness raising, such as the mosque meeting to which Pardis referred.

Such dialogical sites provide room for debate about contemporary political and social issues and in turn produce new visions of statist practices. They thus enable the participants in these local elections to act as empowered agents in the production of the state's institutions, but the discourse and logic of participation is not limited to elections and state politics. Discussions surrounding the politics of elections, candidates, and campaigns engender a consciousness, if not a commitment, among the actors involved in the process and locate the subjects amid a constellation of voices partaking in the production of "the state" and "the rule of law." Although the postreform period revealed the limits of the democratic possibilities, in the immediate aftermath of Khatami's May 23, 1997, election, the political possibilities that emerged through the blended institutions of the Islamic republic allowed the production of new dialogic sites of political and social participation that have had lasting effects on the politics of the state and the discourse of rights in contemporary Iran.

SETTING THE STAGE: THE BUREAUCRATIC ISLAMIC STATE

It must have been about 6:00 p.m. by the time Narges, Hoda, and I got in the car to go to the National Theater in the center of town. We were about to attend a performance of *Richard III*, William Shakespeare's play about an evil king, translated and performed in Persian. Narges informed me that the director, Davood, had wanted to put on this play for the last twenty-five years but was refused permission by the shah. It was only with the new minister of Islamic culture and guidance, Ataollah Mohajerani, that permission was finally granted. The play had been a huge success, with ticket sales filling the house nearly every night of the week, and as such the play was extended through the middle of summer. It didn't hurt that just about every actor cast in a major role was one of Iran's most beloved. And for the first time, women actors were cast without head-scarves. Instead of the scarf, a wig covered each woman's head. As Hoda explained to me, "Khatami's government would like everyone to think of Iran as a country that is advanced and not hundreds of years behind Europe." Narges also commented on the political message permeating the production: "This is because of Mohajerani. None of this would have happened without him. He is fighting those hardliners to change Iranian society."

Indeed, some saw the production of the play as a victory for Moha-jerani, a presidential appointee, and in part explained how well loved he was by the reformers as well as the so-called secular-liberal elites. But it also showed how his actions troubled the religious conservatives. By the middle of his first term in office, President Khatami had made certain changes in the social and political life of Iranians. Apparent in the visual arts of theater and film, as well as in print media, including literature, newspapers, and magazines, Iranians were beginning to feel manifest changes in their social and political lives that appeared to bring relief amid otherwise heavy pressures of daily life. These changes also brought about greater dialogue among Iranians about the state of their society, particularly as they approached the twentieth anniversary of the creation of the Islamic republic.

The state-sponsored production of *Richard III* is an example of the political message about the wave of social changes that were being instituted at multiple levels and on a number of registers that impacted social life. The approval of the play's production allegorically marked a new era in the Islamic republic, one in which the new state formation is a marker of modernity, while that which was deposed, like Richard himself, was a poorly devised and polluted one. As the reformist arm of the Islamic republic speaks to the people through theater, it offers art, in the form of a Western play, as a commentary about what is now good in the Iranian state. At the same time, while a certain state institution, the Ministry of Culture and Islamic Guidance, approved the production of the play, its officials found that these very productions became targets of scrutiny by other state powers, drawing attention to the tensions that lie at the heart of administering of the world's first theocratic republic. What's more, as the state, in its variable factions, sought to enlist modernity in the name of Islam, the very notion of a republic undercut the idea that it is a monolithic entity regulating this new state formation.

Narges, Hoda, and I got out of the taxi and walked over to the open doors of the theater. Couples walked in holding hands, and several university students stood at the door taking tickets. We entered the theater, whose air conditioned interior was a comforting relief from the late afternoon heat. We sat a bit farther back than Narges, who had forgotten her glasses, would have liked. Hoda hushed her mother when she complained about the heat and tugged on her headscarf, grumbling about not being allowed to take it off, "This is why I don't like to go out." Narges, who knew nothing about the play, sat impatiently next to me, her hands clenching the purse on her lap, already prepared to leave. Hoda, however, seemed quite content as she studied the playbill and looked up to see the action on stage as the curtain went up. She had read the play and was eager to see it performed. As the lights dimmed and the actors appeared onstage, a full house fell silent to the first lines of the play.

The stage set and actors' costumes were designed to summon sixteenth-century Europe. The play's producers had even succeeded in obtaining approval for their female actors to cover their heads with wigs rather than headscarves. The play's message, however, was poignantly conveyed by some of Tehran's best stage actors, and likely few in the audience failed to see the connections between Iran's previous monarchical government and Richard III. In case I missed this point, Narges sarcastically whispered, a little too loudly, "This is supposed to be the shah," when the hunchbacked Richard stumbled onto the stage.

. . .

At the end of the play, we quietly filed out. While Narges went to look for a taxi, Hoda and I walked slowly through the park where the National Theater sat, and Hoda gave me her thoughts on the play. Initially she was critical—of the heat, of the acting, of the poor quality of the wigs worn by the actors, and of their overall acting talents. But she was also moved by the sentiment of the play. She saw it as an attack on monarchy, and although she was quite aware of the production's political message, she saw it also as a cautionary tale to the hardliners. "Monarchy is not just through a king," she said. "It's not?" I asked. "No, this play warns us that when a single person makes decisions, then people suffer. So," she said, thinking aloud, "we need to be involved. I don't mean just by voting and political movements. This production is how an artist is participating. He's making a statement about the state." Hoda explained how she didn't know what it was like before, "but the way things are now, it's possible to make some reform if people demand changes."

By now we had gotten into a taxi. Hoda clearly felt inspired by her interpretations, and she grew to think that the play was making a statement about the current system. "Look at what Khatami has been able to do in such a short time. People are talking . . . in the press." She referred to the sudden broad array of opinions in the newspapers, and she reminded her mother that even she now read one or two different papers daily, and that she had participated in recent elections. Narges met her daughter's optimism with disdain, commenting, "What is this nonsense? The reformers are wishful in their thinking. Some people think that one day this can include seculars, but this is just a lie. Even Khatami is an akhund." Narges maintained a very negative attitude toward the government. While she had begun to participate, she still had very little hope that things would go differently because the religious leaders "would never leave." Narges understood her daughter's interpretation of the play as state propaganda. "So, they show you a play about how bad the king was, and it makes you feel that this system is so much better. Remember, they chose the production." Then Narges asked, somewhat rhetorically, "What's the difference between Richard III and Khamenei'i?"

Hoda tried to clarify: "That's what I am saying. This is getting us to think about this system, too." Narges went on: "They created an Islamic government as Khomeini had wanted." Referring to the political sparring that had erupted since Khatami's elections, she added, "These fights are among themselves. In this government, we will never see the day when a real democracy, open to everyone, will emerge."

The play led the women to consider the role of the state and state actors in their lives. What the discussions revealed was that for Hoda and Narges, the production of *Richard III* was a manifestation of the complex political and social conditions that emerged in Khatami era Iran, which provided the conditions for the emergence of these and other new sites of dialogue. This discussion also provides a backdrop for later chapters in which I consider how women like Narges, Hoda, Pardis, Jamileh, and others envision their rights today, because changes in the ways women talk about their rights are also an effect of the dissonant tenor of multiple state factions emerging during this time.

The Age of Khatami: Openings and Closings

By early 1999, when I arrived in Iran, Khatami had been president for a year and a half. Almost every person I spoke with told me how much looser controls on public behavior had become. Among my first friends in Tehran were Roxana and Zohreh, both producers whom I had met at National Television and Radio. As they explained the shift in social constraints, Roxana held out her long fingers, her nails painted in soft pink. "I used to wear gloves everywhere I went. I did not want to risk being arrested for this," she said.

And certainly it was not unusual to see couples holding hands and women revealing strands of hair or wearing obvious makeup in parts of town. It was not what I had expected, but then, what was? Zohreh mused, "People are starting to feel more open. This is a good time for you to be here. The Islamic republic is an experiment. It will just take time for the full effects of democracy to be felt. Look, even in America women did not have the right to vote for over one hundred years. We are also slowly getting to our rights." Then Roxana added, in her understated way when she talked about politics, "They won't be around much longer." As I was still new to the scene, I had to ask, "Who is 'they'? Why is everyone always talking about 'they' or 'them'?" Both women laughed as Roxana explained that the government in charge was full of religious people, many of whom were not chosen by the electorate. "'They' are the ones who created the system and whom we didn't choose. They are the 'ulama who don't like the intellectuals or seculars to govern the country." After a moment she added, "They say we have freedoms we didn't have under the shah, but in place of the old political restrictions there are new ones, social and political. You know, they created a republic (*jomhuri*)." She enunciated every syllable. "That means anyone should be able to participate without investigation (*gozinesh*)."

To gain job security in their government positions, Roxana and Zohreh both had to complete their university-level education, although both also had master's degrees in law and, like all government employees, had passed gozinesh, an examination of their knowledge of Islam, piety, and general moral virtue, in which, in addition to a written exam and interview, the candidate would be the subject of an inquiry among neighbors, friends, and family members. I met a number of women in Iran who had either refused to take the exam or had failed it; in either case, they were left out of government employment. In the Khatami era, both Roxana and Zohreh conveyed, the constraints on social life had indeed diminished, but their participation in and appreciation for the system also brought an awareness of the limits of their freedoms, as Roxana put it, and the rule of law.

Roxana and Zohreh, moreover, could not have been more different. While both were in their late thirties when I first met them in the spring of 1999, Roxana was a well-to-do divorcée from an elite, old-Tehrani family. She was not among the secular elites, like Narges, but considered herself a pious Muslim and had even made the *hajj*, the superexpensive pilgrimage to Mecca. When not working on television production, Roxana spent time with her only child, a son from her previous marriage. She also lived with her widowed mother, who was often called upon to stay with her teenage son when Roxana went out in the evenings. Roxana rarely, if ever, complained about the country's leaders, and yet she flouted every social rule or constraint she could find. She comfortably spoke her mind to the officers who commented on her often *bad hejab*, a reference to an overly tight overcoat or a headscarf that showed too much of her light brown hair.[6] At dinner parties in the homes of friends and family, Roxana displayed the latest fashions from her vacations in Dubai or Ankara. She wore leopard prints and leather with cool aplomb.

Her attitude, as she explained to me, was that she was not doing anything wrong. She would speak with an affectionate tone to the youthful soldiers on the street: "What business is it of yours. If you are a real Muslim, you shouldn't be looking at me anyway." The most interesting thing about Roxana was that she was always right. She followed the constraints just according to the rules and walked just on the edge of what was permissible, but she found a way to live her life as she wanted. She did not feel constrained, she told me, and often spoke of going on trips and to parties, sometimes inviting me to partake. Her son, who had recently been admitted to the best computer science program in the country, regarded his mother with great respect and honor. In all of this, Roxana did not live with illusions about the state of politics in her city, nor did she want to leave it. "Oh, leave them to themselves," she would say and wave her hand away. "They fight" she once said to me, "and the people suffer. You just have to find a way to not be burned by them." And it seemed that Roxana had learned her lessons much earlier in life. When she married at twenty, she quickly found that she could not live with her husband. "Back then," referring to the years immediately after the revolution, "you couldn't get to know the man you were going to marry. There was no way to be together without already being engaged. I was young. I liked his looks and he seemed nice, so I did it." Her lack of attention to details was a part of her plan to live unbridled and to look to the future. In the many interviews and conversations I had with Roxana, her approach was to always consider the lighter side of life, and it was what had given her a life in which she lived richly among the social constraints. Even when a woman could be arrested for wearing nail polish in public, Roxana still wore it, but she wore gloves to mitigate any consequences.

Zohreh, Roxana's co-worker and friend, was altogether different. Zohreh, who was not married, declared herself in love with God, *Allah,* and told me she felt deeply connected to the spiritual world. She felt the joy of being in love when she prayed three times each day.[7] She wore a strict hejab, a black overcoat and headscarf over which she wore a chador that swayed with her every step. In the spring and summer months, Zohreh, so rigorous in following what she believed to be the Qur'anic revelations about pious women, even wore sleeves under her short-sleeved overcoats to prevent any display of her arms. Perhaps to some, like Narges, Zohreh appeared to be among the strict Muslims who support the current hard-line conservatives in the government and assented to making a religious authority the highest official in government. Zohreh undoubtedly fit the superficial criteria, in her dress. But at the same time, Zohreh was extremely private about her views on the system of government, a system that greatly improved her lot and that of many like her. Zohreh moved easily with Roxana, me, and other friends, even those whose beliefs were different from hers. She was never judgmental nor didactic about our "bad hejab." "Each person should dress as she or he sees fit," she had once told me. "This is how I feel comfortable; even if it weren't the law, I would wear my hejab like this. I would feel naked without it."

Unlike Roxana, Zohreh was not a Tehran native and did not have family money. She hailed from the outskirts of a town not far from Kerman, in southeastern Iran, and was the youngest child in a family of four brothers and two sisters. Her family had moved to Tehran soon after the revolution, and her father, a construction foreman who was now deceased, never made much money. The family always rented small apartments in southern Tehran, and one by one Zohreh saw her brothers leave the country. Two were in Europe and one was in the United States, married to an American woman whom Zohreh had never met. Now, Zohreh lived with her mother, as well, in a small apartment but was saving money with hopes of purchasing a small, one-bedroom apartment with government financing from the ministry where she worked.

If Roxana flourished in spite of the strict regulations for women, Zohreh did so because of them. She was an extremely successful producer and traveled all around the country making television productions with a crew of between ten and fifteen men and women, mostly about the lives of rural and underprivileged women. She saw herself as a recipient of the government's casting call for pious Muslim women to show postrevolutionary Iran's attention to and support of women. Her relatively humble background would probably have prevented her from achieving great career success had it not been for the opportunities the Islamic republic offered women and girls like her.

. . .

As the Islamic republic entered its twentieth year, it faced a growing populace of disillusioned and disconcerted people. Indeed the numbers of detractors were rapidly growing as economic hardships were met with increased resentment toward the government. Many blamed their financial woes on the incompetence of the government, whose primary concern was with employing people with proven religious, and therefore political, allegiance rather than skills. But the numbers of dissatisfied were also growing as a very youthful population was coming of age and increasingly finding fault with the system that could not absorb their labor, skills, and training. The latter group, the disgruntled young people, poses a particular problem for the leadership. A large part of this growing segment of the population questions the government's legitimacy and authority on critical issues of economics, social rights, and fundamental freedoms, like the right to free speech. Khatami's succession of Hashemi Rafsanjani began a new era in Iran's political landscape.[8] In the past, the statist discourse on and control over the nation's Islamic identity, especially as it pertained to specific issues such as women's rights, had its detractors, but power came from its very ability to shore up and disseminate a seemingly unified position on critical matters. In such a time, apparent opposition was just that—opposition to Islam, the state, and even the republic. With Khatami in place as a result of a popular, democratic vote, the state agents could no longer assume a unitary voice on matters in question. Now with at least two identifiable state discourses, the conservative and the reformist, rough political sparring had begun. Both sides sought to justify their message and exhibit their strengths. Khatami, the reformer, bandied about as the modern member of the 'ulama, beloved by the middle and, to some extent, even the secularized classes, sought to loosen the reins of social control. One of his first acts as president was to announce that unmarried members of the opposite sex would not be arrested for being out in public together. Accordingly, the revolutionary moral police (*pasdaran*) temporarily tempered their arrests of young men and women.

As Khatami tested the limits of presidential authority, a political power struggle emerged from both his popularity and his actions. His constituents began to have a clearer picture of the complex and contradictory configuration of the state as they saw Khatami's attempt at reform thwarted by his opponents. The limits of his authority became apparent as he was placed in check over and over. In 1999 this power play was evidenced by numerous events, such as the impeachment trial of the minister of culture and Islamic guidance, the closing of numerous newspapers that had been approved for publication by the same minister, and the arrest, prosecution, and imprisonment of moderate or leftist members of the 'ulama and intellectuals who dared to voice their discontent.[9]

The power behind the forces opposing Khatami, his cabinet, and the small majority of reformists in parliament was what the dailies referred to as the hardliners, factions in the government that objected to Khatami's reformist agenda and claimed that it conflicted with Islamic values and the aims of the revolution.[10] The authoritative strength behind the hardliners was a group of nonelected officials consisting primarily of the Council of Guardians and Iran's supreme leader, who held the tripartite republic in check.

In the first twenty months of his administration, Khatami's government had increased the circulation of daily newspapers from 1.3 million to 2.7 million. In 1997 alone, the Ministry of Culture and Islamic Guidance issued licenses for 280 publications, although in 1998, the number went down to 175. The government issued approvals for the publication of over 24,000 books in the same twenty-month period.[11] By the June 2001 election, however, the press was reporting that the conservative factions had closed over forty newspapers or magazines that had previously been issued licenses by the ministry.[12]

The struggle over the regulation of print media and the visual arts (theater, film, and art or cultural exhibitions) is a crucial site of spaces for dialogue for two reasons. First, these media forms, unlike television and radio, fall within the purview of the executive branch of government—at the time, the reformists—whereas television and radio are directly regulated by the offices of the supreme leader. Thus debates over the media and arts depicted the forms and limits of executive and legislative powers and illustrated the ways in which popular power is made to yield to the powers of the Guardianship of the Jurist. Second, the debates themselves reveal the ambiguity of the process of dialogue and debate in Iran. Is a public space emerging through the persistence of a political tug-of-war, or is the political power struggle merely a hindrance to open social dialogue? Even today, the very public character of the struggles between the reformists and the hardliners is a trigger that spurs people to question the social, legal, and political limits of Islamic republican governance, and thus affects the emergence of spaces for public discourse. For this reason, it is no strange coincidence that in the period since Khatami became president, newspapers and individuals I spoke with reported many "firsts":

the first city council elections; the first concerts by well-known female vocalists since the revolution (to female audiences only); the first performance of women musicians on Iranian television; the first CD release of a celebrated musician in twenty years; the first theatrical production by a director who had not produced a play in Iran since the revolution; the opening (and subsequent closing) of the first-ever women's daily, *Zan* (Woman); the opening of Iran's first Internet café; and the most severe violence in Iran since the revolution.

Ataollah Mohajerani: Freedom and Speech

"Some things have improved quite a bit," explained Zohreh. "For instance, we have many newspapers to choose from. I read two or three papers a day. People are more interested in this political system. They are just now starting to understand how it works." Zohreh had invited me to lunch. It was May 1, 1999. We were talking about the impeachment hearing—not the one that the U.S. president had undergone earlier that year, about which Iranians were very curious. Because of the salacious nature of the investigation, many of the details of the Clinton impeachment were left out of the coverage. In contrast, the impeachment hearing of Ataollah Mohajerani, Iran's minister of culture and Islamic guidance, was broadcast live on the radio.

President Khatami's aims for successful governance lay in invitations to his constituents to engage in productive dialogue on the nation's agendas. While some of Khatami's initiatives invited people to seek political changes through the electoral process, he also encouraged wider participation in other arenas of social life that have increasingly led to dissemination of information and to public dialogue on ideas. Soon the international press began referring to a sign of changing times in Iran, and "spaces" or "openings" (Agence France Presse, December 9, 1998). By the fall of 1998 there were tangible changes in the social and political life of Iranians. Reports indicated the abundance of satellite dishes propped on roofs and balconies, even though they were ostensibly illegal. Other reports related increases in the number and circulation of newspapers and magazines in the country, and still others recounted how the opening of Internet cafés allowed Iranians glimpses of the world beyond.

The proliferation of a verbal and print dialogue as well as films depicting social problems owed much to minister of culture and Islamic guidance. Mohajerani, notably, was not a member of the 'ulama, but a historian of Islam, with a doctorate from the University of Tehran. During his tenure, Mohajerani approved the licensing of numerous newspapers and magazines that led to a flourishing dialogue on the state, both in the written pages of text and among the avid readers. His endorsement of so many newspapers as well as other print media, such as literary works and cinema, ultimately landed him in the mire of the political tensions between the reformists and the hardliners. In early 1999 the parliamentary hardliners led a campaign to impeach Mohajerani for approving the production of works that they claimed insulted Islamic values. As fast as Mohajerani could approve them, the newly created Press Court was closing them down. The same editors would then go back to Mohajerani's ministry to receive a license for a new paper.[13]

On May 1, 1999, Mohajerani appeared before a full Majlis to defend himself against a censure motion brought by thirty-one members of parliament (MPs) charging him with mismanagement of the ministry. Mohajerani was called to account for insulting Islamic values by too readily issuing permissions for the production and publication of various newspapers, films, and books.[14] His nine-hour impeachment hearing held the rapt attention of the masses as it was transmitted on the national radio station throughout the country. On that day in every part of the city, radios were tuned to Mohajerani's eloquent response to the accusations. The next day newspapers reprinted his defense in its entirety. Mohajerani stressed that the Khatami administration had a cultural strategy and that its policies would continue. He elaborated that strategy by highlighting the social value of multiple voices: "That in the press (print media) different voices must be heard is a declared policy."[15] Newspapers reported that the minister appeared "calm and cool" as he enumerated his ministry's achievements and his administration's view on the current cultural policies:

> I believe that a thought should be responded to by a thought and not by banning newspapers. The views of the opposition must be heard. If opposition papers do not exist, do you think their will be no opposition (political groups) in the country? Tolerance does not mean the weakening of values. An idea has to be responded to with another idea. The problems of culture in the Islamic republic do not revolve around the minister. Do you think that if I go away the problem in the country will be resolved? If it is so, then there was no need for such a session and I would go away with a slight signal from the leader of the Islamic Revolution, president, or Majlis speaker.[16]

The law office I was working at that day had all but shut down. Staff members had small transistor radio on which they listened to the minister's speech. In the lawyer's office, clients spoke over an audible transmission. Unapologetically, the attorney said to me, "This is very important for us." What was at stake, she felt, was the very viability of the reform movement.

By the end of the afternoon, when Majlis took its vote, the hardliners lost by a vote of 135 to 121, with 7 abstentions.[17] Mohajerani would stay.

The effect of Mohajerani's hearing went well beyond having retained his seat in the ministry. And, although some bemoaned the failure of government officials to televise the impeachment hearing, the multitudes of Iranians who listened to the live proceedings on their radios were elated to witness the administration of justice. After the vote, the minister thanked the speaker of Majlis for handling the impeachment hearing. He also praised the MPs who initiated the impeachment hearing, and thus allowed him to account for his ministry's activities. Through these actions, the minister of culture and Islamic guidance, like the president, attempted to underscore the successful institutionalization of the rule of law in the country.

Mohajerani's impeachment hearing referenced the contradictions embedded in the governmental system. The republican form of government was the recognition on the part of some of the 'ulama, some of whom did not want a republic, that the revolution's success was in part due to the popular support for the overthrow of the shah. As part of this acknowledgment, the new state offered promises and certain liberal freedoms that the shah's government did not. In his impeachment hearing, Mohajerani stressed the basis for these promises, such as the freedom of speech, and argued that the prevalence of such ideas was the Khatami administration's policy aim.

Iran's complex political system combines elements of a Islamic theocracy with republican democracy. The formation of the Islamic republic is the result of political compromises just after the revolution, and now the ongoing struggles between reformists and hardliners. The resulting tensions that emerge and are played out publicly also create spaces for dialogue and further the development of the innovative religio-republican body politic.

THE CLOSING OF SALAAM: LIMITS OF SPEECH AND FREEDOM

The summer of 1999 was marked by the violent culmination of the government's interfactional power play. On July 9, after a day of student protests over the Special Court for Clergy's closure of the latest newspaper, Salaam, special armed forces broke into dormitories at the University of Tehran in the middle of the night and beat and killed a number of students.[18] Riots broke out throughout Iran for several days afterwards, as students demanded accountability for these attacks. At the height of the riots in downtown Tehran, in front of the campus, students held all-night vigils and stood undaunted before masses of armed forces as they demanded Khatami's appearance.[19] Khatami, stories circulated, was afraid because, besides his few personal bodyguards, he had no special forces of his own. Indeed, among the areas over which the president in Iran does not have control are the military and the police forces. Herein lay the uncontroverted power of the hardliners: sheer military might. While Khatami might have popular support, with no military backing, "What power does he *really* have?" asked Narges to her family, sitting at home and, like many, afraid to venture out during this uncertain time. The week of the riots corresponded with Narges's son's departure for Canada. For this reason, the extended family had gathered by the pool in the family's small backyard to bid him farewell. The riots brought many questions to each person's lips. What was happening in the country was truly shocking for those who, like many elite Iranians, obtained their news of the riots from CNN. Nahid, Narges's younger sister, was interested in the situation and what it revealed about the political system. She was a homemaker devoted to her two children and husband and had never participated in anything she would call political. Like most upper-class elites, she avoided constraints imposed by the government by living within the walls of her family estate. The reform movement's victory had brought a glimmer of hope to her, and she had begun to see possibilities for greater change in Iran. Like her sister, she had also voted in the last elections for the first time, even though women had earned suffrage back in 1963. But the news of the riots, especially Khatami's failure as the elected president to quell the violence and meet the students' demands, had paralyzed her hope and the hope of others, both the wealthy and the working classes.

The reformist newspapers had started printing accounts of the riots. Nahid read from the newspapers and explained that to further humiliate Khatami and harden the hardliners' position, newspapers had reported the cynical words of one member of the Council of Guardians: "I don't care if he had thirty million votes; it is we who decide."

Further angered and frustrated, the moderates and their supporters among the working classes—those who could not isolate themselves within their estates—also worried and began to ponder what sort of democracy they really have in Iran. Jamileh and Pardis were among those who worried about the fledgling democracy they thought was emerging. I was at Pardis's home a few days after the riots. Her neighbor's daughter had been arrested a few days earlier. Although she had not participated in the riots and was nowhere near the university when they happened, Pardis explained that the government forces were arresting young people seen in big groups. "Government minivans were in the major centers of town, especially in northern Tehran," where reformists and elites lived. "They were rounding up the kids and taking them to various police stations for no reason other than to harass them. People were keeping their kids indoors, avoiding work and school."

Some, however, were not deterred.

A few weeks after the riots, Afshin, a freelance journalist and also my tutor, came to my house. He had covered the events for a local daily and debriefed me one afternoon. He said that the students claimed that having popular support would make a difference because the people would run into the streets, CNN would pick it up, and the whole world would see. I asked who was willing to run into the streets. Certainly the people I knew were keeping their children indoors. "Look," he said, "the protestors are middle-class kids. Their complaint," he continued, as he grabbed hold of his button-down shirt, "is this. They can't wear what they want; but this is not something they are willing to die for."

As those hot and uncertain days wore on, we watched the situation become defused. Khatami eventually spoke to the students. In nationwide speeches over the following days, he promised to address their grievances and asked that the students cooperate with his administration so that their complaints could be processed through the proper political and legal channels.[20] The reaction to this was mixed. But eventually life in hectic Tehran returned to normal for most. What these months proved, however, was the will of the electorate, which increasingly was seeking changes in the way the laws and their rights were being administered. Whether Khatami had succeeded in moving the debates from the streets into the polls remained to be seen. Elections for the sixth parliament were fast approaching, Khatami reminded the students. The president's addresses, such as the one after the riots, often referred to the power that was in the hands of the people through the political process. In one speech, Khatami stressed that "a kind of mobilization of public opinion has been created which should not be taken as a minor achievement." He noted that "it is important to guide this national consensus toward more fundamental affairs such as institutionalization of the system within the framework of law and safeguarding the people's rights and observing freedom and security with the objective of the society's progress and consolidation of the system."[21]

Significantly, Khatami located that power in law and the political process, not in the hands of the hardliners, or any select groups. He was thereby speaking as much to transgressions of the law by hardliners as he was to those by reformists. Khatami's message about abiding by the law was not just directed to the students, nor was it a message directed to the hardliners. His addresses, constantly locating government and popular action in the rule of law, were part of a political agenda that aimed to expand the legitimacy of elected government officials with an emphasis on rational law and institutions, not as possible sources of power, but as the future of popular rule. The 1999 riots showed Iranians that President Khatami was decidedly not authorized with police powers. And while the comfortable middle classes may not be ready to die for social change, they may be willing to fight for expanding the role of republican and democratic processes through a greater emphasis on legal avenues to action.

DISCREPANT FORMATIONS: LEGAL DISCOURSE AND SITES OF RIGHTS

Negin is Nahid's daughter and is in her mid-twenties. One afternoon after the riots, she came to the house and joined our conversations. She said, "Khatami talks about the law, but he has no powers. They [the hardliners] don't want to establish law, otherwise they will be out of power." Negin, who was studying international law, wanted to work at the United Nations and help with the establishment of the rule of law in Iran. She spoke with authority of the effects of law: "It is part of Khatami's plan to try to undermine their power with more legislation. But after the passing of the Press Law and this attack on the students, it's obvious that they want to show us that the rule of law will not be permitted to overtake their power."

• • •

Establishing a rule of law and enforcing and enhancing customary principles into modern legality has been among Iranian aims at modernity for well over one hundred years. The postrevolutionary emphasis on the rule of law, weighted in Islamic principles, speaks to an expressed engagement with modernity. My discussions about legal rights with Negin and others, however, revealed major discrepancies between theories of Islamic rights and justice and the everyday lives of women and men in a postindustrial country. While there is a great emphasis on family unity, the primary system of redress is the civil legal system. The ideals of the Islamic society are not always accommodated by the civil law approach that operates in the contemporary Islamic republic. Rights that are promulgated in civil legal codes contain no mention of the corresponding duties of other kin. The legal codes that have emerged in modern bureaucratized societies are detached from the underlying principles of their social formation and sometimes leave the women who have social expectations without recourse to obtain them. To understand how the law is mobilized by women in the contemporary era, we must understand how shari'a comes into being as law and becomes part of the bureaucracy of the state.

One of the more profound effects of the convergence of Islamic principles and republican governance is the creation of a codified body of law that takes the shari'a and makes a comprehensive legal code. The effects of this convergence shape and allow for a new kind of dialogue in Iran, one that has the trappings of civil legal liberalism, but is simultaneously sanctioned by Islamic values. Two effects of this convergence have important bearings on women's perceptions of rights. The first is the bureaucratic rationalization of a political and religious space through the promulgation of a hybrid legal system, Islamico-civil law. The second effect, which is an outcome of the first, is increased individuation among people who engage with the bureaucratized politico-religious institutions of the state.

Legal Sites: Law and the Shari'a

Shari'a, which literally means the path, is commonly referred to as "Islamic law." This anglicized moniker collapses the breadth of what shari'a constitutes and reduces it to "legal" signification without considering how the shari'a materializes, literally, as a legal instrument of the nation-state. Though shari'a is classically conceived of as an ageless set of guidelines of God's law, its contemporary application has emerged through a nexus of historical, political, and social conditions. In Arabic, shari'a literally means "the path to the well." As water is considered the source of life, the path, which the shari'a provides, is the methodology for reaching answers to important questions. This methodology, which comprises Islamic jurisprudence (*fiqh*) in the different schools (*madhabs*), allows for rules of explicating sacred texts, for finding solutions to contemporary questions through them, and for determining the reliability of the different sources of explication. The shari'a is the body of rules and regulations that Muslims use to guide their relationships with God and others. For many believers, since the shari'a provides guidance over all aspects of life, there is no need for "man-made" laws. Thus, the work of experts on Islamic exegesis is very important.

The manner by which shari'a emerged into enforceable state law is a rich and uneven practice throughout Muslim-majority nation-states as well as in places in which Muslims are not the majority. Although the sacred texts are theoretically immutable, a diversity of interpretations has led to a multiplicity of beliefs and practices, not just through the various schools, but also through the method of legal process administered in varying degrees by the 'ulama, state authorities, or both. Debates surrounding these practices persist within specialist, ecclesiastical spaces and in the other sites in which legal practitioners or those who must engage with the laws have stakes.

Earlier, Islamic law scholars such as Joseph Schacht (1964) referred to Islamic law as jurist's law, opposing it to judge's law, to note the concern with ethical issues inherent in the administration of Islamic law, about which only those educated in the scholarly pursuits of the science of jurisprudence were knowledgeable.[22] Schacht argued that jurists trained in fiqh had an aversion to a rationalized system of process. As a result, judges, who were not trained in the underlying moral considerations embedded in the shari'a, could not be permitted to enforce the law (Arjomand 1988). Thus, among these early scholars, the administration of shari'a justice was often characterized by its lack of procedural uniformity, recognized memorably by Max Weber's term "*qadi*-justice" (1978).[23] For Weber, moral considerations and a personalized style of process were the characteristic traits of Islamic justice. For early scholars, the idea of Islamic law was troubling because judges used textual explications as tools for deriving legal rules and not a centralized legislative body.[24]

Later work on Islamic jurisprudence and legal systems refuted the idea that Islamic law was incompatible with rationalization (Fischer 1980; Fischer and Abedi 1990; Messick 1993; Rosen 1980–81). More scholarly work in this area in recent years has begun to show a rich history of rationalization within Islamic law (Hallaq 2005; Powers 1994; Zubaida 2005), within Islamic family law (Sonbol 2003; Tucker 1998), and in particular in Shi'i jurisprudence (Gleave 1997; Keddie 1995).

In Iran, where most Muslims are Shi'i, the shari'a is developed through the Twelver or Ithna 'Ashari branch of Islam, whose school of jurisprudence is Ja'fari.[25] Within this school of jurisprudence, there are two major branches, the Usuli and Akhbari, with the Usuli being the primary group controlling the centralized, state-administered legal discourse in Iran.[26] The sources of law in the predominant Usuli Ja'fari school include the Qur'an, the sunna of the Prophet, community consensus (*ijma*), and *dalil al-aql*, which refers to certain forms of logical reasoning that are acceptable to fill in voids in the event that accepted texts are silent with regard to an issue. Within Shi'i Islam, the notion of independent juridical interpretation (*ijtihad*) is a key foundational point as it permits members of the 'ulama to consult their authoritative explications (*tafsir*) and draw from their reasoning skills, which include the process of logical deduction from analogy (*qiyas*, or analogical reasoning). Qiyas can be understood as a corollary to the concept of *istislah*, which recognizes the overriding concern in the shari'a with justice and public welfare and thus allows intervention in the public interest, particularly when analogical reasoning could result in an inordinately harsh rule or when a question arises for which there is no existing rule. Another concept, *istishab*, respects the validity of independent reasoning of the learned scholars. Above all, perhaps, this concept recognizes a core hermeneutical quality of rendering judgments. In its classical iteration, this complex process of independent juridical interpretation and reasoning in the Shi'i school was regularly practiced among the 'ulama and was decentralized.

Even as recently as the nineteenth century, law in Iran, while ostensibly centralized under the Qajar dynasty, was delivered through the 'ulama, the mediators and adjudicators of conflict, who derived their power and their following from decentralized religious institutions (Zubaida 2005). A licensed *mujtahid,* one who is qualified to perform ijtihad, would attract followers who would pay religious tax (*khoms*) to his offices and approach him for questions regarding spiritual guidance of two kinds—those relating to their relationships with God, and those having to do with their relationships to others. In this way it is a "total discourse" (Messick 1993) or, as many of my informants conveyed, offers a framework for answering any question that one might have about life. Important in this context, however, is the idea that, unlike in the Ottoman Sunni context, Islamic principles, while offering guidelines for a Muslim (to submit to the will of God), were not centralized through the state bureaucracy. Mujtahids had a degree of autonomy and were not principals in the centralized political government of the Qajars until the late 1880s when Iran's economic interactions with Europe, particularly Great Britain and Russia, increased. They were instrumental in the boycott of tobacco in 1881 when the Qajar shah sold the British a monopoly on all trade in tobacco in Iran (Keddie 1966). When a constitutional revolution that began in the last months of 1905 forced the consolidation of state institutions, a crisis of power management ensued. Some of the 'ulama felt that a constitution, especially one that authorized a law-making legislative branch of government, would siphon off the power of the 'ulama, not to mention a funding source in the form of religious taxes. However, some mujtahids supported the revolution and even took part in the development of a constitution to address the concerns of the 'ulama (Ghani 2000). But the strengthening of the central government through rationalized civil codes and bureaucratic governmental institutions forever shifted the shari'a from being an ethereal set of guidelines for Muslims seeking the path to perfection to positive law administered by centralized state authorities.

Iran: Centralized Islamico-Civil Law

In the Iranian context, the debates about the role of the shari'a in the centralized legal system have persisted for many years—since well before the 1979 revolution—and continue through today. One important component of these debates was the relationship between the Shi'ism and the modern nation-state (Cole and Keddie 1986). The engagement with modern state formation has spurred considerable discussion about forms of governance and the place of the Shi'i 'ulama in governance (Martin 2003; Soroush 2000), as well as the contests over these issues among the 'ulama themselves (Cole and Keddie 1986), even launching a new epistemology of Islamic law (Dahlén 2003; Salimi 2003). These persistent arguments have not only influenced the configuration of the nation-state, but also shaped the discourse around rights and the contemporary concerns of modern Shi'ism. In all, the processes continue to be dynamic, fluid, and continuously changing. Among other things, the renewed scholarly attention to shari'a jurisprudence shows how gender ideologies inform Islamic jurisprudence (Mir-Hosseini 2003; Sonbol 2003). Such interpretations have also historically shaped gender rights in Islamic family law and continue to shape gender relations. But such interpretations are also produced in state institutions, a transnational discourse on rights, premised on the rights of individuals, and forms of legality that conform with civil legal regularization, such as codes, process, and a *stare decisis* system for following precedent. Recent statements by legislators and activists have called for gender equality under the law and for enhanced legal remedies for women.

In 1979 Khomeini's thesis on Islamic government justified the need for centralized state institutions to implement guidelines set out in the Qur'an and the sunna:

> Any person who claims that the formation of an Islamic government is not necessary denies the necessity for the implementation of Islamic law, the universality and comprehensiveness of that law, and the eternal validity of the faith itself. . . . The nature and character of Islamic law and the divine ordinances of the shari'a furnish additional proof of the necessity for establishing government, for they indicate that the laws were laid down for the purpose of creating a state and administering the political, economic, and cultural affairs of society. (Khomeini 1981: 43)

Khomeini offered an interpretation of Ja'fari Shi'i fiqh to serve as a broker between 'ulama and statist relations when he reintroduced the concept of Velayat-e Faqih.[27] Khomeini further explicated the concept of velayat by recognizing that within Ja'fari jurisprudence, velayat could be practiced in two different manners. First, velayat could be practiced through a conventional fiqh, but another type of jurisprudence, described as dynamic fiqh, could also be practiced. While conventional fiqh is considered more absolute or strict constructionist, dynamic fiqh allows exegetes to consider categories of time, era, and age as well as place, location, and venue.[28] Khomeini believed that time and space concerns were crucial to scriptural explication, and thus to rule making.[29] Through this justification, the shari'a was ultimately codified by a centralized state and thus partially removed from the discretion of jurists.

Codification has its roots in the 1906–1911 revolution, and Iran saw its laws systematically codified in the 1920s and 1930s during widespread centralization and rationalization processes and the creation of a Western-style judiciary (Banani 1961). Refinement of the codes continued throughout the twentieth century as the Pahlavi government sought to form a modern bureaucratic state (Arjomand 1988). After the 1979 revolution and the triumph of the 'ulama, however, the newly formed Islamic republic had to contend with the vestiges of seven decades of the Pahlavi government's modernization programs.[30] With the aim of making Iran a modern nation-state, emulating those in the West, Pahlavi father and son had instituted reforms that consisted of a formal rationalization of the laws through the adoption and promulgation of Belgian and French civil codes. Khomeini's aim in transforming the Pahlavi constitutional monarchy into the Islamic republic was to change the Pahlavi state into a theocracy and to Islamize its judiciary. What is of central importance for this book is the recodification of the newly "purified" Islamic laws after the revolution. For Khomeini, this meant specifically dealing with the rule of law and the legislative branch of the government.

When Khomeini returned to Iran in 1979, one of the first acts that he undertook as sovereign was to repeal legislation that he deemed to be incompatible with the true nature of Islam, including the Family Protection Act that gave women rights in marriage dissolution. Khomeini felt that this and other laws were incompatible with the true nature of Islam (Khomeini 1981). Arguing for a new form of state government, an Islamic government, Khomeini and his supporters also dissolved Iran's Majlis-e Melli for the reason that an Islamic state did not need a legislative body to make new laws, nor did it need Western-style codes to interpret them. In his work justifying this new state, Islamic government (*Hookoomat-e Islami*), he stated,

> At the beginning of the constitutional movement, when people wanted to write laws and draw up a constitution, a copy of the Belgian legal codes was borrowed from the Belgian embassy and a handful of individuals . . . used it as a basis for the constitution they then wrote, supplementing its deficiencies with borrowings from the French and British legal codes. True, they added some of the ordinances of Islam in order to deceive the people, but the basis of the laws that were now thrust upon the people was alien and borrowed. . . .What connection do all the various articles of the Constitution, as well as the body of Supplementary Law concerning the monarchy, the succession, and so forth, have with Islam! They are all opposed to Islam; they violate the system of government and the laws of Islam. Islam proclaims monarchy and hereditary succession wrong. (1981: 31)

What was needed, according to Khomeini, were principles elaborated from the texts of the Qur'an and hadiths of Islam: "The Glorious Qur'an and the Sunna contain all the laws and ordinances man needs in order to achieve happiness and the perfection of his state" (1981: 44). In Khomeini's vision of Islamic government, the legislative authority is derived only from God:

> The fundamental difference between Islamic government, on the one hand, and constitutional monarchies and republics, on the other, is this: whereas the representatives of the people or the monarch in such regimes engage in legislation, in Islam the legislative power and competence to establish laws belongs exclusively to God Almighty. The Sacred Legislator of Islam is the sole legislative power. No one has the right to legislate and no law may be executed except the law of the Divine Legislator. (1981: 55)

When the provisional government of the new Islamic republic attempted to purify the laws by repealing legislation and the legal codes, however, confusion over how to adjudicate the laws of God broke out and caused such an outcry that over time some laws were reauthenticated by the governing bodies of the Islamic republic and codified.[31] With codification of Islamic laws by the Ottomans, Zubaida notes, "The object was to preserve an Islamic or a national authenticity in law, but to cast it in a 'modern,' that is, European form." Codification "denudes the shari'a of all its institutional religious garb, it is 'dis-embedded' and de-ritualized" (Zubaida 2005: 133). More important, "codified law is the law of the state, and the judge is a functionary of the state who has to arrive at a judgment from the codes and procedures determined by it rather than by autonomous judgment through reference to sacred sources and the principle derived from them" (134). The same can be said of the recodification that occurred in postrevolutionary Iran. The codified form of the laws is significant in that it disrupted the historical power of Islamic judges to use a certain level of discretion in assessing the cases before them. Legislative authority, too, was reinstated to an extent, though in a much limited form. For Khomeini, the legislative body is one of the three branches of government, but was to act as a simple planning body (1981: 55–56).

Thus the blended legal system grew through struggles to determine how to put into operation this unique system consisting of Islamic principles and republican institutions and procedures. Not all of the Shi'i 'ulama agreed with Khomeini's thesis on Islamic governance. Some did agree that a final authority on Islamic guidelines should lead the nation, but for others, the features of governance expressed in the republican model, with Islamic laws rationalized in code, were offensive to the essential values of Islam. Notably similar disagreement persisted in Iran's first constitutional revolution, but the thesis of Velayat-e Faqih was intended to address the concerns wrought in the previous era.[32]

This new form of state power was authorized by the people through a referendum passed by 98 percent of the polity in 1979, and it set the groundwork for new debates about the role of Islam in governance, especially with the question of the meaning of the term *velayat*, literally, guardian. At differing points, debates about the role of the guardian emerge: is it a supervisory position or rather advisory?

These contemporary debates are commonly discussed in the press. Public debates about the relationship between Islamic principles, law, and contemporary concerns, such as gender equality and human rights, reveal dynamism in exegesis and offer at least the possibility of achieving practical solutions to current issues. One interesting example from the early 1990s was the need for controlling population growth. Khomeini's own justifications for legitimizing legislation to allow for birth control were based on the interests of the Islamic state, not the Qur'an or the hadiths of the Prophet (Hoodfar 1994; Keddie 2000–01). These debates are interesting not only in that they illuminate the pragmatic possibilities within fiqh, but also for other reasons. First, implicit in the debates about current problems is the idea that shari'a, while perhaps providing a basis for finding solutions, is not, in practice, a limited canon and allows for new developments that are in the best interests of the people. Second, the debates are increasingly carried out by different groups of people, not necessarily only those trained in the specific methodologies of Shi'i explication.

A growth in publications by lay persons, not trained as scholars of Islamic jurisprudence but who consider issues such as the legal rights of women in the Islamic republic, and who contribute to the public debates about the role of women in Iran, evidences this point. One example that has been extensively written about is the monthly magazine *Zanan,* started by a prominent writer and journalist Shahla Sherkat.[33]

Among the women with whom I worked, articles from *Zanan* often figured into our conversations, on everything from teenage runaways to detailed coverage of the women elected to Iran's parliament. These articles guided their thinking on such issues. What was most prominent, however, was the awareness among the women I spoke with of the significance of women's status for the leaders of the Islamic republic. Given that a large portion of the shari'a guidelines deal with the relationships between individuals in familial matters, they also played a crucial role in demarcating women's roles in the Islamic republic. Since the personal status laws re-emerged through a centralized legal system that draws from civil law both in its material form, as in codes and procedures, new implications about women's legal status and rights also emerge.

Important in this context is the fact that any changes to the law occur within a civil legal framework. By referring to shari'a as "law," scholars already conflate a modern legal infrastructure with Shi'i principles but often fail to consider the implications of this hybrid legal formation, particularly with regard to the impact of civil rules of procedure and its relationship to subject making, which is a central concern of this book. Of course issues of implementation and enforcement still concern parties in these matters, but the significance of the interpretations of law is that they occur at the juncture of Islamic principles and the republican state and illustrate how some Iranian women articulate claims using rights-based discourses that are premised on the autonomous individual endowed with rights, a discourse that was considered to be redolent of the Western-inspired individualism.

With the systematic codification of the Islamic law, the weight of the authority of the judge is now compromised by the law's own transparency and accessibility by anyone who can read, for codification has also rendered the law in written form. Pocket-sized copies of legal codes covering areas of law anywhere from property to family law codes are readily available for mass consumption. They can be found in local bookstores and in universities, and they are even sold in the sidewalk bazaars. Weber's oft-quoted notion of "qadi-justice," marking the absence of judicial formalism, is now undone by the rationalization of Islamic law through its codification based on civil legal formalism. This legal formalism offers avenues for lay people to assert their rights in an *Islamico-civil legal framework*.

Greater social individuation accompanies bureaucratization (Adelkhah 2000; Fitzpatrick 1992). In Iran, the bringing together of Islamic principles with the republican state form to create a blended state and legal system has resulted in a rationalization of the religious domains of life as well. In this way, even areas of religious life that appear to be set apart from the rationalized politico-legal order also bring about greater individualization because of increased rationalization. For instance, the ritual that celebrates a girl's initiation into prayer at the age of nine (boys are initiated at fifteen) stresses her autonomy. The feast of duty or devotion, as it is called, is a public performance by girls. Dressed in white veils with crowns of flowers on their heads, they recite the prayer they learned in school. Afterwards, school officials present each girl with gifts, which include a copy of the Qur'an. Of these rituals, which are often televised, Adelkhah notes that individuation is "a mark of social recognition and the value accorded to the child, who is celebrated as a true individual . . . from the youngest age" (Adelkhah 2000: 120).

An increased social rationalization of the ritualized religious spaces led to recognition of women as autonomous subjects. As long as they were properly attired in hejab, women were invited and called upon to participate in most every segment of society, including public office. As a result, the hejab had become every bit a marker of the Islamic autonomous individual woman as it is the international symbol of Islamic piety and homo-geneity, and it started with the training of school girls.

Iranians' contemporary experiences emerge through a new legal and politico-historical moment as the Shi'i Islamic republican state comes into view. In the chapters that follow, I consider some of the effects of the state's rationalized form on the people themselves and show how women's claims to and debates about rights emerge partially from this new era.

CONCLUSION: STATE PLIANCY AND "NEW" SITES OF RIGHTS

> *Regime's Desperate Attempt to Maintain Power*: In a bid to combat flagging interest in daily prayers, Iranian clerics issued an historic decree allowing women to lead collective worship in school, the official IRNA (Iranian Republic News Agency) said. The religious decree, or fatwa, will allow women to lead prayers in girls' schools for the first time since the 1979 Islamic revolution. The education ministry said the measure was aimed at "encouraging school-children to participate." The move comes less than a month after Tehran's arts and culture depart-ment delivered what it called a "shocking" report to the city council which found almost 90 percent of young Iranian stu-dents do not pray daily. Its research also found that 75 percent of the Iranian population as a whole does not perform the daily prayers obligatory under Islam.
> —Agence France Presse, August 1, 2000

Is it an effort to save itself from waning credibility, increased scrutiny, and teeming dissatisfaction that government officials began to encourage wider participation in state-constructed, decreed, and conferred norms on suitable roles for its people? On my first return trip to Iran, Hoda and Narges laughed at my recounting of the article quoted above. Narges opined that before the revolution, she and her sisters went to the mosque to worship on their own accord. "We were more religious (*momen*) before the revolution. Now if we practice at all, we do it in our own homes." And Hoda added, "They can regulate our lives with law; they can even call it 'Islamic law,' but they cannot regulate our relationship to God. That's a separate matter altogether." When worship became too regulated by state actors, practicing one's faith came to be too closely associated with legitimizing the government, and it became a political act. It was then that Hoda and Narges started to separate the individual act of wor-ship with that of governance and sought a distinction.

The conduct of Iran's 'ulama and its government officials takes place in the context of an ideological power play that has emerged in earnest since the election of President Khatami in 1997. Encouragement of greater participation in one site should be considered in tandem with attempts by hard-line government factions to clamp down on meager social liberties afforded to some in the general public when Khatami came into office.[34] In what follows, I consider the conditions that permitted certain shifts (or state pliancy) at the time and inspired what newspapers describe as "openings." What processes contributed to the waning interest in Islam, as the above article indicates, and led to the government taking measures that diverge from a scrupulous application of the methodology of Islamic exegesis?

It is no coincidence that people were coming together in assorted meeting groups, newspapers, journals, Internet cafés, coffee shops, and even places of work to discuss government forces and their effects on the liberties of individuals in urban middle-class regions in Iran at this specific historical moment. While some state officials may have expected that greater daily engagements with Islamic values would push people to further integrate them into their daily lives, the consequences of these meetings produced some inadvertent results as well.[35]

By the latter half of President Khatami's first term in office, his constituents still had not seen the promised improvements that caused them to vote for him. After the student riots in July 1999, some of the president's constituents began to recognize the limits imposed on the republican state system through its Islamic branding, which until the recent manifest disagreements between the guardians of Islam and the republican reformers had not been quite so apparent. Thus it was, in the midst of the uncertainty of the republic's effectiveness and Islam's role in the twenty-year-old state, that power brokers on various sides of the debate saw fit to permit "women to lead prayers in girls' schools for the first time since the 1979 Islamic revolution."

Seeming openings such as women leading prayers and the relative relaxation of social restrictions that accompanied the resurgence of public gatherings are effects of the complex negotiations that social actors were undergoing at the time with heterogeneous and disordered state actors. The intended subjects of the Islamic republic's disciplining initiatives can also push back against state powers, assert their own power, and indeed collaborate with statist projects. Statist disciplinary power has allowed for significant productions of knowledge from nonstate actors. Within new productions of knowledge, statist discourses of rights are always present, even insofar as they are discourses against which nonstate actors, including women, shape their visions of rights.

Attempts by hard-line state factions to discipline subjects failed, on the one hand, as state forces were met with rebelling students and protestors, some of whom were calling for reform through institutional processes, such as the electorate. The electoral process, however, was not the only means through which resistance incarnated productive action.[36] A tide of newspaper articles, meetings held by intellectuals and religio-political scholars, as well as impromptu gatherings in homes, or even the sex-segregated beauty salons and health clubs, helped create the sites in which ideas could be shared and exchanged.

Women also were participating in dialogue and debate, challenging the statist promulgations of their status and roles in numerous arenas, such as newspapers and magazines, but also in other venues as diverse as nongovernmental organizations, scriptural reading groups, the courts, their places of work, and even government ministries. Thus women's discussions and debates about their rights take place in new kinds of hybrid spaces, which are neither bourgeois in character nor aptly understood in terms of the sharply divided public or private spaces. These "dialogical sites" arise as productive effects of the intersection of Islamic and republican principles. In the next chapter I follow the refashioning of one particular type of religious practice, women's Qur'anic meetings, at this very intersection.

CHAPTER THREE

Qur'anic Meetings: "Doing the Cultural Work"

NANAZ'S DREAM

Nanaz opened the meeting with a warm greeting and welcoming words. On a day when a number of new women appeared to be in attendance, she reflected on why she and a small group of friends decided to recommence the Qur'anic meetings. She began with a dream:

> I came upon a poor man reading the Qur'an. He was sitting on a large rock along a rushing stream. I remember that everything was green and fertile. I saw myself watching the man reading very rapidly. At once he looked up at me and cried out, "Are you deaf, dumb, and blind? Why are you waiting for someone else to read it?"

"We are getting together to heal," she said, "and to realize the answers to our problems through the Book." Holding up her own ragged copy, she added, "We want to be advised. Our aim is to improve our understanding of the Qur'an. We read because now we are deaf, dumb, and blind. By learning what the Qur'an is saying, we will permit refuge from the Qur'an to come. We had these meetings before the revolution as well, some of you might remember." As she spoke, she looked around the room to her companions. "But now, here, we must do the cultural work as well."

Throughout Tehran and other urban centers in Iran, women are gathering through Qur'anic meetings (*jaleseh-ye Qur'an*). The parameters of involvement and membership between different groups vary to be sure, but the central feature of each is to engage women in reading and discussing the Qur'an, on their own terms. The women generally have no scholarly background in Islamic theology, but by reading the Qur'an, asking questions, and familiarizing themselves with what Islam as a whole offers them, they are determining and defining how, why, and to what extent Islamic principles affect their rights and roles. The setting at the Qur'anic meetings suggests the interplay between many of the components of women's lives: civil and spiritual, family and individual. As such, the women's Qur'anic meeting is an indispensable component of the emerging sites that contribute to the forging of dialogue within Iran today. The hybrid character of this site, moreover, evidences the false dichotomy between public and private sites.

In what follows, I situate the new interpretive site of the meetings in a broader socio-historical context.[1] Second, I examine how the meetings become a domain for dialogue and debate. In doing so, I explore the melding of seemingly liberal values with scriptural lessons illustrating that what appears as an elision, what some term a reading of rights within Islam (An-Na'im 1995; Mernissi 1987), is more appropriately a commingling of ideas. And it is precisely at this juncture that new possibilities for agency emerge.[2]

Jaleseh: A Vital Site of Rights Production

Qur'anic meetings are not new phenomena, either among the well-to-do urbanized classes or in Iran generally. Indeed, women of this class held the very same kinds of meetings well before the 1979 revolution overthrew the monarchy and installed a theocratic government in its place. These meetings, referred to colloquially as *dowreh*, literally, circles, are an integral part of Iranian social life and have been for many years. The meetings in postrevolutionary Tehran, however, are undergoing changes, both their structure and in the ways in which their leaders and participants conceive of them. The changes are a result of a comprehensive social shift occurring in Iran through a particular kind of political mobilization, one that is effected by the Islamized republican processes. Thus, the shape and form of the Qur'anic meeting are a vivid manifestation of the broader national changes occurring within Iran, to which the meetings' host refers as "the cultural work."

One of the effects of the midcentury demographic shifts that resulted in the formation of large, urbanized cities such as Tehran was the dowreh. By the early 1970s, Tehran was brimming with such meeting groups in which men and women met together regularly to discuss issues of concern. These dowreh were, by and large, meetings held by groups of intellectuals and educated professionals to discuss such topics as Persian literature or poetry, Islamic philosophical thought, or mysticism. Dowreh might also have been held for social purposes as well as gambling. Though popularized by the educated classes and intellectual groups, dowreh were also prevalent in less affluent sections of the city, where a neighborhood akhund might have been leading a group (Mottahedeh 1985: 271). In spite of their urban popularity, Mottahedeh notes, dowreh were "truly Iranian organs of rumination and taste through which Iranians, and most particularly Tehranis, chewed over the vast variety of foods" (271–72). While dowreh were characterized by the social and intellectual pursuits of, for the most part, urban elites, another type of group, the assembly (*hay'at*), was also springing up around the city, mostly among urban migrants.

Migration to the nation's metropoles increased dramatically throughout the twentieth century. At its prerevolutionary height, between 1956 and 1976, migration occurred at such a high rate that the urban population almost tripled. These migrants, coming both from rural villages and from medium-sized towns, often found it difficult to settle, if not survive, in the cities' harsh environs. While migrants spanned from very wealthy landowners to landless peasants, the majority fell somewhere in between and often secured employment in factories or the service industry (Mottahedeh 1985: 349). As migrants settled into the outskirts of the old city, new neighborhoods began cropping up. Far from the centrally located mosque or bazaar, the newest residents of the cities found themselves unable to participate in many of the collective activities of their old lives and soon realized that they were equally hard-pressed to partake in the more esoteric and urbane dowreh. Increasingly, migrant neighborhoods began to find cause to gather based on their common interests. They referred to these gatherings as hay'at, which immediately brought to mind the assemblies of the bazaar that organized around political or business-related concerns. While the bazaar hay'at convened around trade-related issues, the neighborhood hay'at served different interests altogether, as membership was often based on common village or regional ties. But like the bazaar hay'at, the neighborhood hay'at had a strong religious character. At a neighborhood gathering of the hay'at, the designated leader, usually the wealthiest among them, convened the meeting with an invited member of the 'ulama, an akhund. The members of the hay'at would then read from the Qur'an while the akhund corrected their Arabic pronunciation. Where the members were illiterate, the akhunds themselves read from the Qur'an and provided explanations of the verses. The akhund then offered a sermon, and finally the participants posed questions to the akhund. Mottahedeh notes that the kinds of questions the members asked were overwhelmingly about ritual cleanliness, particularly in light of certain temptations that were new to the urban migrants, "the Pepsi-Colas and Brigitte Bardot films" (351). At the conclusion of the question-and-answer session, the participants engaged in the *rowzeh*, the ritual performance associated with the martyrdom of Hossein.[3] At the end, the leader of the hay'at paid the akhund a contribution and adjourned the meeting.

By the late 1960s, an additional feature was added to the meetings—a cassette recording of a sermon by a famous akhund. The cassette could either replace the live akhund or accompany his sermon. Also by that time, the hay'at meetings took on a more political tone, and akhunds became activists concerned with the government's treatment of the masses (Mottahedeh 1985: 355–56).

The hay'at groups were becoming sites in which political expression was increasingly enmeshed and located in religious activity, especially by the lower and lower-middle classes. The upper and upper-middle classes, however, held more humanistic literary or philosophical gatherings with less emphasis on either religious practice or political activism. Such static divisions between hay'at and dowreh, of course, were not always the case. Individuals moved across class categories and also blurred the seeming divisions between hay'at and dowreh. It was not uncommon for an individual to be a member of both a hay'at and a dowreh, inasmuch as the groups met different needs.

The philosophical or literary gatherings of the dowreh frequently included both men and women. But hay'at meetings, particularly because of their religious character, were often gender specific. Women, of course, also had meeting groups in which they participated in religious rituals and organized around political concerns. Fariba Adelkhah (2000: 109) has referred to the "pious gatherings" of men as hay'at and those of women as *jaleseh*. While the linguistic distinction may be imprecise, hay'at literally means assembly or council and jaleseh refers to meeting; the point is that women also held gatherings with aims similar to those of men's. Women's Qur'anic meetings were similar to men's religious gatherings but did not have the same political expressions. This is not to say, however, that women did not have political organizations. In fact, women's anjoman (political councils) have made significant contributions to the Iranian political scene since the first constitutional revolution of 1906–1911 (Afary 1996).

Women's Qur'anic meetings, or jaleseh, as I will refer to them, are quite different from the women's political councils. Jaleseh are loosely organized around the aim of reading the Qur'an and the promise of scriptural guidance. In the past, the aims of the meeting were similar to those of the hay'at, only with less emphasis by the invited akhund on political mobilization of the participants. In the women's meetings, the hostess would usually invite a male akhund, or a woman deemed to be an authority on religious texts, to lead the discussion. The female religious authority, for the purposes of the jaleseh, is referred to as the speaker (*sokhanran*). In most cases, the sokhanran has received special training at a religious seminary and often had close ties to the 'ulama. Such jaleseh are important components of "neighborhood religious sociability":

> The jaleseh are summoned by women of the neighborhood often taking turns, and are generally attended by people of the district. It is not taken for granted that one can pass through the open door into a meeting if one has not been notified in one way or another; the information is passed around in a relatively limited circle. The jaleseh more often than not give their blessing to previously established networks of relationships, but they are also places where people get acquainted; a woman moving into a district will come to fit in especially by

going to the jaleseh. The feminine character of these meetings strengthens their local roots, and it is revealing that the people attending them usually go to the meetings on foot. (Adelkhah 2000: 112)

Qur'anic meetings have informal and neighborly dimensions; they are places where newcomers become acquainted with the neighborhood. The meetings are also a part of the preexisting circuits in which people and information travel and have an effect of unifying certain characteristics of religion by the people themselves. One of the effects of the revolution was to routinize or bureaucratize religion from the top down, but that routinization has been diversified from below through meetings such as these.

Thus the meetings groups are an example of the fluidity between religious and political spaces. National issues do not pertain to a singular religious or political authority, and as they move throughout the city's localities, such issues are diffused and simultaneously infused with local concerns, class, gender, the urban landscape, and so on. Thus constant movements of national concerns manifest differently as they are played out on the various arenas of the nation's local settings. At the same time, however, as the state's Islamico-republican configuration has rearticulated the discourses through which national concerns are expressed, women's Qur'anic meetings, as we shall see, have similarly shifted in the ways they are being held.

TUESDAY JALESEH IN NORTHWEST TEHRAN

The speaker, an engineer by trade, sat upright and leaned forward with conviction. She brushed short brown hairs out of her face as she argued the merits of gender equality within Islam. Her authoritative tone alone evinced deep knowledge of the sacred texts. As she pointed to copies of her newly published book on the coffee table before her, she spoke of the internal logic of God's revelations to Mohammad. From this, she deduced the organicity of the revelations, arguing, thus, for a reading of the texts given the exigencies of life in the present, not some fourteen hundred years ago.

While this was only the second meeting for this group, whose host had, after a twenty-year hiatus, reconvened the meetings in her uptown home, many of the participants seemed to know one another and talked softly as the speaker conveyed her ideas. Some of the women nodded in agreement, while others, particularly several seated in the back of the room next to me, rolled their eyes and whispered their exasperation at the unquestioned insistence of religion in social and political life. For such women, it seemed, there existed a distinction between religious and social life.

I began attending the Qur'anic meetings through the invitation of my friend, Roxana, with whom I had been spending a lot of time. One summer day while at work, Roxana, who by now knew my research interests, suggested that I would benefit from attending the fortnightly meetings in which women discuss the Qur'an and any number of other matters of interest to them. When she invited me to go with her to a meeting organized by her uncle's wife, I jumped at the chance.

One Tuesday evening, not long after our conversation, I accompanied Roxana to a comfortable home in Gheytarieh, a middle-class neighborhood in northwest Tehran and one of the more recent additions to the city's sprawling urban landscape. We left her office together and drove through the busy central district of Tehran to the northwest corner of the city. In the haze of pollution and the bustling city traffic, we made it to the meeting in thirty minutes, mostly as a result of taking the back alleys that only a Tehrani native such as herself could know.

As we approached the front of the house, I saw that the gate was unlatched. A few steps further, I saw that the front door was welcomingly left open. We entered through the open door where the large living room and adjoining dining room of the one-floor house were encircled with sofas and chairs that had been pushed out from the center of the room. Women of various ages, vocations, social statuses, and levels of Muslim faith occupied every seat in the house, having made spaces for themselves on the floor as well. As the session had already begun, Roxana and I made our way to the back of the large room, to a French baroque-style loveseat of tawny satin. The room's color scheme, a beautiful beige and pink, ran through the furniture, the walls, and the three Persian carpets that filled the room and added an extra element of warmth to the greetings already offered by the seated guests. Along one wall, two large dining room tables filled with fruits and desserts offered sustenance during the three-hour-plus meeting.

Weaving between and around the meetings' participants, a young woman served tea in familiar tiny, hourglass-shaped glasses and tempted the women with plates of sweets. The women's ages easily spanned half a century. From preteen to elderly, women sat and either listened attentively to the speaker or whispered asides like a running commentary. I pulled out my notebook after removing my hejab, which consisted of a headscarf (*rusari*) and a long overcoat (*manteau*). Though no men were present, Roxana did not remove her headscarf, only her manteau, revealing a beige knit top and black stretch pants.

The atmosphere of the meeting was one of convicted interest accompanied by a hum of casual mingling, especially among the women toward the back of the room where I was seated. Some were taking notes, while others glanced through the book on women and Islam, which the speaker was now avidly promoting in her remarks. As she spoke, several women quietly conversed to form the buzz that resounded several notches below her voice. Thus was the carefree but concerned air of the meetings—a tone that in no small part was an element of the productive energy that filled the room.

New social spaces or sites result from historical conditions and represent the political use of knowledge. Understanding the presence of preexisting codes permits space to be both read and constructed. Attempting to engage a science of space, Lefèbvre (1991) calls for an understanding of the preexisting codes that regulate the construction of social spaces. The social relations of production (or capitalism) mediate this knowledge in the European context in which Lefèbvre's analysis is located. From the perspective of the Qur'anic meetings, Lefèbvre's work on the social production of space is useful in that he locates power relations within social productions and demonstrates the insistence of hegemonic control of the dominant classes over the less powerful. Applying Lefèbvre's analysis to the Islamic republic, I suggest that hegemonic control of resources, knowledge, and therefore power is not only in the hands of those who own the means of capitalist production, but also in the hands of those who own the means of socio-religious production—the 'ulama, the Council of Guardians, the Assembly of Experts, and so on. In attempting to wrest control of the resources of socio-religious production from the state and its patriarchal band of social producers, women use the Qur'anic meetings as a space of production.

Social space is further defined by class. For Marxists such as Lefèbvre, in the context of capitalist production it is and should be the working classes who organize against exploitation. In considering only the mode of economic production, the relevant mode of analysis is capitalism and thus class exploitation. At the Qur'anic meetings, the issues of concern to women, for instance, greater legal empowerment, are bound within the existing devices of the state's dominant mode of production. In the Islamic Republic of Iran, certain women are increasingly recognizing two dominant modes of social production: republicanism and Islam. Women are grappling not just with their own understandings of Islam, but also with procuring the promises of republicanism, as pledged in Iran's constitution.

Historian Ayesha Jalal (1991) wrote of the failure of upper-class women in Pakistan to aid, support, or join their more oppressed middle- and lower-class sisters as "the convenience of subservience." This commentary, although insightful in many ways, assumed that women's interests in the oppression they share are, first, felt the same way and, second, defeated, or at least organized against, similarly. For Lefèbvre, the concept of shared interests in similarly situated class exploitation yields the same sorts of protests, organizing, and so forth. But Jalal's work does not differentiate the subtle differences of gender discrimination among disparate classes of women.

As discussed earlier, my treatment of urban working- and middle-class women was intentional for the very reason that the effects of the revolution weighed in differently at different venues—be they urban versus rural, or middle versus lower classes. What I examine herein are the responses of a specifically located set of women who may not share everything but at least share common urban residences and range within Iran's middle classes, though along a broad trajectory. The shared experience of the kinds of pressures that women face in the sprawling city guides the meetings' intentions and participants' concerns. In these contexts, "networking" emerges as a strategy for hastening reform (Shaheed 1995: 78). Such groups constitute sites in which women strategize collectively in light of numerous societal constraints and offer ample opportunities for cooperation. Qur'anic meetings, in a renewed format, are forged through societal constraints and provide effective collaborative opportunities.

In interviews with hundreds of women from Tehran, the majority of whom classified themselves as middle class, I asked questions about their perceptions of their rights. Overwhelmingly, the women I spoke with defined the limits of their rights through the societal and familial *control* (same word in Persian) they faced every day, throughout the mundane tasks of daily life. Feeling controlled or under surveillance were the two most common contributors to their sense of feeling disempowered. Over and over, the women I interviewed expressed feelings of pressure resulting from having "a stranger approach you on the street and order you to fix your scarf," or "the obligation (*ejbar*) of having to wear the hejab; it is not the hejab itself that is oppressive, but that it was mandatory (*zarooree*)." That women defined their oppression in terms of the compulsory nature of the dress, not the dress itself, is significant. The significance of reconvening the Qur'anic meetings cannot be understood without recognizing the pressures of the habitus that women occupied in Tehran, which, undoubtedly, are different in a rural village.[4] Thus it was the shared pressures of life in postrevolutionary Iran that led Nanaz to again convene the meetings after some twenty years.

Women engage with their ideas about rights through interpretive arenas that afford them possibilities of agency amid a profoundly regulated habitus. For middle- and upper-middle-class women in Iran, that habitus, in part, is the tight control exerted over their bodies—by their families, by numerous state forces, and, in fact, by society at large. Statist control over women in Iran results from the central role that the trope of "women" occupied in the creation of a new, postrevolutionary moral order, one that is associated with a cleansing of society (Papanek 1994).[5] This habitus is controlled not only by persons other than the women themselves, but by the rigorous methodology for elucidating the rules for women's conduct within Islamic societies, which leaves most women out of the proverbial loop. But the new institutions emerging in the Islamic republic offer sources for putatively native and authentic means in which women participate in determining the parameters of the regulation of their bodies. This, I argue, allows some urban middle-class women to reach out, beyond what Jalal calls the "convenience of subservience," beyond even the reinvigoration of Islamic texts, or even the gender-neutral equality of republican idealism, to formulate a basis for their social and political empowerment at the juncture of Islam and republic.

. . .

At a break, Nanaz sat down to talk more about the jaleseh's objectives with a group of newcomers and skeptics. My first thought was to marvel at Nanaz's energy; after hours of moderating the meeting, she still had tremendous verve. She began by inviting the women to continue to attend the jaleseh, as their spirits would grow despite their doubts. She informed them that the jaleseh is intended for all women, of all age ranges and levels of commitment to Islam. "And, to be welcoming to all women," she added, "there are no rules about clothes or participation." Her desire was that women read the Qur'an together and discuss the meanings of its verses one by one. When a petite woman sitting next to her asked Nanaz to explain the primary intent of the jaleseh, she replied, "There are many purposes, all have to do with your own spiritual growth." Her aim, she stated, was to gather women together to read the Qur'an from start to finish, adding, "This is the duty of every Muslim." She continued:

> If we read it among ourselves, then we can see for ourselves the simplicity and the beauty of the Qur'an. When I decided to conduct the meetings, I spoke with a lot of women about their hopes and aims. From those discussions, I decided to invite speakers to the meetings in order to discuss daily life within our society as well. We have to read the Qur'an in light of the current social and cultural conditions of our lives. Some of us went to Qur'anic meetings before the revolution as well and it was very nice. The meetings are open to any woman who is interested in improving her spiritual life. There is no level of belief that we hold women to; Islam is for everyone.

When I asked Nanaz what she meant by spiritual life (*manaveeyat*), she took me literally and began to explain the inner sanctity (*aaramesh*) that a person has when she is in communication with God.

I want women to be in touch with God and to see that they do not have to be afraid. In this government, many people have become distant from God because they don't like the government, and the government associates itself with God. Many people have stopped reading the Qur'an. But if we read it ourselves, then we take for ourselves the meanings from the text directly; we don't have to take someone else's word for it. Many people are suspicious of the akhunds and do not agree with their readings of the Qur'an. According to the laws of interpretation, the community can read and reach an agreement on the sections of the Qur'an that are unclear. That is what we are doing at these meetings. Some of the verses (*aya*) are clear. We do not question their meanings. Others, though, are not clear. Those verses have to be read within a context. Some akhunds refer back to the time of the Prophet. Now, more open-minded individuals say that we have to consider the context of the day. Among us, I don't know if you noticed, but there is a female scholar on Islam. She helps guide our readings. She is open-minded.

Nanaz's purposeful reinvigoration of exegesis among ordinary women represents a new site where interpretive shifts in knowledge are occurring. In doing so, the women at the meetings engage in their own personalized ijtihad, as one woman conveyed it to me, by reappropriating a community space where they subvert the existing rational methodology for exegesis, and finding the basis for it within the very texts of Islam itself. Nanaz's explanation of the methodology for exegesis—"according to the laws of interpretation, community can read and reach an agreement on the sections of the Qur'an that are unclear"—breathes local agency into the process. Using Islamic principles to legitimize their work, the women at the meetings seek and find paths to individual agency, which lead to a discourse of empowerment and rights that is based on ideas that are expressed in terms like individual liberty, free will, and personal responsibility.

The Qur'anic meetings represent an arena in which women advance their knowledge and, thus, authority on issues that were once apparently out of their domain, issues that nonetheless were about them and bound them to an essential truth, according to their gendered social position. The meetings, then, become an empowering space in which women gain knowledge and authority through the very act of speaking out, a polyvocal exegesis through group discussion and debate.

The significance of women's empowerment through reclaiming issues that pertain to their lives directly should not be underestimated in a society where physical appearances are regulated down to the very fingernail. By saying that women are reclaiming their own issues, I do not wish to convey that men are the sole regulators of women's appearances and movements throughout society. My focus, instead, is on this select group of women who are engaging an intellectual space into which they have tapped, extrapolating from the blending of Islam and republican state institutions.

PURPOSEFUL PARTICIPATION AND EXPLORATION OF THE SELF

Over fifty women could be present at any one meeting, but there were at least twenty-five to thirty women who were regular attendees of the bi-weekly meetings. During discussions with about twenty-five of the women whom I encountered regularly, I asked their primary reasons for regularly attending the meetings. Their responses ranged from serious scholarly interests in Islam to the cynical "My sister dragged me here." Obviously many women offered more than one reason. The most common responses women gave to the question, "Why do you come to these meetings?" were inner sanctity (16); information (ettela'at) (9); spiritual life (6); and to talk with women about life's heartaches (dard e del mekonam) (4).

Qur'anic meetings represent one type of site in which women, by sharing their experiences, develop an authority over themselves in the face of more powerful social bodies. Women's personal status and sense of selfhood in Muslim societies and elsewhere are enmeshed in the complex of identity politics and discourses around the nation.[6] The trope of "woman" is often portrayed as a marker of a nation's identity and vision (Abu-Lughod 1998). An awareness of the "self" among the women depicted here, as elsewhere in Muslim societies, emerges through historical processes (Afkhami 1995).

At one meeting that coincided with an important date for the present government, I walked in as women were discussing how the revolution had transformed their sense of "self." Speaking in a voice that filled the room with emotion, Shahla was addressing the group. Her short red hair conveyed a business-like manner. She reminded her audience of "an age before the revolution," when she was a teen in Esfahan.[7] The words "Pahlavi" and "shah" were carefully avoided, even here, in a private home. Shahla spoke of her childhood naiveté, how she played up to men, dressed as she would back then, in "mini-skirts," sleeveless tops, and, now and then, a "chic chador," running around the streets with nothing to do but attract the gaze of a man. She referred to her childhood self as a mere object and related how society back then encouraged girls to dress "cheap" and to wear lots of makeup. She told her listeners that she was brainwashed until she came of age and began to understand what she was doing to herself, and what society, under the previous government, was doing to women, "making us 'gharbzadeh.'" Then, Shahla revealed, she began to read the Qur'an, on her own at first, but later under the tutelage of an aunt who saw the "direction I was headed." Slowly, she began to understand how valuable women are, and how, in order to be respected by others, one had to first respect oneself. That was when she began to wear the chador, she told the listeners. Little by little she found her own awakening in the chador, and she found that freedom for her meant being free from the constant gaze of lecherous men. "The chador," spoke this impeccably dressed and made-up woman, "provides the buffer we women need in order to be respected in the male-dominated society. I don't think I would ever have realized my worth as a woman if I continued on my way."

Testimonials such as this were common during the latter half of the meetings, when, after having spent an hour or two discussing a certain verse or chapter from the Qur'an, women shared their paths to personal growth in hopes of spurring further discussion and reflection. Other times, outside guests were invited to discuss important issues and events. Reactions to this story and others like it underscore the varied and complex sentiments women have toward the chador, the revolution, and their status, then and now—even among a comparable group of urban, middle-class women.

As Shahla's story was winding down, some women nodded in agreement; others sat silently, only listening, shading their thoughts from view. A woman in the back of the room, lounging in a chaise, rolled her thick eyelashes back and down again. She sat in a cream-colored, ankle-length dress, dyed-blonde hair piled high on her head. I learned later that she was Nanaz's sister-in-law, and the wife of another of Roxana's uncles. She leaned over to me and hardly whispered, "I don't believe in any of this stuff; I only came because Nanaz implored me. I have nothing against Islam. Islam is wonderful, but what these akhunds have done to Islam and this country—this is not Islam."

The insider-outsider viewpoint that my friend's aunt offered was a common sentiment among upper-class and upper-middle-class elites who separated religion from the state, and the state's version of Islam from their own. Clearly for some, the appeal of Islam as a path to spiritual growth was a worthy endeavor. For others, the meetings represented the reorienting of Islam to the spiritual realm from the sullied political sphere it has come to occupy (to them) since the revolution. Still, believing in Islam as the avenue for attaining spiritual comfort proved not to be as uncomplicated as it sounded in those first meetings.

One of the central aims of the meetings was to provide the forum for women to discuss these issues comfortably. While some remained silent, others, like the woman seated near me, whispered their indignation. A few women did speak up and address Shahla with comments that were characteristic of those who did not agree with the theocratic control of women's bodies and their movement. "While your decision to wear the chador was your own, this government has forced all women to dress a certain way. I also believe that girls should be taught to deflect the male gaze, but why can that not be accomplished with a simple code of modest dress?"

Here again, I noted the discourse of control versus liberty. The discomfort was not about the chador, per se, rather, the imposition of an affirmative obligation, the state's control over women's bodies justified by Islam. The woman who spoke believed in the basic principle of public modesty but disagreed with the regulation of it, or at least the manner in which it was regulated. Now, two women spoke at once, as sudden excitement filled the room as the chador issue was further interrogated. "The chador does not mean anyone who wears it is modest. Modesty on the inside is not the same as modesty on the outside."[8] Before this statement could be completed, another woman seated next to her exclaimed, "We have more prostitutes now than ever before, and the problem is that no one can tell the difference between a regular woman and a prostitute." Thus, the dress code, she suggested, actually hinders the intended public modesty.

The issue of the dress code, and the chador in particular, warrants greater analysis, reaching beyond the aims of the present work. What I wish to highlight, however, is that the issue of what women wear in Iran, or in other Muslim countries, for that matter, is much more complicated than women being oppressed or being told what to wear. In Shahla's case, for instance, she associates the donning of the hejab with a political assertion of nationalism, reacting against corrupt and overbearing Western impositions, as has been the case in many countries, such as Egypt, Pakistan, and Algeria. According to some state forces and others (some nationalists, for instance), the wearing of "foreign" attire, such as miniskirts, in public is representative of the impact of immoral Western projects that keep women oppressed and further symbolize the effects of Western influence and power over the people, that is, imperialism, if not outright colonialism.

For Shahla, public veiling was also the assertion of her personhood independent of the sexuality her society assigned to her. Thus, in the veil, Shahla found her "self." By buffering her body from the male gaze, she appropriated her social being in order, as she said, "to be respected in the male-dominated society." Just as important, however, some of the other women cited the right to be free of state dress regulations as assertions of individual personhood. The right to choose to dress however they want is, in their view, a personal matter beyond the right of the state forces to control. Said differently, such women see the state's regulation of their dress as an act that deprives them of their sense of self. And though they may not all disagree with the state's desire and efforts to regulate public modesty, many did see the regulation of their bodies as an illegitimate action by state regulators. In either case, Shahla's as well as the other women's, women discuss their bodies and the control over them as individual persons in possession of their selves.

The conversation above also reveals that opinions about the nature of dress are themselves political assertions, organic ways of viewing the world, and shifting, not only from woman to woman, but also from time to time. The women's responses to Shahla demonstrate the conflicted nature of the issue of dress, where for some the obligation is the most confining aspect and is viewed as a way to keep women from choosing how to dress. The issue from either perspective, however, is that of freedom to choose.[9] This discussion shows that some women equate freedom and liberty with the individual being granted a choice—in this case, to wear what she wants. For others, like Shahla, wearing a chador neutralizes her sexuality, allows her to assert herself independently, and affords her equal status among males in society. The discussion also illustrates the balance that state forces seek to strike between giving women equal status, as their constitutional rights afford, and Islamic standards of public modesty, of which women are the unquestionable bearers.

Later, when the women adjourned, a crowd had formed around Shahla, who was handing out business cards. Shahla, as it turned out, was a certified skin and hair care specialist, having even created her own natural line of cosmetics and creams, which she now pedaled unabashedly at this informal part of the meeting. After her condemnation of the social pressures on women and girls to comport themselves in sexually objectifying ways, her vocation would, at first glance, appear to conflict with her earlier statements. These actions, however, spoke more to the complicated nature of the issues surrounding female sexuality in Iran and the social administration of it through various disciplining mechanisms set in place by the central government after the revolution.[10] Shahla obviously found a need, not to mention a market, for the development and sale of beauty products for women, but she adhered to a rigid binary between public and private domains for the use of her products. Shahla viewed her business as a service to women who have entered into the marital union and have an interest, a duty in fact, according to the Qur'an, to make themselves attractive for their husbands. As one scholar of Islam present at the meetings explained, "Islam recognizes women's beauty and seeks to revere and preserve women's sexuality where other religions try to suppress it." Here she was referring to the idea that Islam does not proscribe sexual intercourse for pleasure.

During her talk, Shahla had conveyed her belief in the integrity that a woman finds when she covers her body; the redemptive value she saw in covering the female body from the uncontrollable gaze of the male. While not all the women agreed with her beliefs, this was a common story that they had either experienced, or at least thought about in their lives. The

stories of girls coming of age during the shah's government, or even after
the revolution, are common themes that women share and express as both
common experiences and underpinnings of identity. Shahla's experience
was a rite of passage, ritualized among women and girls, who, at nine
years of age, are taught in school to pray and to wear the chador.[11]
Whether before the revolution or after, the common themes remain: chador, women's sexuality, men's uncontrollable urges, and the decidedly
heterosexual and biologically determined nature of desire. After only a
few meetings, I began to see recurring themes in women's discussions,
whether they involved how to raise their children, find personal, spiritual
comfort (as in Shahla's example), or simply exist as good members of
society. In doing so, the discussions often turned to how women's roles
have emerged and transformed in recent years, as Iran, through the direction of reform-minded leaders, begins to redefine its place amid a society
increasingly in touch with the Western world.[12]

The Qur'anic meetings permit women to address these issues collectively. This process of exchange contributes to the women's agency in two
ways. First, in situating the discussion of the Qur'an, the women claim
authority over matters that pertain to their everyday lives. Second, the
exchange of knowledge affords women a substantial degree of support
for seeking material rewards and important life changes in various contexts. But how does the process of becoming a social agent actually work?
How does it come to be that by sitting in on the Qur'anic meetings,
women become agents in their lives outside of the meetings? In other
words, how do the meetings contribute to women becoming agents in
their day-to-day lives?

JALESEH, AGENCY, AND THE PRODUCTION OF KNOWLEDGE

The institutionalization and increased rationalization of the religious
sphere, Adelkhah argues, has brought about "the spread of the bureaucratic model in the fabric of society," leading further to the rise of a public
space for reflection and debate (2000: 113). In arenas like the Qur'anic
meetings, state forces not only turn a blind eye to dialogues on religion,
which its institutions try to regulate, but actually sanction them, allowing participants to mete out meanings and conceptions of their own, on
their own.[13]

"Why a Parable of a Gnat?":
The Building Blocks of Islamic Rights Talk

Roxana and I arrived just after the meeting had started. We quietly entered the open door of the home where the meetings were now regularly

held. Nodding greetings to the women standing in the doorway, we slipped into the back room to remove our overcoats and headscarves. Roxana stopped to chat with her eighteen-year-old cousin about the qualities of her most recent suitor, but I was interested in listening to the discussion that was already under way. The women were having a question-and-answer session about their responsibilities, not only to their families, but also to society at large. The question, "Why a parable of a gnat?" was raised by one of the women in response to a Qur'anic verse they had just read.

The women were considering the twenty-sixth verse from the second chapter of the Qur'an, The Cow.[14] This chapter is the longest and accounts for at least one-tenth of the whole book, containing teachings on the importance of one's belief in and responsibility toward God. The twenty-sixth verse, commonly known as the Parable of the Gnat, does not itself contain a parable but considers God's creation of seemingly insignificant beings and things. Nanaz, leading the discussion, enunciated clearly as she read the Qur'anic text in Persian:

> Behold, God does not disdain to propound a parable of a gnat, or of something [even] less than that. Now as for those who have attained to faith, they know that it is the truth from their Sustainer—whereas those who are bent on denying the truth say, "What could God mean by this parable?" (Holy Qur'an 2:26)[15]

Talking in turn, the women discussed the meaning of this verse. They agreed that God is the creator of all things, and that this verse and those following call for an unquestioned faith in God as the creator of all things. The verse and those that follow evince the belief in God as Creator.

> In this way does He cause many a one to go astray, just as He guides many a one aright: but none does He cause thereby to go astray save the iniquitous, who break their bond with God after it has been established [in their nature], and cut asunder what God has bidden to be joined, and spread corruption on earth: these it is that shall be the losers.
>
> How can you refuse to acknowledge God, seeing that you were lifeless and He gave you life, and that He will cause you to die and then bring you again to life, whereupon unto Him you will be brought back?
>
> He it is who has created for you all that is on earth, and has applied His design to the heavens and fashioned them into seven heavens, and He alone has full knowledge of everything. (2:27–29)

Ever the pedagogue, Nanaz asked the women to consider "why a parable of a gnat?"

"In addition to the belief in God's creation," a young observer noted, "we must realize our own small position in the world God has created. We must have humility."

Some simply nodded in agreement, others voiced their thoughts. A small-framed, pensive woman raised a hand and, without waiting to be called on, added, "The reason for comparison with a gnat is to have students reflect on differences between humans and other creatures of God."

The reflection on God as all-knowing tied to the comparison of the gnat brought to light a question of how the human being is different from God's other creatures. Two women sitting next to each other near the front of the room brought up the notion of reason in response to the question posed by Nanaz, "How are we, humans, different from God's other creatures?"

Soheila, sitting closest to Nanaz, spoke aloud. "This verse is about human reason. We are different from God's other creatures because we can reason." A woman who appeared to be in her midfifties, Soheila was among the attendees who seemed to be at all the meetings. She had a well-worn copy of the Qur'an sitting on her lap. Then, pushing her for elaboration, the woman sitting next to her, a friend who sometimes accompanied Soheila to the meetings, asked, "What is reason?"

"Reason is that which God gave to humans, not animals." After a few moments of contemplative murmuring, an answer came from one of the younger women. Maryam, another regular, was a schoolteacher. She was still dressed in her navy blue overcoat and *maghneh'eh*, which she had pulled down around her neck.[16] Having arrived too late for a chair, Maryam was sitting on the floor in the middle of the room. She rose to her knees. As she spoke, her voice filled the room, "Because of our ability to reason, we are different from God's other creatures. We can make decisions for ourselves. In this way, we are independent and unique."

"And God gave free will to humans." Nanaz reminded everyone.

"Yes," Maryam seemed intent on making a point. "We have free will that comes from our ability to reason. But the duties and obligations bestowed on us by God limit our free will."

Significantly the women were steering away from a common misperception (both in Iran and abroad) that Islam does not permit independent thinking or innovation. For Shi'i Muslims in Iran, the issue instead has become who is qualified to interpret the scriptures. Some believe that only akhunds who have achieved the highest level of religious authority, that of *marja-ye taqlid*, can offer valid interpretations. Increasingly, however, who has the authority to interpret is becoming a contested matter, both among the akhunds and among lay persons. The women in the Qur'anic meetings are engaging in their own personal "ijtihad," intent to apply their interpretations to contemporary questions in their lives.

Thus, one of the ways the present Qur'anic jaleseh are different from those of years past is in the manner of textual explication. As the textual reading of this session indicates, the women do not have a male akhund, or even a sokhanran, leading the analysis and discussion of the verse. While at times a female religious scholar was present and would answer questions when directly asked, she was not there to lead the group's reading of the text.

The second way in which the jaleseh was different from those of the past is that most women, if not all, brought their personal copies of the Qur'an with them. It might at first seem an insignificant point to mention that the copies of the Qur'an were quite different from one another in terms of both shape and layout. But from here, the jaleseh reflects two important shifts that are occurring. First, mass production of the Qur'an is an example of the institutionalization and rationalization of the religious sphere that has led to the greater accessibility of religion to the mass population. Increasingly, acquisition of God's message is not mediated by a select group of specially trained akhunds. Adelkhah (2000:108) also makes special note of the mass production of the Qur'an.

Second, women's personal copies of the Qur'an have the Persian language rendering of the original Arabic verses. In most of the women's copies, the pages of the Qur'an were printed on one side with the original Arabic and on the facing page with Persian. Thus, women could quite literally read the Qur'an on their own, unmediated by an akhund who is fluent in Arabic. Adelkhah recounts the prevalence of numerous editions and styles of the Qur'an:

> Numerous editions have appeared and there are differences among them; whereas previously there was some homogeneity in calligraphy, binding, format and Persian translation, a great diversity has taken over. With the help of real effort of exegesis, translations have succeeded each other, and are less literal than before. The believer has a choice of versions which may correspond to differing uses, ranging from the pocket Koran protected by a leather or plastic case with a zip fastener, to the high-value copy meant to adorn the home and impress everyone around. The Islamic Republic prides itself on putting the final touches to the world's biggest edition of the Koran, while micro-Korans are sold, with cases again, to serve as keyholders. (2000: 107)

Of course there is a difference between reading and explicating. Insofar as women can read the literal word of God, as the Qur'an is said to be, their use for the akhund is greatly diminished. As Nanaz carefully noted, in the past the women depended on explication by the akhund because of his ability to read Arabic. Now, however, inasmuch as the women have Persian versions of the Qur'an, they are empowered not only to read, but also to explicate the verses.

The women's substantive analysis of the verses, moreover, is important. Here, the women apply a notion of individualism to the question Nanaz posed, "Why a parable of a gnat?" She justifies her own project of renewing and altering the jaleseh of the past through this reading of the verses. That God requires human beings to take responsibility for themselves is exactly Nanaz's aim in these revived jaleseh.

Mohammad Asad's annotated explanation of the Qur'an also takes up a discussion of the bond that humans have with God. Asad notes that the bond pertains to

> Man's moral obligation to use his inborn gifts, intellectual as well as physical, in the way intended for them by God. The 'establishment' of this bond arises from the faculty of reason which, if put to proper use, would lead man to a realization of his own weakness and dependence on a causative power and, thus, to a gradual cognition of God's will with reference to his own behavior. (1980: 8)

Asad's use of the masculine subject to explain this verse is indicative of a male-centered reading of the Qur'an and does not suggest that the verse's meaning extends only to men. It is indeed significant that the women in the jaleseh use this verse as a point of reference for their own bond with God and underscore their particular human condition.

Asad further notes that this particular interpretation of a human's covenant with God arises from the fact that nowhere else in the passage, either in the verses before or after, is there a mention of "any specific 'covenant.'" Asad suggests that the lack of references explaining the "bond with God" indicates that the phrase "stands for something that is rooted in the human situation as such, and can, therefore, be perceived instinctively as well as through conscious experience" (1980: 8).

The women at the Qur'anic meetings capture this same familiarity with God. They examine this bond as a set of responsibilities bestowed on the individual. The lack of a gender-based dialogue on women's and men's roles, including rights and obligations, which many scholars point out as a normative base in Islam, is not even raised here by the women. It is thus significant that the women's notion of an individual's responsibilities is not based upon or defined by gendered social or familial roles that other interpreters or members of the 'ulama ascribe to the women. When discussing this passage, moreover, the women most frequently used the term "*ensan*," a gender-neutral term meaning a person or human. As the discussion moved on, Nanaz encouraged others to chime in:

"God is familiar and known," said Shahla.

A friend sitting next to her added, "God is the creator of all."

Nanaz clarified, "We all have some capabilities, but there are responsibilities that go with them."

And Shahla again added, "But God sent us different levels of intellect intentionally, so we also have different kinds of duties."

"Yes, that is right. God gave us all special talents, but how each of us uses them depends on the person."

"So each of us is responsible for our own situation," added Tahmineh, a doctor, sitting across the room. She was a longtime friend of Nanaz's and had attended the meetings held before the revolution.

The discussion pressed on. A few women took issue with a notion of uncontrolled individualism. They underscored the need for compassion in a world where people are not always in control of the events that affect their lives:

"But many of the horrible things that happen, happen to the good people," my friend Roxana reminded the group.

"We must be careful not to hurt others, and this is our own responsibility. That's true, and what you give will be returned to you," Nanaz stated.

An elderly woman in a long, flowing skirt spoke up, "I think that these bad things that happen are tests."

After some silence, a newcomer to the group asked, "When the child is born, it is innocent, why does it need to be tested?"

Interestingly, even in a discussion about hardship, the women again moved back to the issue of the individual and the responsibility that comes with their special bond with God. This conversation reveals a blending of fate and individual responsibility, suggesting the correlation between creation and individuals' roles or capacities within it.[17] There is a seemingly heavy burden for individuals to take responsibility for their lives and to be sure not to cause harm to others. Yet there is also a fatalistic view or mention of the bad things that happen to people, in an effort to explain the age-old and culturally boundless question of why bad things happen to innocents.

The discussion the women had around the verse not only affirmed individual thinking but also called for a duty to think and thus act responsibly because they are human beings with the ability to reason. Human beings, the women determined, are different from God's other creatures because they have the ability to reason. This ability is what gives humans individuality and autonomy. The women took the Parable of the Gnat as their starting point for discussing the place of humankind in God's creation. Their conversation began with an examination of the thinking and reasoning sensibilities that God gave only to humans, then shifted to free will, with individual responsibility placing limits on that free will. While this discussion did not focus on the gendered concerns about rights, it is significant in that the women take the Qur'an to be their springboard to personal responsibility and action. Just how that action might take shape is the subject of inquiry in the next section of this chapter.

Notably, the women emerged from the recitation of these Qur'anic verses to discuss their individual responsibility. Ultimately, the capability of being accountable is what distinguished humans from other creatures. The women also highlighted how individuals are endowed with free will, but they qualified that freedom with responsibility by noting that there is an affirmative duty placed upon individuals to use their gifts responsibly. The discussion about free will and rational choice resonates with Western or Lockean liberalism, but the women were not attempting to uncover an Islamic parallel for liberalism nor seeking authentic Islamic or Iranian roots of liberalism. Instead, what is significant in these conversations is the point that faith in Islam does not preempt or prohibit a notion of individual freedom or responsibility but actually necessitates it.[18]

Such arguments cannot but speak to the discussions on individualism as presented by one of the new Iranian state's most highly regarded Islamist scholars, Ayatollah Morteza Mutahhari. Mutahhari was one of the primary architects of Shi'i modern thinking on the family, referenced earlier in this work.[19] At the Qur'anic meetings, then, women are actually subverting Mutahhari's, and in large measure the state's, biological determinism by reflecting on individuality without considering gender. I am not arguing that there is an expression of a Western liberal notion of individual responsibility and free will; the possibilities within these readings of the Qur'an are not the call for or the sanctioning of seemingly foreign concepts. The reading of the Qur'an in this way is an authentication of the women's aims for self-preservation in the context of postrevolutionary, postimperialized Iran.

On some level it must be conceded that some of the women are thinking about their rights within the parameters of postrevolutionary Iran and the newly established Islamic state institutions. At the same time, however, women are not simply employing the Qur'an as a tool of strategic convenience. Many, particularly those in attendance at the meetings—though certainly not all—considered themselves true believers in the Islamic faith. Individual women's relationships to Islam, like any other faith, are varied, multifaceted, and complex. Their readings of the texts in the way that I have described above have empowering effects on the women and in some instances fly in the face of state-instituted practices and interpretations of Islam.

In this way, bringing the Qur'an into dialogue with women's status in the Islamic republic not only gave women agency, as I discussed, but also allowed women to assert themselves as credible social and political actors with knowledge of Islamic texts, practices, and traditions. Thereby they asserted a form of agency that was sanctioned.

This is a crucial step given the lack of credibility afforded to women of this same demographic group when they called for their rights in March 1979. At that time, without having authenticated their calls for certain political and social freedoms within an Islamic standpoint, the revolutionary forces in the country were able to discredit the women as Western puppets. Now, women who study these texts have certain grounding in Islam, but this is not to simply state that women are reading their rights within Islam. Islam is in fact the place of cultural, social, or political authentication for those who position themselves as agents within the state's framework of discourses on rights, for various and divergent reasons, to be sure.[20] The way these rights are enacted or processed, however, is more than Islam at work, as the next chapters will illustrate.

Thus, beginning from the source, that is, the Qur'an, women at the meetings derive their own understanding of rights using the same initial reference point as male theological scholars and various actors of the state. While the Qur'anic meetings provide a place for women to discuss their beliefs, Islam, and their status as women, the discussions lend themselves to approaches to women's rights that are not wholly bound within Islam, or even the state's discourses on Islam, which are themselves multiple and competing. Often women's discussions reveal a medley of ideologies and a commingling thereof. There is, moreover, little concern with finding justification within Islam for every practice or belief. Islamic texts were the source through which women sought access to a program of rights but not the only model for those rights. The women at these meetings certainly accessed the Qur'an as their inaugural source, but they did not seek to find every element therein. Instead, the Qur'anic foundation of human responsibility led them to seek out a program of rights that made sense given their everyday concerns. It was in this way that the practice of engaging their rights, legal or otherwise, came to be a necessary component of their faith. Once the women could establish and agree upon this idea, the meeting could then be opened to a wider set of aims and issues. Other women, moreover, whose backgrounds were not religious, could then be brought within the sway of the meetings. The result of bringing together women with differing ideas about Islam actually made the Qur'anic meetings more inclusive, and the founders could claim that they were able to gain the interest and attention of women formerly indifferent to Islam.

In this section, I have highlighted how women in the Qur'anic meetings use Islam as a source from which to render individual responsibility and social accountability. This is significant because this analysis allows the women to invoke concepts of rights that are derived from the notion of the sovereign individual, such as international human rights, where human actors are individuals in society, self-possessed and endowed with free will. That Islamic texts bestow an ideology of personal responsibility permits other forms of knowledge, which also have personal responsibility at their core, to enter into the language and discourse of rights for women in Iran. This is not to say that women are finding such concepts within Islam; rather, Islam can embrace and inform other forms of knowledge. In the next section, I examine another component of the Qur'anic meetings as an episode of the convergence of knowledge in the enactment of women's rights discourses.

"Rights Talk" as a Vessel for God

As I scanned the room, I observed the faces of the fifty or so women present that day but could not discern the new face that would be Nahid Hajinouri. Impatiently, I listened to a discussion about scheduling while sipping tea from the tiny glass. Finally, the last issue resolved, Nanaz began the next segment with a reminder that reading the Qur'an was only one of the reasons for establishing the Qur'anic meetings. There was another purpose: to discuss issues of present-day import to women, and to invite speakers who could advise women on matters on which they wished to be more informed. The implicit suggestion was that in these meetings, the additional information would serve as further guidance in the women's commitment to Islam and did not run counter to Islamic tenets and beliefs. Like many of the women present that day, I was especially interested to hear Hajinouri speak. We had patiently listened to the conversation about the Qur'an, but many in attendance, like me, were eager to hear what this nationally renowned attorney had to tell them, and an excited buzz infused the meeting.

Finally, Nanaz welcomed the beaming Hajinouri and led her to a seat in the center of the room so that all could see her and seemingly be touched by her grace. When I glanced at the woman Nanaz was addressing, I was surprised to see a woman in a full chador, perfectly wrapped and expertly situated. What struck me was Hajinouri's demeanor. Often, women in chadors appear to be graceful and fluid, a trait frequently mischaracterized due to the fluidity of the draping cloth. But Hajinouri's chador did not wear her; her poise and grace defined her dress. Her flawlessly donned chador revealed only a radiant ivory face. Hajinouri arose and walked to the small pink sofa in the middle of the room. Nanaz then asked her to give a bit of information about herself for the women in the room.

She kept her smile as she began in a strong yet melodic voice, "I am not all that they say. I am just a vessel for God." Hers was a household name in Tehran. A former parliamentarian, Hajinouri had started a well-known nongovernmental organization on behalf of women and the family soon after the revolution. She was also a co-author of several important pieces of legislation pertaining to women's rights. In addition, Hajinouri was a practicing family law attorney with her own private office in northern Tehran. Hajinouri would become a frequent guest at the meetings and would eventually speak on legal issues as they pertained to marriage, divorce, maintenance during marriage, and one of her own legislative initiatives, postdivorce maintenance. By referring to herself as "a vessel for God," Hajinouri was presumably referring to her work as an advocate on behalf of women's rights. Her political and legal achievements notwithstanding, Hajinouri maintained a rigorous bodily connection to God through her appearance and comportment at these meetings as well as in other settings.

Hajinouri's assertion that she was but a "vessel of God" raises the issue of her subjection—not, as Foucault might find, by the state's disciplinary machinery, but by her own voluntary submission to God's will. In her capacity as a Muslim, or one who submits, Hajinouri in one sense overrides the power of the state to discipline her and seeks a higher state of willing obedience (see Mahmood 2001). In the legal process, Hajinouri locates the productive aspects of state power that enable her to achieve this higher state of submission, which is the goal of Muslim piety.

Reciting section 1133 of the civil code, Hajinouri continued, "A man has a right to repudiate his wife without cause." This section of the code allows men to unilaterally divorce their wives. Hajinouri went on, "Section 1133 of Iran's Civil Family Law Code has caused a great deal of trouble for Iranian women in matters of divorce. Men have a right to end a marriage and they may do so without cause. Women, however, do not have the freedom to initiate a divorce. But that does not mean that they are without legal recourse to address their marital difficulties. I am here to talk with you about finding the legal avenues to address your marital troubles."

She spoke confidently and earnestly, "A woman is mother of the family. If a father leaves or dies, the family is still in its place; but when a mother dies, the family is broken." She then read from a single sheet of paper that contained a poem she had written in praise of women. When it was over, Hajinouri paused, looked about the room, and after a few moments, began to speak again, all the while her watery green eyes making direct contact with every single woman there. She described her long list of achievements, the women's organization, the parliament, the private law practice, as well as her educational background, which included a master's degree in law from the prestigious University of Tehran. She had already prepared a specific topic for the day, she told us, and would talk about the bride's portion (*mahrieh* or *mahr*)[21] and maintenance during marriage (*nafagheh*).

Maintenance is currently one of the most litigated issues between couples, while the amount of the bride's portion is one of the most important determinations regarding a marriage contract.[22] For not only is this amount of money the guarantor of a woman's economic security, but in postrevolutionary Iran, mahr has come to provide a crucial bargaining chip in the event that a woman desires a divorce but cannot meet any of the legal grounds.[23]

Hajinouri then began:

> If a woman in her husband's house has a fear of life or honor, she can still obtain housing and maintenance costs. That is, if a husband is suspicious, and his wife's honor is called into question, that is, if, when she does certain things, he is good, but if not, he is bad, she can go to court and, with proof, she can obtain an order from the court to compel her husband to provide separate housing for her and pay her maintenance as well.

Hajinouri then made her point: "Women do not know their rights; that is why they do not get their rights." As I watched her perform, Hajinouri seemed the very embodiment of the Islamic republic. Here she was in her Islamic persona, covered in a chador from head to toe, every bit fulfilling her gendered role, and yet her discussion about individual will and responsibility was strikingly liberal. In instructing the women to "get their rights" by seeking judicial remedies, Hajinouri was calling on them to grab hold of their individuality, to take responsibility for themselves, and thus to perceive of themselves as beings independent of their roles in relation to their husbands, children, families, and so on. She went on, "Rights are not something that will be given to anyone, we women have to learn to go after our rights."

The women in the room listened intently, and some took notes as Hajinouri advised them on negotiating the mahr before marriage and the laws that are in place to help women obtain it. Hajinouri advised women: "Go into the marriage with open eyes and obtain as much information about your potential spouses as possible. Do not use your mahr as leverage during your marriage. One way to do that is to obtain your mahr right away, as soon as you are married. Then it will not hang over your husband's head throughout the marriage."

What Hajinouri was suggesting was rather novel. On the one hand, women do not usually obtain their mahr, and here she was suggesting that women obtain it at the onset of the union. On the other hand, as women do not have the legal standing to initiate divorce, obtaining the mahr early on would do away with a crucial bargaining chip that women have in divorce.

She further advised mothers, both of sons and of daughters, not to forge a marriage contract based on an unusually high mahr, one that the husband could not possibly pay. Many families try to obtain a high mahr in order to obtain some guarantee of the economic well-being of their daughters, regardless of the future of the marriage. In spite of this, mahr is rarely paid out. Obtaining the mahr is often resorted to only as a negotiating tool in the event that a wife wants to dissolve the marriage but has no legal grounds or proof thereof. In such a case, a wife may attempt to execute her mahr and then offer to forfeit it in return for her husband granting her the divorce.

Throughout the room, women were captivated with both Hajinouri and the discussion. She credited Islam with giving women several different avenues to obtain redress for their grievances. But she went even further: she seemed to be telling the women that they needed to take more responsibility for learning what those avenues are and how to access them in order to obtain the desired results in their marital disputes. Next, Hajinouri delved into a technical discussion about the two different ways to execute mahr. Here, I observed that the audience was avidly taking notes:

> One is to go to the civil registry. When a woman does this, however, the man must have the ability to pay, as the civil registry will not garnish his wages or put a lien on his property if he only has one house or car. That is, the government will not garnish unless it is something that can be a security already. The man doesn't go to jail. When the plaintiff receives payment, the civil registry will automatically deduct 5 percent from the reward. So this is helpful in cases where a woman cannot afford the filing fees.
>
> The second way to execute the mahr is to file a court complaint. This route requires putting up a percentage of the mahr. So it is better for women who already have some money. Here, if the man does not pay, he will be arrested and jailed, as long as the claim is not frivolous. The court will give the order to have him arrested and jailed if he does not pay within a specified time frame, about one week. If he does not pay, the police will go get him and send him to jail. If he really has no money, then from jail he would file a petition to say that he cannot pay. If he works for the government, however, he cannot say that he does not have the money to pay. In that case, the court would most likely garnish his wages. They will take no less than one-fourth of his monthly income if he has other people to support as well, such as children. But, if he agrees to a divorce, and there are no children, a wife can get one third of his monthly wages. At court, if you have no money to pay the filing fees, sometimes you can make a deal that when you do get your money, then you will pay the court.

The degree of legal and procedural detail that Hajinouri went into, given the Qur'anic context of the meeting, was striking. Her goal in this presentation and others that were to follow seemed very clear: she wanted to help women see that they were actors or agents and as a result had a legal personhood or identity that enabled them to take some control in the marital dilemmas that they faced. By presenting the issues in sobering legal detail, she made the issues appear to be not only a matter of process, but indeed, principle. Her statements, delivered in precedural legal detail, suggested something new emerging from the effects of Islamization, a transparent legal system that nonexpert women with legitimate marital concerns could access. By clarifying and attending to legal procedures, Hajinouri appealed to the possibility of a seemingly neutral legal arena in which women could seek redress before impartial and disinterested adjudicators.

She continued to advise women on proper behavior during the marriage as well. She told them that when they marry, they need to realize that the way they raise their sons will have a bearing on how they treat their wives. Hajinouri presented the following scenario and asked if it sounded familiar:

> When your daughter comes home and your son is sitting in front of the television, you mothers ask your daughters to go and fetch her brother a snack on her way to kitchen, and to grab his jacket on her way up to her bedroom.
>
> Now, when your son comes home, you mothers ask your daughters to get up from the television to get her brother a snack, as he is tired from having been out all day. Then, when she dutifully gets up, you ask her to hang up the jacket that he has thrown on the ground in his haste to watch his favorite television show.

The women in the room laughed nervously, knowingly, assenting to having inadvertently reproduced the double standards to which they were themselves so opposed. Hajinouri emphasized the need for mothers, who spend much more time with the children than their husbands do, to treat boys and girls equally. The discussion was at once amusing and eye-opening to the women. Although she never ventured beyond the example of a heterosexual male-female couple with gender-assured children, the issues that Hajinouri was speaking about were not just legal rights. While legal rights are an important arena of knowledge that Hajinouri was there to help the women attain, she was also trying to inform the women of how their own behaviors and attitudes shaped those of their children. In this way, Hajinouri's message was also subverting Ayatollah Mutahhari's gender determinism. She was not only telling the women about their rights but was also telling them to think about their roles in shaping their children's lives. If there was an overall message in her presentation that day, it consisted of Hajinouri advising the women to take more control over their lives. She guided them on how to do so by offering information and providing some of the necessary means by showing the legal avenues that existed, that is, through rights-based discourses, or rights talk.

Islam's fundamental concern with justice is increasingly set in the context of legal norms, and the primacy of law is sometimes viewed as a "touchstone" in Muslim contexts (Bulliet 1996: 183). Indeed, law is and has been a primary text and reference point for scholars of Islam for some time, but Bulliet is critical of the textual approach to the study of law in Muslim societies because such an approach fails to appreciate the historical development of law as an important gauge in better understanding Muslim societies. As in other societies, legal scripture does not function as normative, and social practices are extremely diverse. A look at the renewed practices among women in the Qur'anic meetings offers a sense of how the development of newly sanctioned, rationalized legal processes and the increased use of rights talk operate as touchstones of legitimacy in Iran.

Though in the Iranian context historical and popular connections to an increased legal culture are the result of very different processes, the effects of increased legality to attain constitutional promises are now being advanced by people like Hajinouri, who have legal training in the universities as opposed to Islamic seminaries. Hajinouri's position as the exemplary Islamic woman, strategic or otherwise, permits a subjectivity that renders her more suited to make legalistic claims. Her assured earnestness in urging women to fight for their rights by filing legal claims and going to the courts, however, brings into question just what it means to be the feminine model of the Islamic faith.

As elsewhere, in Iran, marginalized groups like women are using promises deemed even by conservative akhunds to be an Islamic version of republican governance, to address their grievances. Thus, the effects of republicanization since 1979 are allowing more and more for legality to be the touchstone of legitimacy, particularly where the founding texts of the state are deemed to be the very texts of an Islamic version of the republic.[24] In Iran, modernity is expressed, in part, through the formation of an Islam-sanctioned republic that allows for increased recourse to the language of liberty, equality, and justice under the law. In this way, Iranians, including disempowered groups such as women, have greater recourse or reference to rights that also arise from constitutional guarantees. Hence Hajinouri's quip, "The rights are there, women just don't know how to use them."

Of course this was hardly the experience of the women in the room. Those with little or no experience using the courts and other legal procedures were dubious and spoke out incredulously against the sanitized manner in which the famed attorney seemed to regard the process.

"But Madam, you are in a different position from us. With your legal training, the judges will listen to you. We are nothing. They do not respect us. They just tell us to go home to our husbands and children and to be good wives and mothers."

Though she did not answer this concern head on, Hajinouri was unrelenting in her support of the legal process, so much so that there seemed to be an even greater agenda in her painstaking enumeration of the procedures for executing mahr. In a meeting with Hajinouri some weeks later in her office, I asked her about her regard for the law particularly given the other women's disbelief that they could obtain desired results, or even just an impartial audience with a judge.

> On some level I agree with these women. But that does not mean that we cannot change the attitudes by telling the judges what the laws allow, and sometimes even require. A couple of years ago, no husband would be jailed for refusing to pay a mahr once it was executed. But now, men are being arrested and jailed. This is due to the perseverance of the women. It was never realistic for a woman to walk away from a marriage and yet obtain her mahr, and though it is still uncommon, it is starting to happen more than before. This Islamic republic is only twenty years old. How long did it take for women in the United States to gain the right to vote?

Hajinouri's interest clearly remained attached to the legal process of a claim. Though there were questionable judges and even unfair laws, the procedural mechanisms provided a security for those who sought to access them. Seeking the procedural remedy is the approach that Hajinouri herself took, and one that she appeared to advocate in her other discussions at the Qur'anic meetings.

When the formal discussion was over, the women broke for refreshments. They gathered into small groups, discussing what Hajinouri had said. Some of the women were talking about how odd it was that she suggested that they try to get their mahr right away. Some joked and said that their husbands would sooner divorce them. Others said that it was just not practicable—it would get the marriage off to a very bad start. One woman said to me, "If I ask for my mahr, my husband will think that I am not in the marriage for the duration." Another told me that the mahr is supposed to serve as a security, "in case your husband wants to divorce you or take a second wife, then what will I do, if I have already taken this away."

Attorneys and other women's rights advocates whom I interviewed often said to me, "Women here just don't know their rights." They were referring to the legal remedies available to women under the state system. In the informal discussions after Hajinouri's talk, women voiced their concerns about the nonlegal arenas of their lives that mediate and mitigate their willingness to follow through on the legal remedies available to them. As I talked with women of various socioeconomic paths, I learned that indeed their concerns grew from the material resources, but also familial matters, concerns with tradition and custom, and education.

A young woman with whom I developed a friendship during the course of attending the jaleseh provided an interesting illustration of how the jaleseh, by supplying religious as well as legal instruction, might serve the women outside the walls of the jaleseh. Knowledge of the Qur'an gave Layla the theological background as well as a certain confidence she needed to protest her arrest for wearing makeup in public two years earlier. After the jaleseh one evening, Layla invited me for tea at her nearby home. As we walked swiftly through the neighborhood, Layla spoke earnestly of her religious convictions. She insisted that just because she wears jeans or likes to line her eyes or lips does not mean that she is not honorable (*mohtarram*). "And," she added, "there is nothing in the Book that says so." But more important, Layla, who is also a law student, felt that the state laws were unfair because there was no transparency in the system. "Once you get to court, you see that they have monetary fines for everything. Mascara is a certain amount, lipstick another, and so on. When I went before the judge, I told them that nowhere in the civil codes does it state these penalties, and so they cannot fine us as such. Because he saw that I was informed, the judge reduced the fine to a third of the original amount."

Layla's personal studies push her to challenge the way Islam is advanced by state forces. She does not hesitate, even in court, to question their interpretations in comparison to those of her own. For Layla, the Islamic republic is not the keeper of the contents of Islam, and Layla is more than aware of the political nature of the state's multiple voices. For her, however, the terms of her allegiance to the state and Islam do not rest on the divergent explanations of Islam alone. Indeed, through her account of the court experience, Layla conveyed an expectation in the civil system of process that the state institutions and agents should afford her, and for which she apparently was willing to fight.

Layla's argument before the judge reinforced her deep understanding of Islam, but her argument was not solely bent on taking religious doctrine to task or finding rights within Islam. She was adamant about obtaining the due process afforded her in the civil system of rights as well. And while the specific claims of rights may be grounded in justifications from the Qur'an, Layla's argument that the system needs to have greater transparency pointed to a deeper understanding of the civil legal system and its inner workings.

Layla, moreover, is one among a massive group of young people who knows, because of her upbringing and education, that this Islamico-republican system affords a space for her to assert her rights. Layla, who did not grow up during the shah's time but came of age after the revolution, is familiar with the claims, just after the revolution, that women who wore makeup were "westoxicated," or Western dolls. Her mother had told her about the early years of the Islamic republic and explained to Layla that women who laid claim to their *rights* were branded whores or puppets of the "West," but Layla, years later, could unabashedly reject those claims out of hand. When I asked her what she thought of those arguments or those people who thought that women who demanded their rights were brainwashed by the "West," she replied impatiently, "I have never been to the 'West,' none of my relatives lives there. Wearing lipstick is not a 'Western' concept. Even in the Qur'an it says the women should adorn themselves for their husbands." She not only rejected the claims that her beliefs were born of Western influence but also refused to place her claims to a certain belief in rights against so-called Western notions of rights, dismissing, then, the Islamic republic's self-definition as in opposition to the "West."

Layla's experience with the legal system demonstrates an effect of the creation of new arenas like the women's Qur'anic meetings: the intellectual empowerment of a greater number of young women who are taking on not only Islamic doctrine but civil laws. Some might say that this emboldening is an unintended effect of the Islamization of Iranian society at large; others might disagree.

Whatever the intention, the result is that new actors are emerging in the production of knowledge about Islamic life and society, especially as it pertains to women and women's rights. It is not now and has never been a big secret that the women members of Iran's parliament have, since the inception of the Islamic republic, been called upon as the experts on women's issues. Soon after the revolution, women parliamentarians formed a commission on women, which is charged with determining women's concerns and presenting bills aimed at addressing them. In this respect, the greater parliament has depended on female representatives to intervene on behalf of women to help resolve important issues. In addition, interviews and meetings I had with various akhunds, both ranking members of the judiciary as well as instructors educated in Qom,[25] told me unequivocally that Islam offers the opportunity for women to participate in interpreting Islamic texts. In the past, however, women have chosen not to participate, nor was there a great opportunity for such participation, as the seminaries in Qom were for males only. In the past thirty years, women's seminaries have opened in Qom and also in Tehran.

That women are participating in the production of knowledge about Islam is significant, but it is not the fact of their participation alone that is significant. What is more notable is that women are moving the space of knowledge production out of the academic arena and offering participation in production of knowledge to *lay* women to practice in the legal and regulatory arenas. But, of course, as we shall see in the next chapter, legality does not work or play out in the same way for all.

Conclusion

Nanaz brought the meeting to an end by bringing her hands up to the air exaltedly and exclaiming that with the wealth of knowledge shared among the women in that room, each can learn to become her own messenger of God's word, and further, no longer be without knowledge. Applause rang out at her words. As the women rose to stretch, some gathered in small groups to converse, while some looked over a pile of French lingerie offered for sale by one of the participants. Others approached the guest with specific questions; still others flocked to the table of fruits and sweets for sustenance. Above the hullabaloo, Nanaz reminded the women that the next meeting would take place in two weeks time when a well-known attorney would be on hand to talk about the logistics of divorce. Another meeting had successfully been brought to a close. Women were enlightened by different aspects of the meeting, and based on their exuberance, one could surmise that each had found some useful insight that would compel her to locate sitters, leave work, and find some personal time to return in two weeks for the next session.

• • •

Women's perceptions of their status and rights are born out of constant discussion in multiple settings in which women are increasingly active participants. The new interpretive arenas like the reformulated jaleseh illustrate women's participation in determining the practical and daily meanings of notions of the rights that the state, ostensibly, has handed down to them. One theme in the meetings that struck me was the consistent referral by women to personal responsibility, whether it was referenced in the Qur'an, by the constitution, or by a lawyer. In all of these instances, the important lesson to be learned was that each woman was an independent being with free will because of her ability to reason. The discussions marked the important need for women to cast off and fight against patriarchy, whether it was in the Qur'an interpretation, the state, the family, or the workplace.

The Qur'anic meetings are one example of a dialogical site in which ideas about rights are emerging throughout Iran. They are a part of the new sites in which women engage in a dialogue, share experiences, and learn from one another, ultimately to find their way in the complex social, political, and religious sprawl of Tehran. As I have shown, dialogical sites such as the Qur'anic meetings afford women agency as they participate in shaping their roles and rights.

One of the main points I have tried to make throughout this chapter is that women engage with statist discourses of rights, and by doing so they create something else, thereby rendering themselves producers of knowledge. I have shown that women's engagements with ideas arise from life experiences. In doing so, my aim has been to challenge the notion that women's rights in the Muslim context are born solely of Islam.

Finally, perhaps there is also a need to reflect further on the relationship between individualism and the "West." Is there a natural relationship between the two, or can one have individualism just by situating Islam? Ashcraft (1996) notes that John Locke's own understandings were shaped and shaded by his own profound faith in Christianity and the Christian's covenant with God. Thus there is no natural connection between individualism and the secular West. Rofel (1999) argues that Chinese factory workers' social identities can be individualistic without being formed by Western liberalism or even failed Western liberalism. Thus in destabilizing the commonsensical notions of an abstract individualism that is implicitly a marker of Western Christian societies, and by noting that individualism is both textual and complex, arising out of various and varied conditions, I suggest that there are emerging "alternative" individualisms. And within Islam itself, there is a polyvocality of individuality as differently situated people draw the boundaries of Islam in different ways.

CHAPTER FOUR

Courting Rights:
Rights Talk in Islamico-Civil Family Court

WHEN HER NAME WAS CALLED, Goli walked into the courtroom. The judge greeted her as he sorted through Goli's filings. At her previous court visit two months earlier, the judge told Goli that her husband had not responded to her petition and that she would have to wait a little longer before he would enter a divorce order (*talaq*).[1] Today, Goli was asking the judge to grant her divorce in light of her husband's failure to provide maintenance.[2] Her argument was based on Article 1111 of Iran's Civil Code of Marriage and Family, which allows for a wife to petition the court to compel her husband to pay maintenance. In the case of the husband's refusal to comply, Article 1129 permits the wife to petition the court to dissolve the marriage. Technically, the judge delegates the divorce right to the wife. But in order for this to occur, the wife must petition the court and provide evidence to prove her husband's breach.

The judge motioned for Goli to approach and spoke softly, never lifting his eyes from her file. Goli followed the dictation of her legal history, nodding and glancing at the secretary who copied the judge's statements longhand. Then the judge looked at Goli and said, "Our society and our religion look very badly upon divorce. It is only in extreme circumstances that a woman can seek to end a marriage, and only if the proper circumstances exist. And this is my job, to determine whether this situation warrants it." Goli, who had earlier decided that this was not a disagreeable judge, began her statement:

> Yes, *hajj agha*,[3] I know. Last time, you told me to wait a bit longer, and if nothing happened, you would issue the order. To this day, I have not heard from my husband. In these last months, I have not even heard from his family. But now I am suffering. I am trapped in this prison of false marriage. He only wanted me so that he could come to Iran every few months or years and have someone. I know that he does not want to live with me. Hajj agha, I do not want anything from him that is outside of the law and I am not asking you to extend me any favor. I am only asking for my right . . . what the law provides.

She reached into her bag. "See," she continued, and pulled out her book of civil codes to a page with a folded edge, "it's all right here. He does not provide me with anything—housing, financial support, nothing. He came to see me two times in the last three years and we stayed at his sister's house. What kind of life is this? I am still—"

The judge interrupted her as she was about to tell him that she was still living in her family's house. "Yes, I know. You stated all this in your affidavit. And you have not heard from him since the last time you were here?"

"No."

"And no one is here from his side today?"

"No. They told me that I could not do anything until he returned."

"That's not so. The law allows it after six months. How long since you last saw him?"

"I haven't seen him in almost nine months."

"Did you contact him?"

"I tried to call, but he never answered. . . .I left messages."

"Yes, well you can file another petition. Did you file a petition for absenteeism?"

"No, I will if you think I need to; I read the [marriage and family] civil code. Up to now, I have done everything myself."

"Yes, yes. I know. You are very persistent, but I have to follow the law. It's not up to me; it's God's will. Do you have anything else for me today?"

"Yes, I have a letter from my sister and one from my neighbor, who was with me last time. You said I should get them to write letters."

"Fine, fine." Looking them over, he added, "Good, they are notarized."

And, then, just before he began to dictate the order granting Goli's petition for divorce based on lack of maintenance, the judge said, "He will probably never pay your mahr. But you can place a hold on his passport so if he comes back, he will not be able to exit the country without dealing with it."[4]

At a break in the proceedings, Goli explained to me that she was filing for divorce just three years after marriage. When her mother died, Goli said, she decided to start a family. She married Ali, who everyone thought was a worthy suitor, despite his age (fifty) and his residence (Los Angeles). Although Goli was willing to move to Los Angeles, for the entire three years of their marriage Ali remained abroad almost exclusively. When she saw no end in sight to this situation, she opted for divorce.

Goli had prepared and filed the divorce papers herself, as she could not afford a lawyer. She laid out her reasoning in both written petitions and oral testimony and drew from the family law code. Goli was optimistic that the judge would grant her petition. Earlier he said that although she had waited the required six months and had presented a plausible claim of nonmaintenance under Iran's civil codes, he would revisit her case in two months. Goli knew she had another claim as well. Her husband's absence of over six months underlaid a second claim, of absenteeism, a basis for divorce stipulated in her marriage contract. Goli explained that since her mother's death and her husband's abandonment of her, she had turned her attention more toward her individual survival. Goli said of her petition, "This is my right; no one will give you your rights, you have to go after them."

• • •

Tehran's Municipal Family Court offers a contrast to the arena of the Qur'anic meetings. At first glance the court may appear to be an inert arena in which agents of the state pronounce dogmatic legal doctrines, but the court is also a site of negotiation and resistance, as well as subversion of statist elaborations of gender roles. The court's significance is not simply as a site of struggle; it is also a place that engenders personhood. The court's blended Islamic and civil configuration produces individuated subjectivities as it requires litigants to perform as autonomous, self-possessed bearers of rights. Through an exploration of legal process, disputes, and modes of argumentation that take place in the family court, I illustrate both the pliancy of the family court as a site and the fluid nature of the subjectivities it produces. While many critics, including pundits in the Western media or theorists of communal Islam, have suggested that women have little power in such matters and are restricted to the indoor spaces (*andarooni*), or that issues concerning personal status laws are confined solely within the realm of Islamic jurisprudence, I argue that the women who use the courts to express grievances bear a legal subjectivity of a rights-bearing entitled citizen. This is the result of the configuration of the Islamico-civil court, which inflects subjectivities that evoke the idealized liberal subject of the civil legal system while allowing the women litigants to perform as Muslims as well. Indeed, as I showed in earlier chapters, the notion of law already points to the civil processes intermingled with the Islamic foundations of these laws.

My aim in this chapter, as in the book as a whole, is to highlight both the changeable nature of statist discourses on women's rights and the ability of some women to penetrate the formal system, not only by participating in the "public" and "private" discussions on rights, but also by forcing state action on their behalf. As a reconstituted postrevolutionary site, the family court exemplifies the unique amalgamated character of the Islamic republic—that it contains principles central to both Islamic values and republican state practices.[5] The practices found therein show some of the effects of a blended state system on the constitution and practice of women's rights. In the end, it appears that the family court and the Qur'anic meetings share much in common, despite the seemingly static and public notion of the former and fluid and private nature of the latter.

DIVORCE AND THE COURT: ESTRANGED BEDFELLOWS

In 1998, in an effort to consolidate all the family law cases of the city, the Tehran municipality moved the family court to a single building in the busy city center, across the street from the Great Bazaar of Tehran. The location of the Family Judicial Complex made sense since the building was also in the city's legal center. Along the same street sat Divan-e Aali-ye Keshvar, the highest court of Iran's justice system. The family court was housed in a corner building resting on a few steps that elevated it from the busy sidewalk where masses of people gathered to obtain information, await their hearings, or tend to unhappy family members.[6] On the streets, people busily hurried in and out of government buildings as vendors sat on the sidewalks hawking their wares, anything from small sundries to fresh fruit brought from family farms on the outskirts of Tehran. Still other merchants sold pocket versions of Iran's civil codes, compilations of specific areas of concern, such as laws of marriage and family, inheritance, and property.

On my first attempt to walk through the open double doors of the building, two armed and uniformed soldiers addressed me, "Madam, enter through the 'sisters' entrance." To my left, I saw a curtained entry where more discerning women casually pulled back the heavy dark drape and walked in. Behind the curtain, several female attendants lightly patted overcoats and reminded women to correct ill-managed headscarves. Attendants scanned the contents of women's bags, inspected their faces and hands for prohibited accoutrements such as makeup and nail polish, and confirmed that they were dressed in appropriate Muslim attire, at minimum a headscarf and long overcoat. For violators, attendants had acetone and tissues on hand so they could, for a small fee, remove the cosmetics in order to enter the court. Men were also inspected upon entering, although their entrance, on the opposite corner of the building, was not covered with drapes. To exit, both women and men left through the central double doors.

Once past the checkpoint, women moved through a second drape that opened toward the dome-shaped foyer of the old building. Here hordes of people walked; some were crying, some walking quickly, some had gathered to talk, sisters with sisters, mothers with small children, parents with young brides, or grooms whose marriages had not gone as planned. The corridors of the building held people full of anger, sorrow, and remorse. A tired-looking man sat off to the side of the entrance hall and directed people to their assigned courtrooms. Three advisors sat in a room and offered free legal information to potential petitioners who were inquiring about their rights or the judicial process.

Once, a friend seeking divorce approached an advisor about the legal process. The advisor spoke swiftly and crudely as she told my friend her legal options: "Boys over the age of two and girls over seven go to him.[7] You can get your mahr if he is divorcing you. You cannot initiate divorce, but if you have a case, you can ask the judge to give you a divorce. First you have to file a complaint and pay the filing fee."

When my friend asked on what basis she could dissolve her marriage, the advisor responded, "If he has disappeared, is a perpetual drunkard or drug addict, impotent, or unable to provide for you financially, and, provided you have proof, you can ask the judge to execute the divorce for you."[8]

I conducted fieldwork in Tehran's Municipal Family Court during the period from February 1999 through February 2000, with follow-up visits in subsequent years. On my initial attempt to gain access, I went to the court's education division where, I had been told by the court's advisory staff, observers had to obtain permission. The person in charge was a young-looking man, probably in his late thirties. He said that he was a judge as well. He asked about my qualifications and what I knew of Iran's laws. I explained that I had studied fiqh with a member of the 'ulama. He and his assistant laughed and said that that did not make me knowledgable about their laws. I further explained my attempts to study Islamic jurisprudence and said that as a result of studying, I had a sense of the Islamic foundations of the laws. The man said that the Iranian civil laws are based on the Belgian and the French legal systems. To this I replied that I had knowledge of the civil laws and had studied and practiced law in the United States, and that I was interested in seeing the law put into practice. With more laughter, but at least now convinced, they sent me off to the head of the Municipal Family Court with a letter of introduction but told me to see the deputy in charge (mauven), Ms. Saidi. When I arrived there minutes later, Ms. Saidi smiled politely and kindly explained that she would be at my service, but that first I needed to talk with the head of the court, since the letter was addressed to him. I went to the second floor of the building and entered the office sitting room, where a young man sitting behind a desk looked at my letter and said, "No, we won't accept any researchers." I asked if he would at least take the letter to the head of the court, which he agreed to do as soon as he was finished with his midday prayers.

A few minutes went by and the man behind the desk told a father and daughter who were also waiting to go home and come back when their court date was scheduled, in two months time. The father, who was very old, wearily looked at the man behind the desk and said that they had been waiting for a year and a half, that he did not think anything more would happen in two months time, and that they did not want to come back because they lived so far away. His daughter added that she had no money or means and needed for the court to bring the court date forward. She explained, "What does it matter, anyway, the man is in prison and I want to get my divorce." Then she further explained that she really did not want a divorce, she wanted financial support for her child and herself. The man behind the desk asked if the husband who was in jail had any money and whether it was even worth going after. The father replied that the man's parents certainly had money, and someone, after all, had to support this daughter and her child as he was too old and too sick and could not. The elderly father then looked to me and said that he could go to the man's parents but thought it best to follow the official process, but, he chuckled, he did not know if he would still be alive when the court finally got to their case. The man behind the desk then disappeared into the office next door and returned momentarily with an answer for me: "Apologies, but no."

My access to the court was eventually facilitated by a journalist friend, Elham, who had conveyed my project to a particular judge whom she knew was open to the idea of having observers. Through Elham, I came to see that neither my request nor my presence in the courtroom was unusual, as law students and journalists were known to seek permission to observe proceedings. I met Elham at her news bureau the day she was going to introduce me to the judge. She was dressed unconservatively in a beige overcoat and jeans. I was surprised at how her unruly brown hair peered out of her loosely tied headscarf. I had specifically worn black and was advised by others to wear black and a long, loose overcoat. "No matter," Elham said as we loaded into the awaiting taxi that would take us to the family court. Elham, however, was on her way to the revolutionary court, a controversial court where state officials adjudicate crimes against the state, which included insulting Islamic values. She also reported on cases in the criminal court.

At twenty-four, Elham had been a reporter for just over a year and really liked it. But then she added, "It's not for everyone. Some people think it's wrong for a female to be comfortable (*rahhat*) with such people as murderers." But her parents were cool with the job, she told me. "They are very enlightened (*roshan-fekr*)." She also advised me not to worry about the judge, that he was not "like that." I was concerned with being from the United States, and Elham told me that I need not tell him that I came from the States. I was a little surprised and told her that I would be taking notes in English. She laughed and said, "He won't be looking at your writings!"

As we pulled up to the courthouse, Elham told her driver that she would be back in five to ten minutes. I thought this was unlikely—nothing could be this swift, as my earlier experiences with the court had evidenced. But to my great surprise, we flew through the security and headed up the stairs, with greetings from all the people Elham knew from when she had covered this beat. We went up to the third floor and walked through a crowd standing outside the doorway of the room. The judge was a small man from the northern province of Azerbaijan. He was dressed formally in a pressed navy linen cloak and white turban (*amammeh*), which nicely complemented his thin white beard. He glanced our way and smiled, to my great relief, as we entered the room. I sat down in a chair along one side of the room while the judge made small talk with Elham. He said that it had been a while since she came by. His soft-spoken yet direct manner conveyed both authority and compassion in the courtroom. Elham explained that she was now covering the other courts, then told him that she had brought a researcher who just wanted to sit and listen. He looked over at me, nodded, and said it was fine—"no problem" (*eshqhal nadareh*). Elham said goodbye, told me to call her at the paper for any reason, and left me alone with the judge. He directed me to sit beside him as he spoke with litigants and dictated his opinions to his secretary, a graduate from the university's law school system (as opposed to a scholar of jurisprudence trained as this judge was, in the Islamic seminary), who would copy them in longhand.[9] A clerk would then take the decision to another room, where the judge's order was notarized and officially executed.

When the first case was called into the room, the judge, to my great horror and surprise, took the legal pad out of the hands of his able stenographer, handed it to me, and asked me to take notes. I looked at him and whispered that my writing was not very good. Utterly confused, he replied, "But aren't you Iranian?" I explained that I was raised in the United States and had lived there all my life, although, yes, I was born in Iran. The judge seemingly took it all in stride and gently took the pad of paper from me, returned it to his stenographer, and continued hearing the testimony before him.

During the months I sat in this court, I heard the proceedings of approximately 140 cases. The proceedings began at about 8:00 a.m. and ran until midday prayers, around 1:00 p.m. I also attended hearings in other courtrooms and visited other kinds of courts, such as custody hearings. Usually two or three hearings took place in the early morning sessions, followed by a break and then another round of hearings in the late mornings. When not attending hearings, I also interviewed litigants in the hallways and spoke with officials of the court.

The judge had disputing parties come right up to his podium. He stood on an elevated platform as he listened to their complaints. At 10:30 or so each day, the judge closed his door for a fifteen-minute break. During these times, the three of us—the judge, the secretary, and I—talked. Sometimes I asked for clarity on decisions he made or inquired about the facts of a case that I did not quite follow. Aware of my legal training, the judge sometimes asked me about similar legal processes in the United States; other times, he asked about social practices.

One day, after a case in which a woman asked the judge to help her find a way to divorce a man whom she had married when she was too young, the judge asked me, "Do boys and girls spend time alone together before marriage?"

"Yes," I replied.

"And is it true that sometimes they relate to one another as a husband and wife, even before they are married?"

"Yes, it is very common, although there are some who would not."

"I see. And are they not arrested or anything, those who do?"

"No, in the United States it is not illegal, and there is a policy that state officials are not supposed to enter into private matters between individuals, although sometimes there are problems, such as domestic violence, in which case, the state would enter into private matters between individuals."

Again the judge nodded. "I see. That is very interesting. I think it should be the same here." After our break, once again the doors of the courtroom were opened and the next case was called in.

. . .

Setareh was a mother of two who entered the courtroom and stood before the judge with an all too common complaint: she could no longer live with her husband. Tearful yet defiant, she claimed that Reza, her husband of seven years, was unemployed and did not come home some nights. Draped in her long black chador, her children by her side, Setareh told the judge that she could no longer endure the shame this behavior brought her.

Setareh had filed for dissolution due to Reza's lack of financial support for herself and their children, and she told the judge that she was asking only for the remedies available to her through the law. She gave three reasons for why she sought divorce. First, she said that her husband was unemployed and so was not financially supporting the family. Second, Setareh claimed that her husband stayed out late at nights and sometimes even did not come home. By this, she was offering proof that her husband was at risk of abandoning her and the children. Finally, Setareh claimed that not having a nice place to live was a blight on her reputation, also a basis for divorce, falling within the category of failure of financial support. Her arguments, while emotionally charged, were also legally sound, based on the nonmaintenance provisions of articles 1111 and

1129. The judge asked Setareh whether she had any witnesses to substantiate her allegations. She instantly produced a list of people who were willing to testify.

The judge also questioned Setareh's husband about his behavior. Reza protested that the three-room apartment he had rented for them in the poor southern section of Tehran was only a temporary situation until his struggling electronics repair business picked up. In a few months' time, he promised, he would rent an apartment that conformed to Setareh's expectations. Reza further explained that he had been staying away from home because he was depressed. The judge expressed disapproval with his response and reminded Reza of his legal duties toward his family. Finally, the judge admonished Reza for having gotten married while financially unstable.

At the end of the hearing, the judge indicated satisfaction with Setareh's evidence and told her that he would grant her a divorce, but only if that was what she really wanted. Throughout the hearing, Setareh had shed tears, and several times Reza spoke directly to his wife, asking her to reconsider. Setareh now looked at the judge and burst out, "What am I supposed to do?" Sensing hesitation on her part, the judge suggested that she could give Reza another chance, but one with a legal guarantee, a written oath (aghd-i kharji-e lazim) that amounts to an additional contract outside of the original marriage contract, the transgression of which would trigger divorce. In this case, Reza was agreeing to an added stipulation that he would move the family to a new living situation within the next six months. Setareh declared that she loved Reza, as he was the father of her children, but emphasized that she could no longer live this way. She would therefore obtain the sworn statement. The judge gave the couple a new court date in six months' time, when he would reassess their situation. If by then Setareh did not have adequate living quarters, the judge said, he would allow her to reinstate her petition. As they prepared to leave the courtroom, Setareh turned to me and said that she was doubtful that her husband would be able to afford a new home, but she wanted both the judge and her husband to see that she was serious. Outside the courtroom I asked Setareh whether she had consulted legal counsel. She said that she had spoken with friends and family about the problems she was having. A friend who had been through a divorce told her how to go about it. She said she also learned about the process of filing the complaint from the advisors on the first floor, and finally that she had paid a transcriber to write it up in the proper legal manner.

A few weeks later I saw Setareh again. She told me that she had withdrawn her complaint. I asked if she was satisfied with her decision. She said that her husband was back at work and had been more agreeable, but she would just have to see. Finally, she said that she has rights and that if he did not respect her, she would to reinitiate her complaint.

For women like Setareh, marriage and family laws are key arenas of engagement with the legal system. A majority of divorce petitions are filed by women, and Iran's national figures on divorce show modest but steady increases in recent years (Osanloo 2006a).[10] Setareh's story illustrates the importance women place on legality, both in the process and in the documentation of it. Setareh had filed documents and made statements before the judge in accordance with the procedural rules of the court. Most important, her narrative clearly addressed specific points of law. The story is also an example of how women use the courts not only to dissolve marriages, but also to renegotiate the terms of marriage or persuade their husbands to comply with the terms of the marriage. As she did so, Setareh also performed as an autonomous subject interacting with state legal forces.

Like Setareh, all the women who enter the Islamico-civil arena of these courts are strictly regulated for Muslim comportment upon entering the court, but as they enter, they are also compelled to use the discourse of rights conditioned by state civil codes and legal procedures. Scholars of liberal legal systems have found that civil legal systems produce the rights-bearing individual subjectivity (Fitzpatrick 1992). The court sanctioned Setareh's subjectivity as an individual rights-bearer and aggrieved Muslim wife.

Setareh's legal pursuit of her aims is indicative of a new historical moment that has relegitimated certain rights-based discourses in Iran. As discussed earlier, just after the 1979 revolution Iran's new leaders declared that such discourses, particularly as they referred to women's rights, depended on an individualism that did not respect the natural differences between men and women and that, in the context of the family, was not in conformity with women's roles according to Islam. Setareh's reliance on the country's civil codes and the legal mechanisms available to dissolve marriage, instead of the Islamic principles that undeniably underlie the legal infrastructure, points to a renewed emphasis on positive civil law, even in familial disputes, which the early leaders of the Islamic republic had rejected.

My aim is not simply to provide a description of courtroom process; instead, I am interested in how civil process creates the conditions through which women's discourses of rights emerge, even in the context of administering Islamic laws. I am arguing for analytically disaggregating the philosophical sources underlying the law—jurisprudence—from its application, civil process, to better understand how the legal process in Iran's family court operates and how it gives women petitioners some rights in marriage and some opportunities to dissolve marriage, despite the overall prohibition on this actual legal right for women. Before moving on, a discussion of divorce is necessary.

MARRIAGE AND FAMILY LAWS IN ISLAMIC TEXTS

Scholars often regard women in Muslim societies as having extremely limited rights in dissolving marriages, and they find that men have a unilateral right to repudiate (*talaq*) their wives. The basis for this idea is said to be found in the Qur'an, the unimpeachable word of God, and so repudiation, many believe, cannot be eliminated. The concept of repudiation, however, must be better situated in the context of Muslim marriage and family laws. Women, or in most cases their families, initiate the marriage offer (and contract) (Bakhtiar and Reinhart 1996). The sole right of husbands to end marriages is sometimes understood as consideration (quid pro quo) for the wife's offer of marriage. This is a primary reason that women have historically had very limited recourse in terminating marriages in Muslim contexts. Since the right to dissolve marriage resides with husbands, wives, in order to leave marriages, ask their husbands to divorce them. If the husbands agree, the divorce is deemed mutual divorce (*khul*). In those cases, women will often pay some sort of consideration, often canceling payment of their mahr. When husbands will not agree to dissolution, or when women do not want to forgo their mahr, women may attempt to wrest away the right of divorce. To do so, women must appear before an authority and show cause in order to have that authority delegate the husband's divorce right to the wife (Coulson 1964; El Alami and Hinchcliffe 1996; Mir-Hosseini 1993). In most Muslim settings today, that authority is a judge sitting in a blended Islamic and civil court.

In the Iranian civil law setting, which has been grafted onto Islamic jurisprudence, claims are made in conjunction with codified laws, related to, but not referencing, shari'a. As petitioners in civil courts, women must prove their cases as litigants through a civil legal process in which judges serve as fact-finders as well. Thus women, unlike men, who need to petition a court with claims couched in specific legal arguments and must back up their cases with evidentiary proof, perform as civil law actors in ways their husbands do not.

Take the case of Sahar, whom I had met in the hallways of the court one afternoon. At twenty-two, Sahar was a veteran of the family court. She leaned against the wall and crossed her arms beneath her chador. "I've been here since eight in the morning," she complained, "and soon I have to pick up my son. Each time I come here, the judge tells me I need another filing, another sworn statement, a witness, or a different form. I have been in and out of the court, up and down these stairs, so much that I know more about the law than the lawyers. Who needs a lawyer?" Sahar was responding to my question asking whether she had consulted a lawyer about her situation. "This is how I learned the law. If you do not follow what they say precisely, then you cannot obtain the result."

As I got to know Sahar, I learned that at age fifteen, she was courted by a man who had seen her walking home from school. The man, Mohammad, sent his mother to talk with Sahar's mother, proving his intentions were honorable. Although Sahar had never seen the man before, when he came to meet her family as part of the initial courtship (*khostegari*), she liked him.

Her family came from southern Tehran. Her father worked in construction but brought home barely enough money to support his wife and six children, among whom Sahar was the eldest. So when a suitor with his own business appeared, Sahar saw marriage to him as a possibility for a better future. Because she was attending school at the time, Sahar had only one request, to continue her education. According to Sahar, Mohammad agreed.

At the start, theirs looked to be a good match even though, at twenty-seven, Mohammad was twelve years Sahar's senior. After they married, Sahar said, they were happy living in a small apartment not far from their families. She attended school and he worked. Soon, however, Mohammad grew tired of her schooling and said he wanted a child. After months of bickering, Sahar told me, they came to an agreement: After high school, she would have a baby and then continue her education after the baby was past nursing. "Since he [Mohammad] was older, I could understand his haste and I compromised." As the baby got bigger, Sahar could see that going back to school was not realistic. When she told Mohammad she wanted to return, he said, "School is for the child." After several years of arguments and fruitless family interventions, Sahar took a bus to the family court. When she went through the checkpoint, she told the guards she wanted to know how to get a divorce, and they directed her to the legal advising room.

From that point on, Sahar began researching the possibilities, first to force her husband to negotiate, and then, if necessary, to dissolve the marriage. One day, she took me downstairs to the legal advisors and pointed to the three seated officials. "They have university degrees, but I learned the law from need. What women in Iran do not understand," Sahar explained, "is that the law is there, [but] we do not know how to use it. What good is having a right if you do not go after it? I will keep coming here and filing whatever papers I need in order to get my rights."

"What are your rights," I asked.

"My rights are mine. That which is mine and no one can take away from me, such as my education or my son."

One of the primary features animating Iran's family law procedures is article 1133 of the civil codes: the husband's unilateral right to divorce. Women, who do not have that right, must seek counsel in the family court. If a wife is able to prove her husband's failure in one or more accepted provisions of the law or the marriage contract and convince the judge that reconciliation is infeasible, the judge may grant her the right to divorce. The same is not true for men, whose appearance in the courts as respondents requires them to have little knowledge of or concern for the substantive and procedural issues with which their wives must contend, first, to obtain a hearing for their grievances, and second, to prove their case.[11] As a result, women's increased petitions before the court in recent years have contributed to their emergence as rights-bearing subjects with greater knowledge than lay men of both the laws and the procedural mechanisms involved in petitioning for divorce. Indeed, my male respondents rarely exhibited the detailed knowledge of court procedures and legal regulations that my female respondents did. Like Sahar, many of my other women informants, who were not legally trained, related how the divorce process had turned them into legal scholars and practitioners.[12]

Islamico-Civil Family Court: Making, Unmaking, and Remaking

Courts are sites that produce subjectivities and allow women, in particular, to contest some ascribed subject-positions as legal processes within courts create new forms of knowledge and meaning (Merry 1990; Sarat and Kearns 1993; Starr 1992; Yngvesson 1993). Courts thus can be sites of resistance (Hirsch 1994, 1998), production and reproduction of culture (Rosen 1989), power (Mir-Hosseini 1993), and performance (Merry 1994). In Iran the possibility that courts offer for challenging ascribed subject-positions exists as a result of the Islamico-civil framework of Tehran's family court and the civil laws it administers. Judith Butler's work on performativity and the formation of subjectivities adds texture to an understanding of how it is that women as litigants in Iran's family court emerge as subjects. Drawing from Foucault, Butler locates subjectivization within the structures of power, not outside of them. Emerging from within governments of power, subjects are enabled even as they contest and forge new possibilities from existing conditions or structures of power (1993: 15). If we take laws to be articulations of a government of power, we see women litigants' engagement with those laws simultaneously reinforcing and yet challenging those institutions, creating new possibilities as well.

Elaborating on Butler's theories of performativity and agency to better understand women's piety movements among Egyptian Muslims, Saba Mahmood offers a critique of Western liberal feminism. One important intervention in this regard is Mahmood's starting point. She does not assume the normative of personhood as the individuated conscious subject. Instead, Mahmood explores Muslim women's exterior bodily practices to better appreciate how the pious interior self is being crafted through these practices (2005: 122). My investigation of women's litigation practices seeks to explore how the courts inflect subjectivity through the exterior bodily practices they instantiate. While Mahmood explores bodily practice to better understand an interior self that is not individuated, my goal is to grasp how such practices produce just such a subject-position.

The following exploration of the recent history of Iran's family court is an attempt to better understand the regimes of power, both Islamic and republican, that condition and constrain the possibilities of subjectivization of the women litigants. Better understanding the civil liberal and Islamic underpinnings of such power structures helps to explain women's subjectivity in these contexts as individuated and autonomous even while expressly pious Muslim, but it does not take for granted this notion of personhood as either conscious or normative.

• • •

In August 1998 Iran's parliament created the Family Judicial Complex in Tehran as a result of a bill that it had passed earlier that year. The bill, which was introduced by the Parliamentary Women's Commission, was designed to remedy a problem that arose from a previous law that gave General Courts broad jurisdiction over all legal actions—everything from penal to familial matters (Mir-Hosseini 2000: ix).[13] Thus, when the Family Judicial Complex opened in the center of town, the only issues that its courts entertained were matters relating to marriage and divorce. The laws from which judges make decisions are interpreted from shari'a and codified in Iran's civil codes, which have existed since the late 1920s. In the fall of 2002, a new complex was constructed just outside of Tehran with branches in different parts of town intended to accommodate the large numbers of cases and reduce the distances people had to travel throughout the city. A brief look at the judicial arena, both its courts and laws, reveals how the resulting system is neither wholly Islamic nor wholly civil, but an amalgamation thereof.

Islamico-Civil Family Laws

When Ayatollah Khomeini and other religious leaders who participated in the founding of the Islamic republic made the decision to Islamize the judiciary, they retained the civil codes of the previous era as the tangible expression of the law. The religious leaders found that the civil and commercial codes addressed issues in Islamic law to a satisfactory degree, so postrevolutionary revisions to those sections of the codes were modest. The major revisions came in the area of family law, which some of the newly empowered 'ulama condemned as fundamentally opposed to the laws of Islam. Only two weeks after Khomeini returned to Iran from fifteen years in exile, he suspended the Family Protection Law (FPL) of 1967, which had been revised in 1975.

When the FPL was first enacted by the prerevolutionary parliament in 1967, its advocates hailed it as a major piece of legislation that protected family life by restricting practices that damaged the stability and health of the family in a modern society (Paidar 1995).[14] The FPL addressed inequities among men and women in the family laws by means of three primary changes in the law: procedural limitations on the unilateral right of men to divorce their wives, a restriction on polygamy, and a qualification of men's presumptive rights to child custody.

First, the new law required the initiating spouse, whether it was the husband or the wife, to petition a family protection court before a divorce could be granted. Prior to this, men only needed to register their divorces. The intent and effect of the law was to require divorcing parties to enter formal mediation under the supervision of the court before a marriage would be dissolved; this is not to suggest that men's unilateral right to divorce was repealed, only preempted by a formalized judicial process. That is, men still had the right to divorce their wives without cause. The new law simply required parties to partake in a formal process of mediation to try to resolve their differences. Second, under certain conditions, women could petition the court for a divorce, even if such a stipulation was not stated in their marriage contract. For instance, if a woman's husband took a second wife without the permission of the first, the first wife could then petition the court for a divorce, even if this stipulation was not in her original marriage contract. Third, divorcing couples were compelled to make formal arrangements for custody and maintenance of their children before a divorce could be granted. As one commentator stated, the FPL did not give women rights so much as it limited men's unilateral rights to polygamous marriage and divorce (Vatandoust 1985). When it was amended in 1975, the FPL raised the age of marriage for women to eighteen and for men to twenty, with some exceptions. The revised version of the FPL also allowed either spouse to petition the court if the other was deemed to be engaged in employment considered detrimental to the family, whereas the 1967 version of the law had given this right only to husbands.[15]

While these changes were hailed as advancements in the protection of women and the family, the laws were also conspicuously shaped to conform to the tenets of Islamic law (Higgins 1985).[16] Also, article 17 of the FPL noted that the conditions under which both parties could petition the family protection court for divorce would be included as a stipulation in the marriage contract. The legislators' purpose in crafting article 17 was to openly recognize that a woman's right to petition for divorce was a condition in the marriage contract, ostensibly granted to her by her husband before the consummation of the marriage. By inserting this legal contrivance, the legislators indicated that they did not abrogate section 1133 of the civil code (1928, revised 1931) that gave men the unilateral right to divorce in accordance with Islamic law. The FPL thus attempted to retain its concordance with Islamic law.

The majority of akhunds at the time did not react negatively, but Ayatollah Khomeini disagreed, and from exile in Iraq he delivered a sharp rebuke of the FPL, published in his book on clarifications of religious questions, *Resaleh Towzih al-Masael*:

> The law that has recently been passed by the illegal Majles under the name of the Family Protection Law in order to destroy Muslim family life, is against Islam, and both its originators and implementers are guilty before the *shari'a*. Women who are divorced in family courts should consider their divorces as null, and if they re-marry they are committing adultery. Whoever marries such women knowingly is also an adulterer, and should be punished according to the *shari'a* by whipping. The children of these men and women are illegitimate and are not entitled to inheritance. (1981: 314)

When Khomeini returned to Iran on February 1, 1979, his plan to revitalize Islam through the creation of a newly improvised Islamic state began by addressing matters pertaining to women and family, issues that he felt were at the heart of a true Islamic society. Thus, upon returning to Iran, one of Khomeini's first steps toward achieving his vision of a true Islamic society was to suspend the FPL on February 26, 1979. Women's protests delayed the complete abandonment FPL until August 1979 when Sadr Haj-Seyyed-Javadi, the minister of justice in the provisional government, announced the formal abrogation of the FPL (Paidar 1995: 272). Ironically, the invalidation of the law effectively returned legal issues involving the family to the 1931 civil code, which was intended by Reza Shah as an attempt to modernize the shari'a.

Family Law Courts

One of the bases for the nullification of the FPL was that the Family Protection Courts, which the law had created, were deemed to lack jurisdiction to issue verdicts on matters pertaining to divorce since, under Islamic law, men did not need a reason for divorcing their wives. In October 1979 the Revolutionary Council approved a proposal to replace the Family Protection Courts with Special Civil Courts.[17] The new courts were authorized to preside over cases in which couples had disputes. Thus, despite being deemed un-Islamic, the Family Protection Courts were effectively retained, although renamed, and continued to function much as they had before the revolution. The verdicts of judges, who at this time were both members of the 'ulama and secular, were supposed to conform to the old civil codes. In cases in which consent to divorce was said to be mutual, husbands were only required to register the divorce in the presence of two male witnesses.

In March 1981 a new bill was presented by then prime minister Mohammed Ali Rajai that called for the Special Civil Courts to refer to Khomeini's religious opinions on matters for which no guidance existed, either from the Council of the Revolution or from Majlis (Paidar 1995: 273). The bill had the effect of multiplying and confusing the sources from which judges could obtain the reasoning for their decisions. Another wrinkle added to the confusion of laws when, in August 1982, Khomeini called for purification of the laws among judges. Disgruntled by the enduring existence of Pahlavi era *"taghuti"* or "Western" laws, Khomeini ordered primacy of the shari'a on matters for which the existing civil codes suggested a different result (Paidar 1995: 273).[18]

Yet another complication arose at the level of judicial forums. A special civil appeals court was established in 1985 to determine the validity of decisions based on erroneous readings of the multiple and often differing laws. Still another type of court, the *shari'at* court, was soon established to reckon with the enormous backlog of cases created by the confusion of laws and forums. When this tactic alone was insufficient, the judiciary allowed public courts to hear family disputes where Special Civil Courts were not available.

After much protest and calls for coordination of the laws, the judiciary invalidated the informal shari'at courts and denied public courts any further jurisdiction in entertaining family disputes. In the early 1980s, government agents held seminars to discuss women's concerns with the uneven handling of family disputes. In response to one of those seminars, then public prosecutor Ayatollah Saanei declared that the civil codes were indeed in conformity with Islamic law. In consultation with its women deputies, Majlis formed a Committee on the Family in 1984, and with the help of NGOs acting in support of women, the committee sent proposals for remedying the confusion of family laws to the judiciary (Paidar 1995: 275). Soon thereafter, the failure on the part of the state institutions to give women their rights became the subject of commentary in the pages of a woman's weekly magazine, *Zan-e Ruz* (Woman of Today). Among the judiciary's failures, the paper's editors cited ambiguous laws and unsystematic decision making. The stories of women in the courts told of unfair treatment of women by court officials. Responding to these assertions, the head of a unit in charge of decision making in the Special Civil Courts, Mohammad Ali Ebrahimkhani, stated in an interview with the magazine that the biggest problem with uniformity of laws and regularization of judges' decisions was the lack of legislation to fill the gaps in the family laws created by the abrogation of the FPL. Mr. Ebrahimkhani lamented that many judges preferred to rely on their own personal interpretations of the shari'a while some did not allow secular lawyers to represent their clients (Paidar 1995: 276). This was a plea for greater formalism.

ISLAMICO-CIVIL FORMALISM

A brief overview of the family court's making and unmaking reveals the extent to which the leaders of the new Islamic republic were facing questions to which they did not have ready answers. Many important religious figures complained of the confusion over the laws. Women, parliamentary representatives, and even members of the judiciary called for regularization of the judicial process for family law disputes. The significance of these complaints is that they expressed the moment in which a crucial shift was taking place in what was emerging as a blended legal system. As Iran's new leaders brought the republican state together with the ideological underpinnings of the shari'a, a unique situation arose in the administration of justice through law: the need for a more uniform system of administration was taking precedence over the moral idealism of Islamic law.

For this reason, calls for uniformity of the family laws signaled not only a historical but, indeed, an ideological shift in the administration of Islamic law. Arjomand notes, "After the revolution . . . , the triumphant Shi'ite heirocracy inherited the political and hierarchical judiciary organization of the Iranian nation-state, as formally rationalized by seven decades of Western-inspired modernization. The declared aim of Ayatollah Khomeini had been to transform the Pahlavi state into a theocracy and to Islamize its judiciary system" (1988: 184). State actors within the Islamic republic ultimately answered the prayers for greater legal uniformity, and hence transparency and predictability, by making what Arjomand (185) calls a "historic" decision. The religious leaders of the new republic decided to administer the shari'a through the European civil law system, the model of judicial organization inherited from the previous government. The ironic result of creating an Islamic state that aimed to return Islam to the people was that the merger of the shari'a with a civil legal process ultimately brought about the end of the traditional system of Islamic justice.

That the area of family law played a large part in the systematization and rationalization of the legal order is significant because of the critical role the laws of the family have played in the recent Islamic context. In the past, public and criminal laws were deemed to be within the purview of the state agents, or the ruling shah, but family laws were thought to be the sole responsibility of scholars of jurisprudence (Arjomand 1988: 184). The codification and legislative administration of family laws brought the issues of family out from being the sole province of the 'ulama and into the emerging public sphere. As attempts to integrate shari'a into a uniform set of civil codes led to a more systematized body of law, they were accompanied by appeals by religious leaders, members of parliament, journalists, and others for women to determine what their rights are and to learn how to use them (Najmabadi 1998a).

By 1989 a seemingly more uniform set of family laws was collected from the various sources of law, including the abrogated FPL. A host of developments since the 1980s have reinstated many of the old FPL provisions, even the articles that were most offensive to the 'ulama. And, although religious judges replaced the secular, the new judges were better trained in the features of civil administration and were aided by law clerks trained at the universities instead of in religious seminaries.

In 1999 women again were able to stipulate the right to initiate divorce should a husband take a second wife without obtaining the permission of the first. The husband must sign each stipulation in the marriage contract individually. When he does, the signed stipulation amounts to a delegation of the divorce right to the wife, in effect, to divorce herself. Of course the legal process requires the wife to prove to a judge her husband's failure to comply with a particular stipulation. In this way Islamic divorce has become increasingly bureaucratized.

While the lawmakers did not outlaw polygamy altogether, they did take a policy stance in favor of monogamy. As then-president Hojjatoleslam Rafsanjani argued that since the male population in Iran was about 5 percent higher than the female population, there was no justification for any man to take more than one wife (Paidar 1995: 285). Rafsanjani stressed that monogamy should be the norm, and that polygamy should be practiced only if absolutely necessary.

In the years just after the revolution, husbands were permitted simply to register their divorces when there was no dispute between the parties. In 1992 Majlis enacted a new law, Amendments to Divorce Regulations, which once again compelled both husbands and wives to petition the court before being able to dissolve a marriage, forcing parties to enter into arbitration. Again, state administrators pointed to a policy decision against divorce because Islam placed marriage in the highest regard.

Other important developments of the 1992 law included a provision that provided for postdivorce maintenance (*ojrat al-mesl*) for women, a legal form of redress that was not previously thought to be provided in the shari'a. In addition, a provision that was written in as a result of much concern by women's groups, NGOs, and women parliamentarians was the appointment of women advisory judges to work in cooperation with the male judges (Mir-Hosseini 1993: ix).

Another important cause of action that arose in the mid-1990s was the equitable division of the couple's marital assets. In the event that a husband decides to divorce his wife without cause, she is entitled to half the wealth and property of the husband. This rule places yet another limitation on men's unilateral right to divorce. While the shari'a principle prohibits legislators from requiring men to give a reason for divorce, the newly devised laws compelling arbitration, postdivorce maintenance, and equitable property division seek to proscribe specious divorce claims by men and to protect women, at least to some financial extent, from the otherwise unencumbered unilateral right of men to divorce.

The broadening of stipulations that trigger the delegation of the divorce initiatives to women are justified in the shari'a through the concept of *osr va haraj*, literally meaning poverty and cruelty. The items stipulated in the marriage contract and codified in the civil codes are the expression of the heretofore-accepted grounds of hardship in which women can petition a court for divorce. This of course leaves the possibility of further developments in this arena. In the event that a husband makes life unbearable for his wife, and where she has no previously expressed legal remedy available to her (i.e., as stipulated in her marriage contract), she may initiate a petition based on the general rule of hardship, at least theoretically. Of course it is up to the judge to decide whether the grounds upon which hardship is claimed warrant a divorce. Nevertheless, some legal experts see this provision as offering possibilities for a divorce petition where none of the legally defined grounds exists.

A legal strategy increasingly used by the courts to protect women is for judges to preside over the signing of an *aghd-i kharji-e lazim*, a binding outside contract between the husband and wife, as was used in Setareh's case above. The additional contract allows a woman to obtain written guarantees from her husband to cease a particular behavior that is offensive to the wife's reputation. In effect, the wife can obtain a written document in which the husband transfers an additional right to divorce to her, in the event that he transgresses the proscribed activity.

Furthermore, in 1997, after much protest and deliberation, parliament qualified the child custody laws so that in the event of divorce, if a woman could show that her husband was unfit to care for the children, the court had the power to award the children to the mother (Mir-Hosseini 2000: x). Obviously the extent to which the remedies, new and renewed, may be able to address some of women's grievances remains to be seen.

The aim of the discussion above is to situate the context in which lawmakers in the Islamic republic have attempted to Islamize the family laws in Iran. At first it appeared that state administrators were intent upon abrogating Western-inspired law, both procedurally and substantively. In attempting to do so, however, state actors actually revisited, re-created, and reinstated many of the innovations of the FPL, initially condemned by Khomeini as taghuti laws. In this context and amid the post-1979 legal developments discussed above, it is important to note the increasing shift toward a legal arena to adjudicate divorce. The shift is significant, even if the space for negotiation is small, given the starting point of men's unilateral right of divorce. Increasing laws, regulations, codes, and contracts move the concept of divorce away from being the sole and arbitrary purview of men into an arena where women can express themselves and force men into negotiation. The courts thus may not offer women the equal right to divorce but may offer an arena in which women can bargain and men must come to the bargaining table, when they did not before.

In the end, the agents in the Islamic republic retained the civil courts as a system of adjudication, reinstated the laws, and re-created the formal expression of the law in civil codes. Why would the religious leaders, in an attempt to Islamize state institutions and recover a past that was presumably unblemished by Western imperialism, remain content with a systematization of the laws that echoed the very process that Khomeini had nullified and invalidated? Arjomand writes, "I suspect that before embarking on this project Khomeini and his followers did not realize that the attainment of these goals would entail a legal revolution in Shi'ism. But embark on this project they did, and the legal revolution they initiated was in full swing" (1988: 184). Mir-Hosseini observes,

> It is interesting to note that the *ulema* did not openly challenge the secularization of the law when the governments started to introduce reforms which severely limited the scope of the shari'a. Some felt that it would be better to keep the shari'a intact than to interfere with its substance by codification; thus its

replacement was deemed a lesser evil. Others, with modernist views, favoured its incorporation and collaborated in its codification in the sphere of family law. (1993: 12)

Indeed, the blending of the laws was a subtle acknowledgment on the part of the 'ulama of the conditions of their rise to power. They recognized that the overthrow of the shah came about as a result of the collected efforts of multiple groups and political parties. The combination of shari'a and civil law was a reflection of the compromises among various groups. It was also an effect of the final outcome of the revolution: that the entity that came to fruition after the revolution was not a pure or traditional expression of Islam nor a copy of the European state model, but something different, something new, which ultimately offered some women the means with which to challenge the roles ascribed to them both socially and privately.

SANCTIONED SUBVERSION

Tehran's family court is an important point of intervention for examining how women make sense of their rights, not only because of its nature as a legal venue, but also because of what the concept of the family, and women's crucial role within it, came to symbolize for the revolution and for the Islamic republic. Family courts throughout the world have effects on gender, family, identity, and subjectivity (Lazarus-Black 1994; Lazarus-Black and Hirsch 1994; Merry 1994). In the Iranian context, revolutionary forces, both state and parastate actors, mobilized the image of women as the symbolic bearers of virtue who represented the nation's honor and hence needed to be saved from Western corruption (Mogha-dam 1993: 88). The return of women to their proper stations—as wives and mothers and the bearers of national honor—became the explicit goal of many high-ranking officials in the newly formed Islamic republic (Moghadam 1993: 171–76). Thus the current increase in the divorce rate as well as women's increased petitions for divorce have proven to be vexing matters for state agents, as women appear to challenge these state-inscribed roles.

The Virtue of Courts

"Are you a virgin (*dokhtar*)?" the judge asked the young woman, attempting to ascertain whether she had consummated her marriage. This case involved a newly wed couple in which the bride, a twenty-four-year-old self-described housewife, had filed a petition asking for divorce on grounds that her husband was clinically depressed and could not provide for her. Alternatively, citing her husband's impotence and poor emotional state, she asked that her marriage contract be rescinded (*faskh al-nikah*), an action similar to annulment, in which the marriage is erased from records.[19] She also petitioned to execute her mahr. Her husband had followed up with a response indicating that he would grant a divorce if she pardoned her mahr. He denied both impotence and poor emotional state.

Initially both parties filed into the room, the husband with his father and lawyer, a relatively uncommon phenomenon, and the wife with her mother. The families sat on adjoining sides of the room. The judge had initially attempted to have the families sit together, but the parties declined. After everyone was seated and the parties had identified themselves, the judge stated the cause of action: "This is a petition for faskh al-nikah based on the husband's depression. There is also a petition asking for the execution of the mahr. The couple has been contractually married for one year and two months." At that moment, the judge looked up and asked the parents to exit the room so that the young people could speak without embarrassment. Then the judge began to gather the pertinent facts by posing questions to the parties.

"Are you a virgin?" He asked the young woman.

Evidently aware of what he was getting at, she responded, "From a medical perspective, yes, but I lived with him for five months." Her tall yet slight build appeared even smaller hidden beneath the draping brown manteau. Her sitting posture revealed blue jeans underneath. And black hair poked through the top of the scarf, gently grazing her forehead.

"Why are you still a virgin?

"He is sick."

"Well, are you asking for an annulment or your mahr?" Generally, when a woman opts to have the marriage contract rescinded, she is not eligible to receive her mahr. In one exception to this rule, a woman who has not consummated her marriage can obtain half of her mahr in the event of rescission, provided the basis of it is the husband's impotence. So when the judge asked this question, he was also trying to find out whether she wanted a divorce, in which case she would still be eligible for the entire mahr, or would rather save social face by opting for a rescission of the marriage contract, in which case she would receive at best half of the mahr.

"I do not know the difference. He is so depressed that he cannot function. He is unemployed and drinks, and he is impotent." The young woman had obviously been advised by someone and had drafted her petition to obtain the most financially beneficial outcome: divorce and her mahr as opposed to rescission.

"You are *doosheezeh*, yes?" He asked, double-checking that she was still a "maiden."

She nodded, and the judge turned to the husband, seemingly worn in his tattered flannel shirt and faded blue jeans. He sat arm over arm slumped low in his seat with his left ankle hanging over his right knee.

"You are willing to give her a divorce?" the judge asked, looking down at his paperwork.

"Yes."

"And," flipping through the file, the judge continued, "what about the mahr?"

The husband shifted one leg over the other, looked briefly at the judge, then, staring at the floor, stated that he would divorce his wife provided she pardon the payment of the mahr.

In dissolution proceedings, often the judges try to work with the petitioners to come to a mutual decision, in which case the divorce is termed *khul*, separation by mutual consent. Here, generally, to gain consent, women often give something in return for the divorce, such as their mahr. This is what the young man was angling for.

The judge looked over to the woman and, with a voice that indicated that he already knew her answer, asked, "Are you willing to do that?"

Angered, she said, "He took my youth, my life, came forward with deceit. His mother told us he lived in Germany and was a successful businessman, but she did not tell me that he had been in the hospital four times and had tried to kill himself twice. He cut his own tongue." The young woman, by making a case for his failure as a husband, through impotence, was making the strongest case possible for a marriage dissolution by judicial process (*tatliq*), in which, with proof, the judge will delegate the husband's divorce right to the wife.

But now the judge seemed annoyed, "What do you mean he took your life? You just said you are a virgin. So why do you say that?"

The woman stood up, faced the judge, and shouted, "I lived with him! I will be a divorcée; I will never find a husband." By now tears ran down her face. "He ruined my life. I am only twenty-four years old. All I wanted to do was finish my studies, but he would not leave us alone. He fooled us all. Now I will never be able to marry."

"But you are still a virgin, yes?" He asked for the third time.

"Yes, medically speaking."

"Is there any other kind?"

The judge told the husband that the wife wanted a divorce; she would not break the marriage contract. The husband's lawyer had advised his client to break the marriage contract because that way he would not have to pay the mahr, as she was still a virgin. The judge then asked the husband and his lawyer to leave the room so he could speak with the young woman privately.

When they left, the judge turned to the woman and said, "You know there is a problem with your case. The legal physician's report said that the doctor could not ascertain whether he is impotent. It states that he is only a slow starter and needs encouragement. So if he is not legally impotent, then you do not have cause to make the divorce petition. You may still petition for your mahr, and see if he is willing to divorce you. If you are a virgin as you say you are, he would only have to give you half of it. But the medical report says this is unclear. Your hymen is of a kind which does not make it possible to know."

She nodded. The judge moved from behind his podium to open the door of the court. He invited the husband and his attorney back into the room and then asked the women to leave so he could talk with the husband.

"She claims she is still a virgin and the doctor's report is inconclusive. If you agree to pay her half of the mahr, it will be all over. She does not want to break the marriage contract because she lived with you, and since both of your medical reports are inconclusive, I cannot break the marriage contract. Do you understand?"

"There is nothing wrong with him," the husband's attorney said. "The doctor's report says that he needs encouragement. That's all."

It then became clear that the issue the husband's attorney was trying to bring forth was the wife's legal duty to submit sexually to her husband (*tamkin*). His wife's failure to sexually submit would prevent the husband from having to pay any portion of the mahr. But the judge did not buy the argument. He asked, "She lived with you for five months?"

"Yes."

"You slept in the same bed?"

"Yes." That was all he needed. The judge invited the wife back and said, "Unless the two parties agree to go to the mediator, I will make my decision.

The wife replied, "I will leave it up to you."

"It is not up to me. This has been the law for fourteen hundred years, since the time God spoke to the Prophet. Even during the shahan-shahi [the previous monarchical government], this was the law; a girl gets half the mahr."

He told them to come back in a couple of days to pick up the written decision and order. The parties thanked the judge, stood up, and filed out. What became apparent in this case was both parties' apparent knowledge of the legal issues and their strategic maneuvering in the courtroom. The husband, reticent and uncomfortable, had brought an attorney with him to help mediate, but he seemed to lack resolve. The wife, who had been advised of the complex legal permutations of the relief she sought, seemed to play down her knowledge of the law and her obvious strategizing. When she spoke, she emphasized her lack of knowledge, although her petition clearly outlined her demands. She expressed her deference to the judge, despite having shouted at him. In the end she said she would trust in the judge's decision, but not before having made strong claims about the status of her marriage and her right to relief.

At the close of the hearing, the judge hinted at the likely outcome. Should the couple not come together in arbitration, he would order the husband to pay half of the wife's mahr and would execute a dissolution order, as opposed to an annulment. In stating that the decision was not up to him, the judge underscored his role in implementing God's law, although he also interpreted the law and acted as fact finder, reminiscent of the investigating judges of civil legal systems. The judge's statements and actions reflected the blended nature of the codified civil Islamic law; it is the message of God and it is standardized, transparent, and constant.

Finally, the woman's strategy of opting for the mahr as opposed to the annulment was noteworthy given that she would have saved social face by opting for the annulment, something her statements suggested she was concerned with. But had she done so, she likely would not have received her mahr, since the medical reports about her virginity and her husband's impotence were inconclusive. Thus, despite her worries about not being marriageable after divorce, she did not seek to remedy it if it meant not getting any portion of her mahr.

Because women cannot execute or initiate divorce, the family court becomes a key site in which women express their grievances and resist different aspects of patriarchal authority, be it that of state agents or the male head of the household. Sometimes women also use the court to renegotiate the terms of their marriages, entering into this sanctioned arena where they can bargain as rights-bearing, entitled subjects. The blended Islamico-civil context of the court inflects subjectivities that may not be available in other sites, such as in the home, where the husband is the legal and spiritual "head" of the household.[20] Indeed, use of the family court as the site for such renegotiations is especially noteworthy given that the family is so sacred in Islamic life.

These narratives show that the space for intervention might be small, but that the scope of the family court increasingly allows women room to maneuver. Indeed, women's increased use of courts as a means to seek changes in their domestic situations evidences their greater willingness to employ the political and legal institutions of the state to obtain state-sanctioned promises. And, as the primary petitioners, women give Iran's Islamico-civil family law greater form and substance through their engagement with it. In doing so, women use state-sanctioned means, the courts and civil laws, to access and obtain justice as allowed.

Mir-Hosseini has suggested that women's confident and articulate performance in the courts is "largely the legacy of pre-revolutionary reforms which provided a legal frame of reference in which women were treated on equal grounds with men" (1993: 30). In contrast, I find that the current composition of the court allows women to access and enact a discourse of rights. The prerevolutionary reforms to which Mir-Hosseini refers, such as the FPL, were abrogated as illegitimate, Western-inspired laws. The fact that post-1979 laws went through a process of "Islamic purification" has given the existing legal apparatus the legitimacy that it did not have before. The resulting system is neither solely Islamic nor solely civil. Women's confidence does not arise from prerevolutionary nostalgia or, in many cases, even remembrance, but instead results from something new emanating from the sanctioned blending of the shari'a with certain civil legal norms, and against a backdrop of an increasingly transnational circulation of the language of rights since the latter half of the twentieth century.

CIRCULATION OF RIGHTS TALK

Anthropology of law scholars Sally Merry and Mindie Lazarus-Black have each written about women's rights talk in contemporary court settings, Merry in Hawaii and Lazarus-Black in Trinidad and Tobago. Merry (2003) examined the use of law and legal mechanisms among battered women in Hawaii, finding that women's positive encounters with law gave them a heightened sense of their rights. Lazarus-Black (2001) came to a different conclusion in finding that it was not women's use of the law or experiences with the law that gave them greater consciousness of their rights, but rather the law's very existence and society's acceptance of it. In this discussion I am interested in the conditions that allow what appear as rights-bearing subjectivities to emerge in Iran also, in a very different legal context.[21]

In her studies of Kenya's Islamic Kadhi's courts, Susan Hirsch (1994, 1998) explored the place of resistance and discourses of rights among Swahili women litigants. She found that women's increased use of the courts reflected a "quiet resistance to the patriarchy," but not a "collective or conscious resistance articulated by women on explicitly gendered terms" (1994: 219). Unlike the Iranian women I worked with, the Swahili women who used the Kadhi's courts, according to Hirsch, rarely characterized the courts as spaces in which women could obtain their legal rights. There, instead of resorting to rights talk, women litigants focused on Kadhi's courts as among the few venues available for resolving conflicts (1994: 219).

In distinguishing women's use of Tehran's family court as potentially part of a collective, though not necessarily conscious, resistance to state practices, I stress the politically and historically situated position of both Kadhi's courts in Kenya and Tehran's family court. Kadhi's courts are among a small and decidedly religious and ethnic minority group in an otherwise liberal, secular state configuration. The people who access Kadhi's courts are an acknowledged minority population of Swahili Muslims. And Kadhi's courts exist as part of a larger project by the Kenyan state to control and monitor a group whose ethnic and religious diversity places it outside of the formal legal jurisdiction of the state authorities. In contrast, Tehran's family court is a branch of the central state's legal system. The regulation and control of the court is directly administered by the central state government. As such, women's increased petitions to the court, their increased use of the legal process and greater reliance on a discourse of rights[22] pose challenges to statist patriarchy and compel the courts to implement women's state-sanctioned rights.[23] Thus, women's discourses of rights in Tehran's family court could be seen as part of the resistance that is informed by state-approved and legitimated Islamico-civil rights. As part of a collective discourse, whether conscious or not, women's rights talk is derived from a broader network of communicative and interpretive strategies of which the Qur'anic meetings provided one example. Women in Iran's courts not only express themselves in rich narratives, as do the women in Kadhi's courts, but use a language and tone, as inflected through the rights-bearing, entitled subject, that has a particular place and effectiveness in the courts, but not necessarily beyond. Beyond the court, conditions that produce the subjectivity of rights-bearer may not always exist or may be a last resort because of the stigma attached to using the legal process for family matters (Mir-Hosseini 1993: 15).

CONCLUSION

In the early years of the revolution, the overt changes in Iran, particularly in women's dress and mobility, became symbolic of the "return" to tradition, Islam, and some ordered past. The nature of the government, systematization of the laws, and appeals to the polity to become acquainted with their rights, however, suggested the emergence of something very different. As the discontent with the administration of justice became more and more apparent, statist attempts to regularize the laws evinced recognition by some state actors that the people had a voice and were beginning to use it. The merging of the European civil law system with the shari'a, just as the Guardianship of the Jurist was blended with the French republic, reflected a new kind of governance in Iran, one that had never before been seen.

Iran's legal system takes shape through a mingling of the civil legal system and the shari'a, neither of which is homogeneous. Hybrid legal systems, sometimes also referred to as legal pluralism,[24] are often theorized in the context of colonialism, emphasizing the way different legal systems "intersect within fields of power relations" (Merry 2000: 18). Such studies stress the role of law in furthering cultural transformations and build on earlier critiques by British social anthropologists who failed to take into account the effects of colonialism on law (Merry 2000). Scholars today increasingly refer to the notion of interlinking legal systems as "not benignly 'plural' but as imposed normative orders that reflect power relations of colonialism and postcolonialism" (Hirsch 1994: 214). I distinguish Iran's civil legal system from that arising from an imposed colonial order and suggest that in Iran, both during the time of the shah and in the establishment of the Islamic republic, the adoption, importation, and ultimate retention of the civil codes was a willful political step toward modernization, on the one hand, and legitimization, on the other. I consider the legal and social transformations that are occurring through the merger of Islamic law with a civil legal structure but also regard the willful nature of the adoption of the civil system. In doing so, I highlight a different kind of power relationship evident within discourses of rights in Iran's family court and examine how this Islamico-civil system conditions the ways in which women make claims, discuss grievances, and ask for redress.

Lawrence Rosen has argued that civil laws are an arm of the central state and not a separate branch of government. In civil law systems, he suggests, law is not imagined as a counterbalance outside of the central authority (2000: 55–57). In examining civil law in the Islamic context, however, Rosen highlights the laws' intended indeterminacy (57–58). Here, Rosen expresses a view different from that of Ziba Mir-Hosseini, who, exploring Iran's civil system, suggests that the hybrid system creates an odd result, one in which the fluid shari'a "open to interpretation and capable of accommodating individual needs and circumstances is ossified by its codification."[25] As such, "not only has the traditional equilibrium between the shari'a and the state-administered law been upset, but the shari'a, for the first time in its history, has been given a definite legal force" (Mir-Hosseini 1993: 11). While I agree with Rosen that civil laws do not exist outside of the reach of the central authority, I have found that the concretization of the law that occurs with codification permits greater accessibility by the common people, who can then demand greater accountability of state forces. Definite legal force and transparency also bear on the way claims will be made.

I have noted that configuration of Tehran's family court positions women as autonomous subjects, even as it also positions them as being observant of the requirements of Islam. The subjectivities that emerge from the courts are contingent, not fixed but socially, historically, and politically negotiated. Thus, I have found that the codification of Islamic family law creates the situation where Iran's Islamico-civil law (1) is part of the state's central authority, (2) has transparency and a definitive quality in its codified form, and (3) allows for modern, rights-bearing subjectivities. This subjectivity, however, does not shift seamlessly to different contexts. In different settings, women must reckon with numerous other contingencies in performing their roles.

In the "official" legal setting of the courts, the merger of civil law and shari'a law becomes most apparent. This imbrication permits a hybrid discourse based on civil laws and Islamic principles to enter into discussions of rights and justice. Some scholars have argued that Iran is a Muslim country or a theocracy; others, often attorneys I interviewed in Iran, told me that, in fact, Iran has a civil legal system, and for that reason they were not bound solely by Islamic doctrines. It is this apparent discrepancy that led me to seek clarity on the subject and to find the sources of this contradiction amid political and legal state apparatuses. In the next chapter, I continue to explore the language of legality in family matters by looking at lawyers' conversations with their clients and offer a glimpse of how the language of motherhood or wifely duty, while based in Islamic principles for many, is, in these contexts, readily translated to actionable civil legal language.

Women's use of a language of rights and their engagement with the legal process provides, perhaps unwittingly in some cases, a mirror of legitimization back to the state. That the institutions of the Islamic republic create the possibilities for citizens to employ a discourse of rights, a tangible and transparent legal process, and material results further legitimates this new form of governance while also partially constructing it. This is particularly significant given that state agents took on the "woman question" just after the creation of the republic and made the social and moral rehabilitation of women a national project and symbol of its urgency.

CHAPTER FIVE

Practice and Effect: Writing/Righting the Law

Ms. Tabrizi's law offices looked like any other: waiting clients cast their eyes down, seemingly contemplating the shoes on their feet. Others anxiously scanned the room and tapped their heels as they waited in the small reception area of the ground floor office located in north central Tehran. Several young women in short overcoats, small scarves, and painted nails ran to and fro calling clients, serving tea, and answering phones. Here I, too, waited. I was seeking a meeting with a well-known attorney, a woman in her early forties, who had been active in working to fashion new legal claims where she and other advocates were facing major difficulties during and after divorce due to a lack of legal framework. The problem was not solely that the laws were discriminatory, but that there was a lack of legal apparatus to address issues that were arising as a result of increased divorce. In this chapter I consider some of the ways that women's rights advocates were attempting to bridge certain gaps in law, especially as they affected women's rights in marriage and divorce. In exploring the conversations in this law office, I show how some lawyers attempt to put the new corrective laws into operation as well as educate their clients about the importance of contracts. I also consider the broader context in which the discriminatory laws are situated, addressing lawyers' and advocates' attempts to seek remedies. In doing so, I consider some social consequences women face for going after their rights.

A few people were ahead of me: an older man stroked his worry beads while a stylish young woman stole a look at herself in the adjacent mirror. As clients were called in one by one, an assistant led them through the long narrow corridor to Tabrizi's office. The mirror in the entrance of the small waiting room gave the room an illusion of expansiveness. Below the mirror, a small calligraphic sign displayed the cost of a thirty-minute consultation.

After a short time, I was called in to meet with Ms. Tabrizi. Her jovial receptionist led me down the hall to the room at the very end where four green paisley chairs faced a large, dark green wooden desk. From the angle of my low-sitting chair, Tabrizi appeared larger than life, sitting regally behind the elegant mahogany desk. Over her chador, beneath which not a sliver of hair was revealed, she sported a sleek black leather jacket. Beyond pondering the logistics of putting on such attire, I mused at how multifaceted Tabrizi looked in this outfit: at once the symbol of Muslim traditionalism and yet the modern lawyer zealously campaigning for the legal rights of her down-and-out clients.

Even before going to Iran, I had heard of Tabrizi, whose name was prevalent among Iranian women's rights advocates. Once I arrived in Iran, her name continued to come up.[1] Tabrizi's well-known advocacy on behalf of women attracted clients of various backgrounds. Women ranging from the deeply religious to the secular as well as those who shunned the Islamic republic spoke of her as a leading advocate of women's rights in Iran.[2] The primary purpose of my visit with Tabrizi was to ask her about the intellectual and legislative history of the law that permits wives to obtain postdivorce maintenance (*ojrat al-mesl*) in the form of the economic value of the services they rendered during a marriage, in the event their husbands seek dissolution. This ojrat al-mesl was, at that time, a new way in which women were obtaining something akin to alimony. Tabrizi was not only an advocate of this bill, but also one of a handful of women who construed this legal right from scriptural texts.

According to Tehran's Bar Association, there are more than 700 women licensed to practice law in the city and over 2,500 in the country. Some lawyers, like Tabrizi, train in the university system, while others, mostly men, are able to obtain the requisite training through the Islamic seminary system. Tabrizi had moved to Tehran as an adolescent. She attended law school in the early years of the revolution, when the universities had reopened after having been closed for retooling by the new government. Her father was an akhund who had studied in Qom, and her family supported the removal of the monarchy. Like many, Tabrizi emphasized the political reasons for her family's support for Khomeini: "to free the country from imperialism." Her family had sent soldiers to the front of the war with Iraq and, like many, had lost relatives in the war. She was fortunate in all of this, she told me, to have had a chance to focus on her studies. Like most students who earned legal training through the university system, she took courses such as jurisprudence, civil law, civil procedure, criminal law, criminal procedure, and business law. Before receiving her license to practice law, she had to pass her exams, then complete two years of internship at a law firm. Finally, for her specialty in marriage and family law, she also had to intern an extra two years. In the years after her initial training, she continued to work in other law offices, gaining more training until starting her own practice almost ten years later. By the time I met her, she had also served as an advisor to the Women's Affairs Division of Majlis as well as in several ministries.

Legal (Re)formations

"Before the revolution, we had mostly Belgian and French laws," she explained.

> But after the revolution, everything changed, mostly in family and penal laws. We were confused for a while. Imam [Khomeini] had ordered that laws against Islam should not be executed. But now we are slowly seeing laws that we had in that previous time. For instance, a recent presidential decree to parliament stated that law students with a bachelor's degree can practice law—set up an office, go to court, see clients, and so on. This was a law proposed to Majlis nearly forty years ago—and it was refused.

Her manner was professional, yet accommodating and friendly.

> I work with other advocates to bring needed changes to the laws, and we are required to do so through our religion because it provides us with guidance. We are working on bringing about equitable results for families in our society. People, mostly foreigners like you, think it is only the women who are suffering. But it's not true. Sometimes it is the men. I have a case in which the husband, who was much older than his wife, did not work because of his age and ill health. His wife had a good position in the government. She contracted a very bad illness, leukemia, and died soon after. When she died, her pension ended. Now her husband had nothing to live on. But in the case where a woman loses her husband, she will continue to receive his pension until she dies. We are trying to address these inequalities as well.

Then Tabrizi quickly moved to the legal issue I had asked her about. Ojrat al-mesl, she told me, was conceived in response to the law that gives men the unilateral right to divorce. "When we saw the state in which this left women, we were bound to do something about it," Tabrizi told me.

> Ojrat al-mesl allows a woman to petition the court for compensation for the domestic services rendered during the course of the marriage if her husband seeks dissolution. It is based on the fact that in the shari'a women are not required to work in their homes. When we first proposed this, some women protested, saying, "We are getting paid for work we do in the house, but in our own homes," and "We are not prostitutes." But advocates like me felt strongly that we needed a counterbalance to this unilateral right of men to divorce. If the law provided for them to divorce their wives without cause, they should at least have to compensate the women for their lost time.

She went on to explain that the codified version of the law that allows men to divorce their wives arises from a very specific verse in the Qur'an and therefore cannot be repealed. For that reason, she and some other women legal scholars researched Islamic jurisprudence for a theoretical basis to compensate women for the unevenness in the law.

"*Ojrat*" (an Arabic word), she explained, "means compensation (*mozd*)." In reply to my question about the theoretical basis for the law, she said,

> There are three different Qur'anic bases from which we were able to deduce the legal concept of ojrat al-mesl. First, there is the basis that says a woman who gives her child milk from her own breast can be compensated monetarily. Second, there is the matter of obedience (*tamkin*). In Islamic jurisprudence, a wife's only obligation to her husband is obedience.[3] And the husband's only obligation is payment of the mahr. These are the duties associated with being a couple (*zojeeat*). And third, we use an analogy with the concept of bride's portion in-kind (*mahr al-mesl*), which is the legal concept that if there is no mahr, then the wife should get an estimated amount "like" (*mesl*) that which is befitting to her station.

Tabrizi's arguments should be contextualized in her practice as an advocate, but whether her advancing of these arguments is merely strategic is not at issue. The effect of codifying this law severed it from its jurisprudential sources, which, on the one hand, provided for hitherto absent postdivorce maintenance, but also brought about an uncomfortable logic in raising such a claim. The advocates of this law did not get exactly what they had asked for, however. When the final version of the bill passed in parliament, there was an additional burden placed on women: they had to prove that they were not at fault. "Men use this a lot. Sometimes a man will simply say that he is 'suspicious' of his wife, in order to suggest that she is not virtuous," Tabrizi said. "They try to get out from under the law by saying that their wives somehow caused the problems. But we are saying that when it is the husband who wants to divorce, it has nothing to do with fault, and the wife should be able to obtain compensation for the work she has done."

Contests over women's virtue, amid policy and legal changes geared toward extending women a greater degree of social protection in the event of dissolution, have raised many an eyebrow. The symbolic value of women as the bearers of virtue, both national and familial, cannot be overlooked in the legal administration of redressing grievances, even if the ostensible goal, as here, is for the benefit of the women themselves. Nonetheless, new hybrid legal formations have made possible new claims and remedies. I remained in my seat that day and for months after as Tabrizi called in her clients one by one.

ACCESSING RIGHTS

A few weeks later, I saw the law of ojrat al-mesl animated when Mitra, a married woman in her mid-forties, walked in. Her warm smile and gracious personality belied heartache, abuse, and separation. After the necessary pleasantries, Tabrizi asked, "How can I be of service to you?" Mitra, who had already been to another attorney, was seeking a second opinion for a matter that seemed to have no simple solution. Her husband, Ali, had become physically abusive in the later years of their marriage, and Mitra simply could not take it anymore. The couple had met while they were both students in Shiraz, he in engineering and she in English. They were very young, in their early twenties, and he swept her off her feet. They were very in love. He wanted to go to the United States for advanced training; his family, a very conservative religious family, thought it best that she remain in Iran. She refused and went with her husband. They stayed in the United States for ten years. His family blamed her for keeping their son away. They returned only recently when he was offered a terrific job as a university professor. The work and stress of the new job had affected him. One night he came home and spoke sharply to her. She was used to this—over the years he had grown increasingly gruff in his tone, and he always had a temper. Harsh words were something she had grown used to, and she would normally walk away. But this time, she explained, she spoke back to him, accusing him of having affairs, something that she had known about over the years but had kept to herself. When she responded with her accusations, he hit her. She struck back at him and things escalated. She ran into a room, locked the door, and called the police. When the police arrived, she filed a complaint against him. This gave her a basis for initiating divorce.

By the time of her visit to Tabrizi's office, she had been away from the house for some months, having spent a month at a friend's house before securing her own apartment. The children were with her husband, who, because of his work, traveled a lot and left the children with his sister. To punish her for the complaint, he refused to let her see the children and had her name put on a list that prevented her from traveling abroad. In order for her to see her children, he demanded that she withdraw her complaint and sign a piece of paper that would give him full ownership of their property in the United States. If she did, then he would also agree to divorce her. Now Mitra sat before Tabrizi, almost childlike in the large green chair as she looked up to Tabrizi for her opinion. "I give in," Mitra said wearily. "I hope you do not try to convince me to fight for my rights. I just want this to be over." Tabrizi did not relent. She advised Mitra not to take back her complaint against Ali. She also advised her not to sign away all her rights and not to pardon or give in (*gozasht*) in order to see her children. She explained to Mitra about the recent process that allows a child, at the age of puberty—nine for girls, fifteen for boys—to obtain an order of majority (*hokm-e rosht*), which is a ruling from the court that permits the child to decide which parent he or she would like to live with. Mitra was surprised: she had no idea such a thing was possible. Tabrizi asked to see the piece of paper that Ali wanted Mitra to sign. Mitra responded that she did not have a copy. Ali would not give it to her, but maybe he would show it to Tabrizi if she [Tabrizi] asked him. Tabrizi advised her not to sign anything that she did not have a copy of, explaining, "He has something to hide if he won't give you a copy," and so there was no point in having a lawyer look it over if he could just change it at will. Tabrizi added that she would not contact Ali as she did not want to be insulted by him if he was as belligerent as Mitra described. Tabrizi then told Mitra that she should add some stipulations of her own before finalizing the terms of the divorce. Mitra was incredulous. "It's up to him. Everything is in his power. I can't ask him for anything. What can I ask for?"

Tabrizi suggested that Mitra not give up on her property in the United States. She told her to say that this was the only way she would be willing to withdraw her complaint. But Mitra said that she was afraid to tell her husband this. She sat for a moment and reflected on the unexpected difficulties of marriage. Tabrizi stared at her in silence. Mitra finally responded, saying that she would try to talk to him about her suggestions. Then she thanked the lawyer, nodded in my direction, and walked out of the office. Tabrizi turned to me and said, "You see, women don't know their rights and even when they do, they don't go after them. Our women are taught at a very young age to give in."

A few days later, Mitra returned. She told the lawyer what Ali had told her. She said that Ali was willing to remove her name only if she agreed to give him five million toman (about four thousand dollars), which she refused. Tabrizi again told Mitra not to give in, that Ali wanted something to hang over her head. Tabrizi explained to Mitra that her power came from the new law, ojrat al-mesl, that she had the power because she had lived with Ali for almost twenty years and was not at fault, and that she had a basis to initiate divorce. "It's he who must give you money," Tabrizi explained. Again, Mitra left with indecision and doubt.

I continued to correspond with Mitra during the turbulent course of her legal process. After her second meeting with Tabrizi, Mitra called her husband and conveyed the lawyer's suggestions. Ali screamed at her through the telephone and told her that she had made his life hell. Mitra hung up on him. On another visit to the lawyer's office, Mitra said that Ali's behavior was an indication that he was growing weaker. Through her better understanding of her options, she seemed to feel that she was growing stronger. She had even convinced Ali to let her see her children one day a week.

In the following weeks, Mitra went to see yet another lawyer, a third one, seeking assurances about the law and whether she really had the options the first two had told her about. This lawyer gave her similar advice. He told Mitra to give her husband conditions: first, that she would not sign anything for which she did not have a copy; and second, that she would not to sign anything she did not first have her representative read. He also explained that if she did, her husband could otherwise just change the document. This lawyer also told her not to give up on her rights. He explained that Mitra should demand a bank check in the amount of her estimated ojrat al-mesl—then she and her husband could go to the notary (*mahzar*) and sign the agreement only after they first went to the bank and the court to finalize the divorce. This lawyer told her that she "could do everything."

Again, Mitra called and spoke to her husband, trying to tell him what, by now, three lawyers had told her. He was difficult and began posturing on the telephone. But she told him that she did not want his advice, that she trusted her lawyers. Mitra said that when he started yelling at her, she hung up on him. And that was that. "And now it is up to him," she said. She said she was glad that she placed some conditions on him and that she was "standing up for herself now." She did not speak about the children but only expressed that she was not sure to what extent he would use them to pressure her.

In terms of her divorce, Mitra told me that they planned to go to the mahzar to register the divorce. The money that he had agreed to give her, which is only a fraction of the entire ojrat al-mesl to which her lawyer told her she was entitled, was about thirty-three million toman (at the time about $23,000 dollars). The plan was for her to register the divorce at the mahzar, which would finalize things, at which time Mitra would receive her money. She was nervous and happy and sad and all around impatient. She awaited word from her lawyer, who called and told Mitra that she had a letter that had been faxed to her from her husband's attorney. Mitra did not know what it said and it made her uneasy, yet another potential problem that could postpone things. She said she just did not know what Ali's problem was. It turned out that he wanted a check for the thirty-three million just in case she failed to withdraw her complaint or to sign over her rights to the property in the United States.

In the end, Mitra decided to sign away all of her rights to the property and monies that she might be entitled to. This she did in return for her divorce. She bought her divorce, she said. She was permitted to see her children but once a week, even when Ali was gone or in the United States, which was sometimes months at a time.

Even though her husband had behaved terribly toward her, she thought that he did not want a divorce, not because he loved her, but because for him it was a symbol of failure. He was the one who always preached to his family that he could keep his wife and that they should learn from him. In the end, he was a monster, she said, and the reason they stayed together as long as they did was that Mitra had become subjugated (*mazloom*) in the time they were married. She was afraid of him, of talking back to him. She told me that this developed over the course of a long period. It was not until the incident when she stood up to his insults and attacks and spoke back to him that things really changed. Now that she was divorced, she wondered how it would affect her and her children in society (*jame'eh*). The questions that Mitra had about who she is and what people would think of her and how that would affect her socially were the same questions that many of the divorced or soon-to-be divorced women I encountered expressed. This was a concern independent of whether women had rights or made use of those rights. Indeed, the concern with a perception (anonymous and writ large) of moral depravity was a major factor that troubled women who got involved in legal issues surrounding private and family matters; Mitra's concerns in this respect were hardly unique.

COURTING VIRTUE

That some new legal rights have been awarded or at least afforded women through the creative thinking and hard work of people like Tabrizi is not to be underestimated, but the question then becomes one of access. By access, I refer not merely to the economic feasibility of filing claims, but to the social feasibility, the politics of accessing the laws. Who are the women filing claims in the courts, and how does the social discourse of women in the courts affect the status of women outside the courts? What are the specific subjectivities of the women in the courts, and how, if at all, do the subjectivities that women assume in the courts interact with their subjectivities outside the realm of legal process?

The debates about women accessing laws in family matters are an instance of the uneven and shifting nature of law in society and law as a domain of culture (Sarat and Kearns 1998). Law, as many have pointed out, has the power to make meaning because laws enter social practices and shape social consciousness, all the while seeming invisible, natural, or benign (Silbey 1992). The cultural influence of the legal domain has been a major component of the modern nation-state, bearing on the construction of the free-willed, rights-bearing, individual subject, the imagined social contract, and the insistence of boundaries and boundedness (Fitzpatrick 1992). Law, however, is created in a social context, amid existing social relations. The meaning-making of law then, is, as Sarat and Kearns (1998) regarded it, "a moving hegemony"[4] rendering meaning differently across and within societies. The liberatory promises of civil legality have meaning in limited circumstances or settings within a society, such as in the civil court system in postimperialist societies.[5] Thus, in what follows, I highlight the unevenness, impermanence, and distinctiveness of the cultural productions of law. What are the specific relations that constitute the cultural production of law in Iran? The lively contestations of the religio-liberal courts over women's rights, roles, and duties are a set of practices distinct from the kinds of contests that occur outside of the courts, and which do not necessarily entertain the possibilities inherent in the modern nation-state in the same way the courts do.

While the domain of law has its own cultural productions, it provides for a certain kind of subjectivity and certain kinds of arguments, which are much less accessible in other contexts—even within that society—that do not bear the markers of modernity in the same way as the courts. The modernizing process itself is thus distinct and uneven. The moving hegemony of law does not always move in the same way in all arenas of social life. In Iran, the legal structure is a moving hegemony throughout the courts and other sociopolitical offices, and as such it does not play out in the same manner in, for instance, familial contexts where the individual is met with naturalized gender roles (Yanagisako and Delaney 1995).

The aforementioned ojrat al-mesl law became one of concern for women, who, while advocates of change and improvement in the status of women, were also concerned about what it could mean, appear as, or translate into in greater society: a woman being paid for the domestic duties she performs for her husband. "That makes it sound as though we are domestic servants in our own homes!" a woman exclaimed one day in the lawyer's office.

Indeed, the attention paid to appearances and "what that could mean" is an enormous issue in the search for solutions to improvement in women's status. Most everyone agrees with the idea of improvements of women's status and rights, but what exactly that means in practical terms is where disputes emerge, and the debates are drawn not at all neatly along categories of gender, religion, class, politics, or tradition. In fact, what it means to improve the status of women in Iran is itself highly contested.

In the specific case of legal rights, as revealed in the courts, women, on the one hand, seek and fight for legal rights, while in their home lives women also struggle for respect as mothers and wives, and the two do not always coincide. Women who make use of the legal apparatus of the state may actually be risking their social capital, honor, and dignity, with respect to their families and communities (Hirsch 1994). Women's subjectivities shift through the different settings in which they move, and their perceptions of rights and the social relevance of such rights are deeply influenced by their settings, and they change just as their settings do.

One day while interviewing people in the corridors of the court, I asked a gentleman standing alone if he would mind discussing his situation. "My situation?" he repeated, bemused. "I am married. My wife is at home. She is a good woman. I am here today accompanying my cousin. He is getting a divorce. I am sure he will be happy to speak with you when he is finished in court, but he does not have a story that will interest you. He and his wife came to a mutual agreement and have remained friends. They just came here to finalize the divorce." Roxana, who was accompanying me and who was herself divorced, stated, "That is a good thing. Coming here, running after your case, can be so awful. The women (*khanumha*, literally, ladies or gentlewomen) here have it really hard, especially when their husbands do not cooperate or show up."

"That's right," the man replied, "this is a very difficult place to have business, but really, some people get themselves into these messes, and sometimes it is just what they deserve. I mean, look around you, I don't see one gentlewoman (*khanum*) here." Shocked, I looked at my friend to get her reaction. Roxana looked at me, unmoved. We were suddenly interrupted by the call to prayer, signifying the beginning of the end of the day's court hearings. The man said goodbye and walked away.

"He's right," she said, scanning the faces of the last remaining men and women. "The women (*zanha*) here are not gentlewomen. They can't be, after what they have to go through."

I understood, however, that Roxana meant something altogether different from what I understood the man to be saying. There is a social transformation that the soon-to-be-divorcée goes through when undergoing the ordeal of getting a divorce. The woman is no longer in the delicate protective armor of the social innocent. I recalled a commonly expressed sentiment, "A gentlewoman must be delicate (*khanum bayad lateef bashad*)."

Virtue and modesty are key indicators of a woman's respectability in Iran and in much of the world, the United States not excepted. In Iran, these values are characterized in numerous ways and have become signifiers of the revolutionary woman's character. Just before the revolution, when those in favor of the revolution complained that Iranian society was permeated with decay, the effects were most dramatic and visible upon women who, it was said, dressed up like Barbie dolls in short shirts, heavy makeup, and so on. Then, when the revolution occurred, women again were made to be the symbols, the terrain upon which the ideological fight against imperialism and Western decay was played out.[6] Civil society and state control over women's bodies through the enforcement and regulation of the modest dress code became important markers of the changes that occurred in Iran after the revolution. The revolution, inasmuch as it was said to be about cleansing the corruption of Western decadence from the soul of Iran, looked to women as that soul, as the core and primary spiritual agent of the family. For this, women's virtue became the virtue of the nation as well, and regulating women's virtue was a nationalist as well as populist enterprise.

But the acts of women divorcing their husbands, executing their mahr, and filing complaints for economic support had slowly crept upon the state. At first, the relevant state actors looked upon these actions as petty annoyances, but as the stories grew into well-constructed narratives in newspapers and magazines, on television, and eventually in the courts, they began to consider these cases in earnest. Still, the women themselves were often scrutinized and blamed not only for their behavior in the homes, but also for bringing such claims, which were thought to be belittling to the family's honor, to the court, and taking time away from the women's "real" duties to their families. Although a number of women had had winning experiences in court, when they left that arena they returned to lives over which they still did not have full control.

LEGAL CLAIMS AND THEIR SOCIAL COSTS

That "bad" women go to court certainly resonated with Roshan's experiences before the judge in Rey, an ancient town along the silk road, now considered a suburb of Tehran. I met Roshan at an attorney's office. With her ivory skin and black hair, she reminded me of a sad Snow White. At thirty-three she was twice married and once divorced. She was now sitting before her attorney seeking legal advice about a husband who had, she claimed, abandoned her. I asked her why she had decided to seek out the help of an attorney with her case. She replied that she needed legal advice about when and how to file a complaint to the judge, but since she did not have a lot of money, she would do the footwork herself.

"Since I know my husband is not coming back to me," she said, "I want to know how long I have to wait before I can file my petition against him. I have no money, and I at least want to get my mahr from him."

"But if you don't know his whereabouts, how will you be able to get your mahr?" I asked.

"I know that he wants to leave the country and they will not permit him to leave once his name is placed on a list of disappeared (m'afqhood *al-asr*). He will be arrested at the port on the spot. Then at least he will have to make my situation clear." She continued to describe her situation, stressing that he only married because of family pressure. The lawyer tells her that she has to accumulate six months of not receiving maintenance before she can file a complaint for lack of support, which will then presumably also be the basis to initiate divorce proceedings.

Roshan also made passing mention of legal representation: "The court officers and the judge are not as mean to you." "How so?" I asked. She explained that even though more and more people are getting divorced, they still make it really hard, "especially for the women, because the society still does not want to accept that women are initiating divorces," even though in her case, it was her husband who had left her. She said that when she went to court the first time, the judge was talking to a woman in front of her. "He was yelling at her and telling her that she was a bad woman for seeking a divorce. The judge was really abusing her, shouting that no woman should leave her husband under any circumstances. The woman was crying; it was a terrible scene."

Roshan then said,

> It is not that the woman was not granted her divorce in the end, but the authorities are so abusive to women, and it should not be that way. They are doing nothing wrong; most women wait until the last possible moment to look into divorce. It is not something that any woman wants because afterwards you are nothing, nothing at all, and you have no life. Even me, I was a divorced woman, and look what I got, a man who does not come home at night, who, it turns out, just wanted to keep me around so his family would think he is a decent family man. Iranian society still has not come to accept this—that women seek divorce. We have always been taught to *besooz o besauz* [colloquial phrase that means to burn and make do].

The Islamico-civil subjectivity that I suggested earlier, in which women perform as entitled citizens endowed with rights in the court, is now seen as a transient subjectivity. Despite the effect of the law, the subjectivities women take on in court, while empowering, often are not carried over in the household or other contexts of daily life.

For instance, Layla, the law student we met in the previous chapter, applies her well-versed individualism in most aspects of her life, but she questioned how this individualism would affect her personal life. When the discussion turned to marriage and family, Layla, only twenty-five, had severe doubts about her marriageability because, as she put it, "I don't agree with the typical duties expected of a woman in the marriage." At first she listed a range of duties associated with the legally defined rules between husbands and wives. When I noted that many of these rules could be set aside in the marriage contract, Layla expressed concerns arising out of a more complicated dialectic between law and society. The duties of a wife are enmeshed in a social context, which, despite existing legal caveats, are extremely difficult to transgress, and if transgressed, are done so with certain serious consequences.

"For instance," she explained, "when I get married, my husband has the right to prohibit me from working outside of the house, leaving the country, or continuing my education. Despite contractual agreements we may have in the marriage contract, if I don't comply with my wifely duties, I could have a very difficult situation with my family, my husband's family, or otherwise."

"What do you mean by wifely duties?"

"Wifely duties are the daily chores that are expected of a woman once she enters into marriage, cooking, cleaning, and submitting to sex. Men have a legal expectation that their wives will carry out these duties. If women do not submit, husbands can refuse to financially support their wives."

Thus, the legal identity—or legally constructed duties and benefits—compete with gender roles that are naturalized and said to be ordained by God. In this way, legal identities constructed by and contained within the laws are not bounded entities in and of themselves but are fashioned and fomented in changing and varied contexts, such as the court, the middle-class urban households, the all-girls middle-school, and so on.

Women's shifting subjectivities, moreover, are not pendulums, swinging between legal constructions and naturalized gender roles alone, but are inflected amid a range of values and beliefs, like class or ethnicity, among others. Layla's story can be understood in the context of the life of a middle-class, urban woman with a college education. Her story can be contrasted with the multitude of stories from women who live in the southernmost parts of Tehran, where the ghettoes of the city exist. This is where I met Parry, who comes from a relatively poor family. Her first marriage ended in divorce when her husband told her, after only four years of marriage, that he wanted to take a second wife, and that he did not love her. Parry told me, "I did not know what to do; I was only twenty-one at the time." When he told her he was going to take a second wife, Parry had the option of giving her consent and remaining married to him, or getting a divorce, her husband having agreed to give her one. On the advice of her family, she obtained a divorce.

Parry explained that her family's attitudes toward her changed once she was divorced, despite being divorced on their advice. "My aunt and uncle no longer allowed me to come to their house. As a divorced woman, my aunt now saw me as a threat to her teenage sons." Parry was mortified by the insinuation that she would tempt her cousins, with whom she was raised, into immoral acts and thoughts. Parry found that the attitudes of everyone around her had changed. She found that not to have a man's "shadow over her" caused her to be a threat to her social and familial group. When her parents introduced her to a suitor, she opted to marry again. She wondered why this forty-something man had never married. Once she was married, Parry's suspicions were confirmed. Hossein was a heroin addict. When I met her, Parry had been married to Hossein for over seven years. She had a five-year-old son whom she supported entirely from her work as a custodian. Her husband did not work; he received only a small pension, which he used to support his habit. Though she knew she had the legal right, Parry told me that she would not seek a divorce despite her family's advice that she do so. Parry felt that knowing the consequences of being an unmarried woman, twice divorced, no less, she was not willing to return to this marked category in her social group. Parry's story can be juxtaposed with Layla's to show how the currents of law and society bear differently on differently situated women. In addition, Layla's and Parry's stories demonstrate that the kinds of legal negotiations that women make have far greater consequences and implications than simply obtaining the legally available remedy, and the concerns surrounding these negotiations involve much more than the law. Thus, the legal realm is but one arena of negotiation, and only one way in which the women I interviewed found themselves negotiating their roles and perceiving their rights. And in most cases not only are those arenas shifting, but women's identities are also in flux, changing through different contexts over time.

Accessing Law: The Role of Contracts in Marriage and Family Laws

Fereshteh worked in an attorney's office in central Tehran. She was in her late forties and had been divorced for many years. She had strong opinions about women's status in marriage through her own experiences with the legal system. The first thing she said to me when I met her in the summer of 1999 was, "The only thing I want for my daughter is the divorce right," referring to the stipulation in the marriage contract that gives women the right to dissolve marriage. She explained that it was not until she ran into problems with her marriage that she realized how naïve she had been about her rights. She said, "Despite what people say, there are laws in Iran, but few know how they work. Only a small number of people understand that the laws, while working to protect the state's interest in keeping families together, give men an incredible degree of power over the members of the family." She said she learned how the civil laws guiding family issues worked only after her husband began treating her badly and she needed to leave the marriage. "Only after the troubles started," she said, "did I realize how very powerless the laws made women, especially after the revolution when Khomeini repealed the marriage and family law."

"The law made you powerless?" I asked her.

"No, you must understand, my own lack of interest in the law made me powerless." Fereshteh explained that she came from a working-class family in Tehran who had supported Ayatollah Khomeini's calls for wealth redistribution. "We were told that we would have oil dividends delivered to us, that we would not pay for gas and electricity. Of course we thought our lives would improve. Instead all they have done is bring us this," she said as she tugged on her headscarf.

Fereshteh nonetheless maintained her lack of interest in politics, "What did it matter to me? I was young, without money. I was married to a government worker and had a newborn. I wanted economic improvements. Now that I am on my own, I understand why those women protested. Social rights and economic rights cannot be separated. I learned this when I went through my divorce. Back then, it was much harder. Judges did not look at you as an individual with rights. They did not care what you had to say. You had to find a way to get your husband to agree. That was what I did."

"What did you do?" I asked.

"I conceded everything. I said, I don't want any mahrieh, you can keep the dowry (jahaz). I even left behind all the jewelry they gave me as a gift. All this so he would agree to divorce me."

"So in the end he divorced you?"

"That's how it was back then. I had no avenue to initiate divorce; I didn't know how things worked. But now I do." Although not trained as a lawyer, Fereshteh, who worked at the front desk primarily as a receptionist, had learned a great deal about the laws regarding divorce and often entertained questions from the clients waiting for their appointments. As with many women who had had dealings with the legal system, Fereshteh saw knowledge of the law as the avenue to getting her rights and put this in the context of Islamic law: "Islam is about justice. But you can't go and tell the judge, give me justice, even give me my rights—you have to know enough to be able to convince the judge that *this* is justice. In order to do this, you need to know how the system works. You need to go to court and know what to say, what evidence to provide. In that respect, it's no different here than in France or America." For her, going after her rights consisted of some tangible actions, such as learning what the legal codes permit, what the legal process entailed, and what the procedures for filing claims were. Knowledge of the laws permitted greater leverage in negotiating, which, as I learned from attorney-client meetings, were crucial skills women needed to develop because of the importance of the written contract in private matters, especially marriage and divorce.

The focus on negotiating and bargaining emphasizes a key component not only of gaining rights, as Fereshteh believed, but also of expanding the laws by developing them in new contexts and fostering a pattern of behavior that ultimately comes to be viewed as a customary practice of law. For instance, when I spoke with Fereshteh in 1999, the stipulation that she spoke about, the right to initiate divorce, was an important concern of a mother whose young daughter was about to get married. Only a couple of years later, the stipulation was standardized and officially added to the official marriage contract. The marriage contract itself has evolved from being a ritualized document that was signed ceremoniously between parties as part of the larger marriage process to being viewed as an actionable contract in which parties recognize legal provisions to which they are acceding.

Omid was a conscript in the midst of his two-year mandatory military service. While on furlough he went to see Tabrizi. He and his wife of three years were talking about divorce. Aware of the laws of equitable property division, he asked Tabrizi if he could avoid splitting the property by placing it in his mother's name. She asked him why he wanted to do such a thing, that this was his two-year-old daughter's mother. He answered that she had a very high bride price and if he paid it, that would leave his young wife with enough to live on. He said that he was just beginning his life, and due to military service he had barely even lived with his wife, so it wasn't right that she should get part of the property that was in his family for generations. In spite of her counseling to the contrary, Tabrizi conceded that there was no law preventing him from doing this. As he walked out of her office, Tabrizi told me the law is in motion—it is always changing from these exigencies. "Several years ago we worked hard to find an equitable solution to property division. Now people are finding ways around this, and now, again, we need to find new solutions." Indeed, the individuals or families who came to see Tabrizi frequently asked for her guidance on getting around the law. As she and her clients pushed the limits of the law, they sometimes undermined the legislative aim to compensate women for the discriminatory legal framework. In such cases, Tabrizi tried to appeal to a greater sense of justice, speaking more broadly to the foundations of the legal provisions, the shari'a and Islamic jurisprudence.

Tabrizi compared this man's situation with that of another client she saw—a distraught, love-struck artist who had been to see her several months earlier. Majid, in his mid-thirties, had been married to an "angel" for almost a decade but had recently realized that his feelings for his wife had changed. He told Tabrizi that he sought her advice as an older, wiser, world-traveled "sister." She thanked him, expressed her wish to properly advise him, and asked that he explain his situation. He told her that he had married about nine years ago. His wife is in her early thirties. They have no children. They had tried to live together but realized that they did not have a lot in common, so they separated and were talking about divorce. In the meantime, during the separation, he met and fell deeply in love with a much younger woman. She was about twenty. Shortly thereafter, with the intervention of both families, he and his wife were convinced to get back together. He tried to break it off with the younger woman but just couldn't. He and his wife had again separated because they could not live together, but he felt sorry for his wife and explained that he really did not want to abandon her. Meanwhile, the young woman's parents did not want their daughter to be with this man who has another wife. They did not want their daughter to be anyone's second wife—she was too good for that. They wanted her to have a good life with a devoted husband. This man was confused and did not know what to do. Tabrizi looked at his problem as a puzzle. She asked him what he thought he should do. He said that he cared deeply for his wife, but not in a husband and wife sort of way, and he didn't think she cared for him in that way either, but that they liked and respected each other. So he thought he should divorce her and kindly give her all that is hers, including her mahr. Then he could be free to marry the other woman, and her parents would be willing to give their approval. Tabrizi laughed and agreed that it seemed like there was a straightforward solution available, and she did not see why he was avoiding it. Tabrizi explained that this man was doing the honorable thing. Of course, she said, lawyers never know everything that is going on, but sometimes when people go to her to obtain advice, they already know what they are going to do; they just want approval that what they are doing is legal and advisable. Tabrizi's clients also seek clarity on the written laws in order to get the maximum benefit from them.

For instance, on one occasion, a young woman in her late twenties came to see her. The young woman said that she had a problem and proceeded to explain the disintegration of her marriage of ten years. Her husband, she explained, said he had a university degree when they married, but over the years she realized he did not. They lived together for over eight years, but, she explained, he was frequently away, and eventually he just stopped coming home. In the beginning, he said he was traveling to look for work and sometimes sent her small amounts of money, but in the last year he had given her almost nothing to live on. She told Tabrizi that she sold her jewelry and other gifts from their marriage, but now she was running out of money.

Tabrizi jumped in, "Do you want to separate?"

"It doesn't matter to me. Either he comes back or he needs to divorce me and give me my mahr. I need something to live on. I have children."

Tabrizi told her that she had some legal avenues and verified the amount of time her husband had not been supporting her. "Has it been six months?"

"Of course. More than that."

"Where are you living now?"

"I am still in our home. But soon I will have to leave and go back to my family. What choice do I have?"

"You may file a petition in the court."

Then the client revealed a bit more information. "I already have one pending. It's been almost two years now."

"What do you mean?"

"I filed a petition. I went to court but my husband ignored it. The judge told me that he could not do anything without seeing my husband. He told me I have to get him to come."

Tabrizi noted this and explained that sometimes it is difficult when young women go by themselves and that she must be persistent. Then she added, without great detail, that after a certain amount of time, the judge will have to make a decision. Noting the obvious problem in the case, she asked the young woman if she knew the current whereabouts of her husband.

The woman said that she could probably reach him through his brother but did not know whether he was in the city.

Tabrizi thought for a moment, then said that it appeared the woman still cared for her husband, and asked if she really wanted a divorce. The young woman responded that she was not sure how to answer because she could not remain in a marriage all by herself. Tabrizi nodded and explained that it would be in the woman's interest if she could somehow get her husband to meet with her and an arbitrator, explaining that the judge would require it in any case, but that this way she could explain, in a less combative manner, what she needed. And the arbitrator could explain her husband's financial responsibilities. Tabrizi explained how the law worked with regards to *nafagheh*, maintenance. "Your husband is required by law to pay. If he hasn't paid and it is over six months, then you can complain. Have you left the house?"

"No, I still live there."

"Then he needs to keep paying to support the family. That's his responsibility. He must give you nafagheh as long as you are staying in the house." Tabrizi began to explain the process for filing a complaint for failure to pay the nafagheh. She was interrupted with the woman's worry about her children. She was afraid that she would lose her son, or that her husband would use the children against her.

Tabrizi explained the terms of another legal reformulation, one having to do with custody of the children. One of the most discriminatory results of marriage dissolution is custody. Unless the couples make a custody determination on their own, the law that takes effect grants the children to the husband. "How old are the children?" Tabrizi asked.

"My daughter is five and my son is seven."

"It is our law that the husband obtains custody of girls after they have reached the age of seven and boys at two.[7] There are some exceptions we can consider. Now we can try to get the court to consider what is best for the children. This is very difficult, but sometimes we have good reason for giving the children to the mothers. The best way always is to negotiate with your husband. In your case, it is good that you have not left the house. Your daughter would stay with you, at least for two more years, but once she reaches the puberty, she can make a decision for herself. Here the law allows a nine-year-old girl to make a decision, if the court sees her as mature enough. You can go to court to obtain a *hokm-e rosht* to get the children. In any case the daughter will be able to get it around age nine. It's a bit more difficult for the son, but we can discuss this more another time."

Tabrizi sees many custody cases. Parents, she says, often use their children in their disputes. In her office, a distraught woman in her mid-fifties explained that she gave up everything that was due to her—mahrieh, everything—in order to get custody of the children. She had been divorced for two years and had primary custody of her two sons, ages sixteen and eight. The children were supposed to visit their father each week. The problem was that her former husband was insane (*mareez-e ravanee*), she told Tabrizi. Her eight-year-old son did not want to see his father, so she wanted to find a way to get permanent and total custody of him. Tabrizi waited until the woman was finished and said, "This is my advice: file a complaint on behalf of your elder son and say everything that his father does to bother him—hits him, insults him, whatever." This complaint is called "Cease to Bother" (*Raf-e Mozahemat*), and it is basically a restraining order. Tabrizi explained that they would need to obtain notarized affidavits to support this.

"How many do we need?" asked the woman.

"The more the better, but at least four. Also, get a tape recorder and record what the father says or how he bothers the son. There must be proof. And with this information, you can cut the ties, both mental (*manavee*) and physical (*jesmee*), between the father and son. Your son is competent/mature (*rashid*)," Tabrizi stated more than asked.

The woman's brother, who was accompanying her, asked, "What will be the outcome?"

"If you do all of this, then the court will issue an order for Raf-e Mozahemat. If he is still bothering you, he can get a jail sentence of up to one year."

The woman's brother weighed in again, "We had to take the boy to the hospital the last time. His father beat him and he had to see a specialist."

"You can use the records from the hospital as evidence. The boy can even use it to file a complaint against his father."

The woman was outraged. "I do not want my son to put one foot in the court. But what about the pressures on my son to see his father, not just from his father, but from their family?"

"Tell him it will make him stronger."

"Can people's actions change?"

"It depends on the person. It will be in your son's best interest for now. You don't want him to turn out like his father. If he learns to stand up to him, he won't."

The woman's brother then asked, "Will you file the complaint for us?"

"I have no time."

"But we want you to do it."

Tabrizi looked at them, and slowly a smile brightened her face, "Okay," she yielded hesitantly. She clearly did not want to get in the middle of this family's troubles. "I will do it, but in ten to fifteen days, and you need to get the records together and bring everything to me." Heads bobbed in agreement. "On your way out make another appointment."

As a legal counselor, Tabrizi often emphasized the written laws and the importance of contracts. She, like many other women, stressed that women's rights in marriage must be secured at the time of marriage. She often counseled young couples before they were married. One day, a young woman who was getting married came to see Tabrizi. Her mother, she said, had suggested this and had come with her. She said that she was in love with her fiancé, but due to her own mother's preoccupation with the terms of the marriage, they decided to come see Tabrizi. They had heard about Tabrizi's talks to women's groups, she explained. The young bride-to-be said she wanted to know about the stipulations in the marriage contract. Tabrizi pulled a sheet from a file. It was the standard marriage contract, with standard stipulations. She handed a copy to the client, who looked it over with her mother. Tabrizi explained that one area where women have lots of rights and power and never make use of them is in the initial stages of marriage.

"But at that time, the young women are so excited about their grooms and are trying so hard to make a good impression that they forget," said the young woman's mother.

Tabrizi responded that "Law is about contract. There are many possibilities in negotiating the terms of such contracts, if people will only pay attention early on before the emotions of love carry them away." In the case of women's rights in marriage and divorce, it was clear to Tabrizi and others attorneys whom I had met that women needed to secure their rights at the time of marriage and state conditions in the marriage contract. Tabrizi clarified, this is where women can secure their rights. Then if something happens,

> you have a contract that legally obligates their husbands and states the conditions of their marriage. Women do not realize this when they are in love. When negotiating the terms of the marriage contract, instead of fighting for five thousand toman more for the mahr, which most women never obtain anyway, women should be smart and ask instead for additional stipulations in the terms of the marriage. One can always add more stipulations in the marriage contract, beyond the standard ones that are listed.

Tabrizi told her client how the courtship is an important family negotiation that bears on the laws and women's rights in marriage and, if necessary, in divorce. She explained that these negotiations were the way toward a mutual understanding. "Khostegari is not an insult to women; women are the choosers. It is the woman who comes forward in Iran. It is not like in other countries, where people date openly. Here, this is a way couples can see what they are getting. Khostegari is acceptable in a society like this where you just don't know. It's not that in other societies you know, but here there is less of an acceptance in hanging out with strangers. Instead, people hang out a lot with their relatives who are known to them." Tabrizi turned to me and added that this was "a safe way in our society to make friends and to get to know people."

The women in the meeting expressed reservations about this approach to marriage. "So I was wrong about how I went about finding my fiancé," the bride-to-be said, adding sarcastically, "I was supposed to look at marriage with a buyer's eye, as if I were in a market."

Tabrizi laughed and said, "You will thank me later." Indeed, contracts and negotiation play out in key family meetings such as marriage, death, and divorce. Such meetings are so ritualized that they often obscure the crucial legal aspects of the family relationships being forged. Not surprisingly, Tabrizi and other lawyers I met kept advising their clients to be aware of the legal elements of these meetings and to press for more transparency through documentation. With her client still in the room, Tabrizi turned to me and said, "You see, women in Iran have lots of rights, they don't realize it."

The lawyer's part in trying to get women to realize they have rights was to focus on the terms of the marriage. That is, like in any relationship built on contract, to obtain good terms *prior* to the start of the relationship. One of the big problems that Tabrizi encountered, she told me, was that women often came to her after the terms of the contract had already been determined. For that reason, when Tabrizi lectured or was invited to speak at various functions, she often spoke about the marriage contract (*aghd nameh*), which is negotiated during the courtship, often by the parties' mothers.

COURTSHIP

When I entered her room, Bita was blow drying her long, dark brown curls. She had flipped her hair over her knees and was sitting on the edge of her twin-sized bed. Dressed in a knee-length, blue-and-white polka-dotted dress with a matching cropped jacket, she was prepared to greet her possible new in-laws. Bita's desk sat adjacent to her bed, and her desktop computer took up almost the entire space. Next to the keyboard was a photo of the man whose mother and sisters were coming by this day to see Bita. When the doorbell rang, no one moved to answer it. Her family members had gathered to meet the family of her suitor, but they stood back even as the second set of rings chimed in the foyer of the three-bedroom apartment. Her mother finally rushed in and hissed, "Bita, come on now." It was clear that Bita had to open the door. Unfazed, Bita stood up and shook out her hair, straightened her skirt, and swished toward the door. She opened the door to three relatives of the would-be groom—the mother and two sisters. One of the sisters lived in the United States and wanted to see the would-be bride to report back to her brother in Houston, Texas. Her family was interested in Bita, who was considered a suitable candidate because of her looks; she also came from a good family and was well educated.

Bita met the family through a mutual friend at the gym who brought in a photo of the wife-seeking bachelor, an engineer with his own house in the United States. Bita, who was twenty-four years old, had recently finished her studies in computer science and was intent on completing at least her master's degree, and perhaps even going on to get her doctorate. The man in the photo she was given had short black hair and a mustache. He was wearing a brown leather jacket with a black-and-white plaid shirt underneath. He was clearly quite a bit older than Bita. Thirty-six, the woman had told her, but Bita thought he looked gentle. She wasn't really looking for a husband, she told the woman at the gym, but for several weeks the woman gnawed at her resolve. Bita gave her e-mail address to the woman to give to this man in the United States so they could begin a correspondence. She also gave her telephone number to the woman so she could pass it on the man's family in Tehran. The correspondence gave way to a series of meetings with the man's sister and mother in Tehran, and thus the khostegari had begun.

Soon after she had begun corresponding with the man, his mother called her. After speaking with Bita, the man's mother also began speaking with Bita's mother. They spoke about whether Bita would be amenable to moving to the United States, and how her parents and siblings would feel about that. The man's mother also assured Bita's mother that her son was extremely respectful of women, that he had not had any previous fiancées, that he was financially successful, and that Bita would be well taken care of financially and could return to Iran as frequently and for as long as she liked. Finally, the man's mother suggested that it would not hurt for them to meet to see if their families were compatible. Bita's mother first checked with her daughter. Bita, who had been corresponding with the man in Texas, had agreed, and the family, through the mothers, scheduled the first meeting, a second meeting, and now a third. The third meeting was important because the man's closest sister, who lived in Los Angeles, had come to Tehran and wanted to meet Bita.

On the morning of the visit, I arrived just a few minutes before the suitor's family, and Bita hardly had time for conversation as she ran back and forth to the kitchen to bring drinks. The guests had requested blended milk-and-banana drinks (*shir moze*), instead of the tea that Bita had already served them. She ran to the kitchen to make the drinks. Over the sound of the whirring blender, the women chatted with the others in the room. The women, along with Bita's aunt, younger sister, and brother, nimbly picked at the overflowing spread on the coffee table: baskets of fruit—peaches, pears, apricots, oranges, and apples—garnished with smaller plates full of pastries, dates, and nuts. Bita's father was decidedly withdrawn, standing in the farthest corner of the room, smoking a cigarette beside an open window. Bita was doing all the work, showing her hospitality and warmth, not to mention that she was mature enough to serve in the role of hostess. The mother of the groom eyed Bita the whole time—her gait, her demeanor. She watched almost eagerly, perusing the young woman she was considering for her son. In the kitchen, Bita joked about being looked over as an object, as a vessel for children, and told me that she did not feel very strongly about this family. When we were outside of the kitchen, she appeared very polite, serious yet warm.

The first two meetings had brought the families together to talk about the kinds of people they are, about their family, social, economic, and spiritual backgrounds, and about Bita herself—what her hobbies are, what kind of family life she would like, and how she sees her role as a wife and mother. The man's mother told Bita that her family is *ba hejab*, a term that denotes modesty and faith and, in common parlance such as this, indicates an observance of the dress code, which was evident in the three women's brightly covered headscarves and overcoats, which they did not remove in the presence of Bita's father and brother. Bita had already twice told the man's mother and sisters that she is not ba hejab, meaning that she does not cover her head in the presence of males who are not close kin, but the women said that they are not bothered by this—what counted for them was what was inside.

In this third meeting, the mothers of the betrothed began to openly discuss the terms of the relationship, a prelude to negotiating the terms of the marriage contract. The groom's mother, clearly impressed with Bita's skills as a homemaker, asked how many children she would like to have. Bita answered that she would like two, a boy and a girl, but not anytime soon. She would like to finish her studies. The mother and the sisters, both of whom worked outside the home, had no reactions to this. They continued to talk about the importance of family and children. They also talked about education, especially how important it was for girls. "Boys always find a way," said Bita's mother. They spoke about the necessary skills for being a good mother; the importance of raising children, whether it was boys or girls, equally. "And Bita dear," her potential mother-in-law turned to her, "what would you do once you arrived in the States? Would you like to work or stay home?"

"First, I would finish my education, and I would like to find a good position after that. I would like to have children, too, but only after I have clearly established myself."

One of the older sisters replied, "It's always easier to say than do. I found that once I had my children, I preferred to stay home with them."

Bita was diplomatic, "I will have to see once I get there."

Questions about lifestyle continued—how often the family goes on vacation, where they go, what they do, where the children when to school, their parents' expectations for their children's future. It was clear the man's mother was doing most of the questioning and was trying to get a clearer perspective on Bita's family. From Bita's perspective, she was pleasant and amicable, but not at all desperate for marriage. When the question of the mahrieh at last arrived, Bita's mother barely hesitated and said it would be no less than two hundred gold coins, at that time worth about U.S. $60,000. In some ways it was a rather high mahr, but for a seemingly well-to-do man who lived in the United States, it was just scratching the surface. Everyone in the room also knew that there was little chance that Bita would ever see such a sum. The negotiation was about status, with which the man's family was clearly concerned. The high amount for the mahr sent the message that Bita's family, while not rich, were also not desperate to give their daughter away. "Clearly in this day we never know what the future holds. I have to think of Bita's dignity and integrity."

The suitor's mother hardly showed any reaction. Looking at her own daughters, she said, "I know how you feel, I am the mother of two girls, as well. These days the future is very unclear."

In this meeting there was no signing on the dotted line, no ceremonious announcement of families joining together, but it was the beginning of marriage negotiations by the mothers on behalf of their children who had never met in person. The conversation was cordial and casual, almost completely obscuring the contract terms being negotiated at this early stage.

In the end, Bita did end up marrying Ahmad. After the positive report from his sister, he continued greater correspondence with Bita until about six months later when he finally arrived and the pair met, in the company of relatives on both sides, at a dinner given by Bita's family. Over several months, Bita and Ahmad got to know each other, went on walks, to museums, to movies, and to restaurants, and finally agreed to get engaged before the end of his visit.

The importance of these initial contracts and negotiations was also evident well into marriage. As the next section will show, in the face of omissions to contracts, family members had little legal protection despite the intentions of the law, which the supporters of the system tried to explain.

ARBITRATION

"Women in Iran have no rights," protested Jamileh. Pardis, Jamileh, and Ali had invited me to a family gathering at their house one Friday afternoon to discuss the division of property associated with the recent passing of Mohsen, Jamileh's husband and Ali's father. Pardis and Ali had gone to meet the bus that was dropping off their son from school, and Jamileh and I were sitting in the kitchen sipping tea. The steam rising from the samovar gave the already hot room an added mist.

"What are you talking about?" I was stunned by her comment, as Jamileh had so faithfully voted for her candidates and made strong statements about her participation and how much it mattered. "When my husband died, what did I get? I was living with him for fifty years and what was I left with? Nothing. I have this house, and my children all want to sell it to get their portion. I deserve more than this. I worked all my life and now my children say they need the money."

Jamileh's concerns were hardly unfounded. Her husband had died suddenly of a heart attack several years earlier, and her four children—two sons and two daughters—wanted to discuss the division of the property among themselves. "I told Mohsen to put everything in writing and in my name so that I would have something, if something were to happen to him, but he never thought too far in the future." Jamileh was no amateur when it came to understanding her legal rights in this case in which her spouse died without leaving a will.

According to the inheritance laws, daughters receive half of what sons receive, while widowed spouses only receive one-eighth of the physical property, not including the land. First the widow receives her portion, then the remainder is divided among the children. Thus, in Tehran, where land is at a premium, this leaves widows with very little in terms of assets.

Jamileh's concerns thus seemed quite valid, and the disproportionate share given to the children, especially the sons, seemed unduly harsh and unjustified. I was reminded of a conversation about women's rights that I had had with a women's affairs representative at a government ministry just a few weeks prior.

"Iranian women have more rights than women anywhere," she said, especially in Europe and the United States. "Iranian women," she told me,

> are taken care of within the family because they take care of the children and their husbands. Women don't have to work outside of the home unless they would like to; if they do, they can keep their earnings for themselves. The reason why male relatives receive twice as much as with female in testate cases, for example, is that the males are expected, culturally and legally, to support the females. An unmarried sister can at any time go to her brother and say, "I need financial support." A man cannot do that.

She went on to explain the legal discrepancies in terms of a broader social framework and opposed this to a society that is highly individuated. "Our society draws from Islamic principles that value women as mothers and wives first. In Iran, if a woman is left without means, for instance, if her husband or father dies, she can go to any of her male kin and demand maintenance and support. She should never be on her own and without support." She also framed this view through a dialectic of entitlement and obligation. "But women also have duties, and this is how Islam provides for everyone, sees that everyone in the whole society is cared for."

Having been debriefed in much this same fashion several times before, I stated, "But this does not happen in reality."

"You are right," she conceded. She attempted to give an explanation for the discriminatory laws.

> And there are many reasons for this. Sometimes women do not know their rights, and sometimes they do not know their obligations. Of course we live in a different kind of society now than in the Prophet's time, and unfortunately women do not always have the family situation that allows them to obtain the financial support that Islam requires. But, these discrepancies are also the issues that we in the government, along with local and international NGOs, are work-

ing to improve. For instance, Majlis just passed a law that allows widows to obtain the full pensions of their deceased husbands, when before it was just a percentage. We are also trying to pass a bill that creates the legal category of "head of household" for widowed or divorced women. This will allow them to obtain full government benefits when they do not have male guardianship. It's a matter of developing the values of our religious and cultural system to match the modern industrial society that we are living in.

When I recounted this story for Jamileh, she scoffed. "I don't care about these ideas. Islam is about justice so those people running the country need to be fair first of all. You have to look at how people are living, not how they ought to live." She emphasized "ought" and continued, "I am an old woman. I raised four children and lived with my husband for fifty years. I am entitled to more than this. Now I have to ask my son to provide for me? This is my right that I want, not benevolence."

"But she said you have a right to get your family to provide for you," I attempted.

"That's not true. How? If my children decide to sell this house, I have nothing. My daughters have nothing." Jamileh pointedly referred to her daughter, who had dropped in while we were in midconversation. "Look at her."

A year before Jamileh's husband died, her eldest daughter Shahla had lost her husband. Shahla was struggling to manage her finances in spite of the fact that her husband's wealthy family was not making any claims on her. But Shahla and her husband had rented a posh apartment that he financed through his European import-export business. Without the European remittances, Shahla was not able to continue making the expensive payments and had already moved three times to find suitable housing for herself and her three children.

CONCLUSION

For several years I returned to the law offices of these attorneys. When I went to see Ms. Tabrizi on a trip in 2004, I reminded her that she was initially convinced that women did not know their rights, and I asked her how she saw the state of women's rights. Sitting in a brand new locale, with a large, open waiting room complete with new red chairs and oversized mirrors, several offices for herself, a young partner, and numerous law clerks, Tabrizi, from behind her desk, raised her hands and signaled for me to take in the breadth of her practice.

"Well, in my opinion, women know their rights too well, now they do not know their obligations."

Interestingly, this lawyer, who had for as long as I had known her advocated for legal reform on behalf of women and litigation for women to achieve their rights, now seemed puzzled by the increased number of women and men seeking out judicial redress. Her surprise also emphasized a common effect of increased legal rationalization, that of the separation between the law and the social principles that underlie its creation. Women were now forgetful of the fact that behind these positive legal rights lie obligations, perhaps tied more closely to the principles in the shari'a, specifically in texts such as the Qur'an or the sunna. Now, the increased legality with which women pressed their claims produced, even for this advocate, too great a discrepancy with societies' mores and social codes.

In the following chapter, I move beyond the "grounded" arenas of the previous chapters—the Qur'anic meetings, the family court, and the law office—to examine the space of human rights, specifically statist performances of human rights, which act at once as a politically and historically specific discourse yet also aim to partake in a transnational language of rights to express modernity in a broader context, the global.

CHAPTER SIX

Human Rights: The Politics and Prose of Discursive Sites

THE UNMARKED DOOR OPENED to a dim reception area where a family sat waiting. A man turned to me, seemingly responding to my silent confusion, and said, "Yes, this is the right place." Verifying, I asked, "This is the Islamic Human Rights Commission?" He nodded, adding, "Supposedly." I first went to the Islamic Human Rights Commission (IHRC) to interview one of its staff attorneys in the summer of 1999. Located on the posh upper northwest side of Tehran, the IHRC is housed in the lower level of an imposing high-rise residential building at the north end of Africa Street, one of the city's most elegant strips, where one can find shops with exquisite European designs and prices to match. The taxi driver, gracious in his persistence to find the obscure address, dropped me off inside the underground parking garage of the apartment building that would lead me to the IHRC's elusive entrance.

Once inside, I was greeted by a receptionist who notified the attorney with whom I was to meet. In minutes, a young woman with a round, pale face engulfed in a black chador entered the reception area and greeted me. She asked me to follow her and flowed down the hall back to her office. There was little small talk as we seated ourselves and I began to ask about human rights in Iran. Just as we were starting, a distraught young woman with a child in tow entered the doorway of our room and yelled, "Where is the foreigner having an interview on human rights in Iran? I want to speak to the foreigner. You should interview me, not her." She stood in the entryway and pulled her child tight, then shouted, "There are no human rights in Iran!" and swiftly moved away. Ms. Tazeh, the attorney, sat silently through it all, seemingly unmoved. Coolly, she clarified that the woman was disgruntled about her housing situation and sought help at the IHRC, which was powerless to provide living accommodations. At the time, the intervention seemed little more than a failed attempt at provocation, one that my host casually dismissed. The disruption, however, showcased how narratives about human rights pass through multiple discursive registers—political, social, gender, and historical. It emphasized how even my role as a person researching human rights partially shaped the discourse about Iranian human rights and also animated how human rights practices, both inside and outside of Iran, are produced in reaction to politicized imaginings about Iran's place in the greater geopolitical landscape.

Today, questions about human rights in the Muslim MENA region often ponder the relationship between Islam and human rights, taking each as separate and distinct entities a priori. Instead of beginning with this premise of opposition and coexistence, I consider the coconstituting nature of such discourses. Instead of seeing these ideas as binaries, I explore dialogical processes that exist in various contexts of on-the-ground human rights practices. For this reason, the methodology for this chapter is different from the previous ones, which explored specific places as interpretive spaces through which notions of rights emerge. The physical space through which human rights discourses emerge in practice is elusive, like the location of the IHRC itself. Human rights, Louis Henkin famously said, "is the idea of our time" (1990: ix);[1] although grounded in philosophical tracts and legal treatises, the tangible quality of human rights emerges as a discursive formation given numerous local contingencies. In this chapter I thus highlight my discussions with numerous Iranian state actors to show how they also construct the idea of human rights through multiple layers of discourse, including the transnational, which is ostensibly secular, but also discourses that invoke "culture," "religion," and "tradition." The questions I consider are: what do human rights mean to the state actors I spoke with, and what conditions have given rise to and form their discourses of human rights?

Certainly some have attempted to appraise the country's record on human rights from the standpoint of the international treaties to which Iran is a signatory (Afshari 2001); others have attempted to compare the legal apparatus of human rights in Iran with that of the international (Mayer 1991). Such studies, however, have little regard for the evolving and established on-the-ground networks of human rights through which those practices travel, and sometimes they even dismiss local practice as political ploys used to avoid international scrutiny. These assessments fail to seriously consider the politics surrounding the "idea" of human rights, particularly, the politics of human rights in Iran as they shape understandings of human rights more broadly, both inside and outside of Iran. Indeed, some studies have attempted to take the political nature of Iranian human rights into consideration, but they place human rights in a reductive framework of Islamic practice (Mokhtari 2004).

Instead, I seek to include geopolitics as part of the broad concerns that give human rights its local meaning in Iran. I consider how productions of law, in this case human rights laws, emerge in practice—in new iterations and in various contexts. I seek out the dimensions of the discourse of "human rights in Iran" amid the multiple landscapes—domestic, regional, and international—in which "human rights" is the object of a

broader understanding about the legitimacy of a nation-state. Pronouncements about human rights often appear fixed and play a performative role
in a wider geopolitical terrain, for instance in the media, where Iran serves
as a rogue state, and as such, as a foil to democracy or modernity. These
fixed terms then circulate from one discursive context to the next. As they
do, they also serve as nodes on an ideological network that communicates
a set of ideas. For example, with the notion of rights, human rights, their
meaning is considered to be common knowledge or self-evident, as in
Henkin's statement above. There are, however, a whole set of assumptions underlying these ideas that are not investigated by mainstream
human rights assessments. By seeking to understand human rights as a
discursive practice, with an ethnographic approach, I seek to open up
"human rights" to identify the ideas and assumptions that are embedded
in the term. In this chapter, then, I seek to unpack some of the assumptions
that are built into the object—human rights—in the Iranian context.

It should be noted that I am not advancing a "cultural relativism" argument. The claim of relativism, hurled at scholars who argue for a context-
based analysis, carries with it the charge of apology or moral softness. In
fact, this approach allows for the possibility of a more direct challenge
and more rigorous critique of state practices because it calls for analytically exploring human rights systems. And that which exists in Iran, as a
condition of its own insertion in the system of nation-states, by virtue of
its deliberate participation in the apparatus of supranational law (i.e., the
United Nations), makes it more accountable to the international community, not less.[2]

In Iran, a country in which in 1979 revolutionaries stood up to the
imperialism of Western values, local discourses of women's rights and
human rights are still manifestations of broader globalization processes.
Indeed, claims by some Iranians or Iranian state agents of ideological
opposition to the "West" reveal Iran as already acting from within the
international political economy. For a better understanding of these issues
and assessment of the problems, I suggest a different approach from one
that simply appraises Iran's human rights from a seeming vacuum of legal
and political abstraction, because discourses of rights manifest amid ongoing relations—social, political, and economic—are contingent and in
need of contextualization. Local practices need to be contextualized in
the intersecting spaces of transnational and local politics.

FROM HUMAN RIGHTS AND CULTURE TO HUMAN RIGHTS AS CULTURE

Commenting on the events of September 11, 2001, *New York Times* col-
umnist Thomas L. Friedman wrote, "Osama bin Laden has triggered the

most serious debate in years, among Muslims, about Islam's ability to adapt to modernity."[3] Even before September 11, some journalists and scholars had attempted to explain the relationship between Islam and modernity as one of binaries, opposites, dualities, contradictions, and, of course, clashes. Perhaps Friedman's well-intentioned prose aimed to make complex issues clear for the uninitiated, but in the end, the bare-boned explanations of the sort he offered only further obscure the issues, leading readers to believe that modernity and Islam are at odds.[4] What Friedman and others categorically misperceive is that modernity can and does take forms different from those he appears to identify as occurring only in the "West." Indeed, as I have discussed, Iran's nation-state and its laws are a product of modern forces. Writing on Islam and the modern state, Zubaida (1989: ix) made a similar argument: "[C]urrent Islamic movements and ideas are not the product of some essential continuity with the past, but are basically 'modern.' Even when they explicitly reject all modern political models as alien imports from a hostile West, their various political ideas, organizations, and aspirations are implicitly premised upon the models and assumptions of modern nation-state politics."[5]

Commentators living in the United States are not alone, however, in setting up the intractable oppositions based on religion, tradition, and ultimately culture—state agents in Iran may do so as well. For instance, at a meeting with the women's affairs advisor at the Ayatollah Khomeini Complex's Organization of Culture and Islamic Relations, a conservative research and policy group in north central Tehran, the representative, Dr. Kermani, similarly indicated a belief in an unattainable understanding on the part of Western observers. This she made plain in our discussion about human rights: "When I am in America, I cannot explain human rights to Iranian women and when I am in Iran, I cannot explain human rights to American women. The culture is different. Customs, likes, relationships, education, everything, even the method of eating is different. The UN cannot come in and say what is what."

This seemed odd to me, coming from a woman whose Ph.D. degree in philosophy from an American institution clearly translated into the Iranian educational system, not to mention a very high-ranking government post. Dr. Kermani went on to explain that the realm of culture is best understood by the people within that culture, and that they are in the best position to understand the social problems that exist, such as "the difficulties women might have."

When I asked her whether the effects of globalization would bring greater understanding and change to societies, Dr. Kermani answered with her own rhetorical question: "What does it mean? Globalization. Is this just another way for the 'West' to force their beliefs on us? They tell us that we have no right to export our revolution, but then I say, 'America, why can you export your culture to others?'" Dr. Kermani's statements about the distinctive qualities of cultural practices also mobilized the concept of culture for political ends as an expression of a nation-state's sovereignty (Pollis 1996). The political mobilization of culture notwithstanding, it bears tracing the politics surrounding international attention to Iran's human rights in order to unpack some of Dr. Kermani's reflections: her distrust of the UN and her use of the term "culture." In this context, how might international monitors assess Iran's human rights practices, given that Iran *is* a signatory to many international human rights accords? And why is it that Iranian state actors who argue for a distinctive culture still mobilize the concept of "human rights" instead of something else, like justice, for example, when, I was told again and again by state agents, Islam is most concerned with justice?

Iranian state actors who made claims about local productions of "human rights" actually positioned the institutions of the state further within the purview of international accountability. By evaluating state actions in terms of "human rights," even if they tie those actions to indigenous beliefs, such actors referenced a specific genealogy that devised a transnational framework to oversee the treatment of individuals and groups by state forces. In the following pages of this chapter, I approach the Iranian discourse on human rights from a standpoint that considers the multiple voices that give it form and content. Given the dialectical processes of its unfolding and its on-the-ground meanings, I note that these voices are not merely state actors, but among them are the voices of numerous women who have legitimate claims on state institutions for protection, like the attorney at the IHRC.

Conversations I had about human rights with Iranians, both state representatives and nonstate actors, show the myriad possibilities that exist in negotiations about the nature of human rights in the Islamic republic. Such discussions cultivate new ideas, engender responses, spur activity, and generate statist and nonstatist technologies and apparatuses in the production of human rights discourses. Discussions about the status of transnational laws take place at local levels, and as they do, they literally create new local spaces for practice. While the universality of human rights may be an ideal, it is ever the exigencies of local practices that give form to its principles, and it is significant that even in Iran, the language of human rights is "the idea of our time."

WHY "HUMAN RIGHTS": FROM ISLAMIC JUSTICE TO RIGHTS TALK

Soon after the revolution, a debate sprang up between the multiple groups that had built a coalition to overthrow the shah over what the name of the new country would be. Nationalist and secular groups wanted the new name to include the word "democratic." Khomeini, however, stood firmly by his rejection of the term, a "vulgarity" to Islam, he called it, the very essence of which is justice (Arjomand 1988).

Shah Mohammad Reza Pahlavi's modernization programs, however, had included Iranian participation in numerous multilateral agreements that guaranteed human rights. Indeed in 1945–48, an Iranian representative was among the eighteen delegates sitting on the Economic and Social Council's Commission on Human Rights, headed up by Eleanor Roosevelt and charged with the drafting of the Universal Declaration of Human Rights.

In that pre-1979 period of international organizing and building of legal infrastructure in consideration of international human rights, the Iranian parliament ratified numerous treaties, including the triumvirate, the Universal Declaration of Human Rights (signed December 10, 1948), the Convention on Economic, Social, and Cultural Rights (June 24, 1975), and the Convention on Civil and Political Rights (June 24, 1975), which together comprise the International Bill of Human Rights. It also ratified the Convention on the Elimination of Racial Discrimination (August 29, 1968). After the revolution, parliament ratified the Convention on the Rights of the Child (July 13, 1994).

The term "human rights" gained prominence throughout the world after World War II and acquired a meaning associated with the transnational legal system that was created in its aftermath. After the Holocaust, the term "human rights" came to express the now legitimate concern of an international community, with a sovereign state's treatment of its polity. In June 1946 representatives from eighteen countries, including Iran, came together under the auspices of the Commission on Human Rights to draft an international bill on human rights. This process initially brought the term human rights to the attention of elites in the Iranian polity. In Iran as in other postcolonial societies, however, it was not until the mid-1960s that the language of human rights gained greater prominence. Nationalist and leftist groups critical of the shah, Mohammad Reza Pahlavi, began to mobilize human rights language to bring worldwide attention to the government of the shah, who many saw as a puppet of Western interests, especially the United States, in that period.

Interest in nation-states' observance of human rights gained greater international attention after the 1977 election of U.S. President Jimmy Carter, who made human rights a cornerstone of his foreign policy. With regard to Iran, Carter encouraged greater leadership by the shah on human rights. With increased signs of the monarchy's weakening, the shah, whose feeble leadership depended in large part on U.S. support, felt it necessary to allow for U.S. appeasement on human rights issues, despite his concern with feeding the nascent revolutionary movement (Cottam 1986). Some scholars have cited Carter's insistence on the shah's attention to human rights as a turning point for the growing opposition, which was able to capitalize on the U.S. president's criticism of the shah and bring international attention to the dictatorial government in terms of human rights violations (Munson 1988).[6] While this faction of the opposition consisted mainly of an older generation of leftist intellectuals who sought to reform and liberalize state institutions, other, more radical groups in favor of revolution also emerged. Among the opposition's leaders was then-exiled Ayatollah Khomeini, who joined the chorus of criticism hurled at the monarchy's human rights abuses and those of his paymasters, Great Britain and the United States (1981: 213–15, 218).

It is significant that in the time leading up to the shah's overthrow, Khomeini used the language of human rights when citing the violations of the government and in describing the role Islamic scholars could play in people's lives (273). Just after the revolution, however, Khomeini threatened to withdraw Iran from its international commitments. In the end his advisors persuaded him not to do so. Khomeini similarly based this disavowal of the international legal order on the idea that there is no need in an Islamic polity for the creation of liberal state apparatuses, particularly those that make the new government accountable to Western imperialist forces.

According to Khomeini, with justice at its base, Islam was all the people needed. In the debates by the provisional government to draw up the new state institutions, Khomeini argued against the creation of a legislature. Iran's national legislature had been dissolved after the revolution, and in its place a new polity, the Islamic Consultative Assembly, was formed. In the end, the Islamic Consultative Assembly was given the functioning power of a legislative organ, but one whose laws and members were to be vetted by a group of experts on Islamic law and jurisprudence, the Council of Guardians. Given Khomeini's views, the retention of executive, legislative, and judicial branches by the transitional government, while controversial, is all the more significant in that they mirror those of Western republics.

With the revolution's anti-imperialist tone and the rejection by Khomeini and his supporters of Western liberal state polities and the language of rights, one must consider how, in the aftermath of the revolution, the language of "human rights" has reemerged as an important way to give expression to the language of Islamic justice, and how Islamic justice produced the various Islamic Declarations of Human Rights. Certainly scholars like Mutahhari had been influential in their scholarship that engaged with the human rights language, but Mutahhari (1981) rejected the UN's

Universal Declaration of Human Rights because, according to him, it failed to account for the biological differences between men and women.

In the aftermath of the revolution, Iranian state authorities came under even greater fire than during the shah's time. Scores of writings have brought this point home. And over the last two and a half decades, actors in the government have also voiced disdain for the biases inherent in the Western human rights infrastructure. In April 1999, at its annual meeting, the UN Commission on Human Rights had issued a resolution criticizing Iran for its continued human rights abuses. Iranian Foreign Ministry spokesman Hamid-Reza Asefi denounced the resolution as politically motivated and claimed that it failed to appreciate the dynamics of Iran's Islamic republic. Asefi declared that Iran relies on its Islamic and cultural values to promote human rights.[7]

Since the 1970s, well before the revolution, Iranian state agents have been on the defensive against claims about their lack of attention to human rights. Many informants complained bitterly to me that when they had called on the United Nations to intervene at various points during the shah's monarchy, human rights monitors gave little or no response, but now the attention placed on Iran's human rights record, they felt, is based on political posturing and often fed to the international organizations by exile groups who had not returned to Iran and were seeking regime change.[8] For these reasons, government agents whom I interviewed felt that these issues gave them good reason to be suspicious of attacks on Iran's human rights and further led to the need for development of an indigenous human rights program.

Comments about the UN's interference further suggest that Iranian human rights were produced in relation to its defiance of international political pressures since the revolution, despite claims to indigeneity. The UN's checkered history of attention to Iranian human rights is part of the dialogic of responses to outside claims that Iran does not have regard for human rights. Thus in our conversation, Dr. Kermani stressed international power relations as she identified the outside concern with human rights in Iran. That is, the human rights discourse about Iran, by its state agents and sometimes others, is often produced in this self-conscious awareness of having to respond to outside pressures and encroachment. It is through such historical events that many hard-line state actors associate human rights with imperialist aims and are suspicious of the agendas of nongovernmental agents who come into the country under Iran's obligations to international treaties to report on human rights in Iran.

That some Iranian state officials simultaneously critique the international discourse of human rights alongside a production of legal apparatuses and institutions serves a developing local human rights discourse. This occurs with the increase of scholarly works on Islam and human rights, including philosophical explications of Islam's compatibility with human rights and politico-historical works that question the aims of international attention to Iran's human rights record. Nonetheless, such works legitimize the importance of human rights. Contemporary Iranian scholars, such as Abdolkarim Soroush, have written about the importance of the discourse of human rights and its connection to modernity and legitimacy: "As we have stated before, a religion that is oblivious to human rights (including the need of humanity for freedom and justice) is not tenable in the modern world" (2000: 128).

Some modernist 'ulama have also recognized the important connection between the legitimate nation-state and human rights. For instance, Hojjatoleslam Mohammed Mujtahid-Shabastari, who trained in Qom and teaches modern theology at the University of Tehran, stated:

> If we accept that modernity is a global phenomenon today that is not exclusive to the West and that the West differs from other parts of the world only in the spread or limitations of modernity, then we must accept that the composition of human relations today requires new construction and planning on a global level. In this sense, human rights have become a global issue. (2000: 229)

Nor has this connection been lost on hard-line factions of Iran's state who seek to promote the legitimacy of their vision of Islamic justice by mobilizing discourses of human rights. I had a conversation about law with a judge in the nearby town of Rey, just outside of Tehran. In explaining the concern with justice in Islam, the judge, a member of the 'ulama noted that in principle, there is nothing about Western human rights that is not contained in the values embedded in Islam. He then repeated a statement that came to be a refrain among state agents—mostly reformers but also some hardliners—with whom I spoke: "Islam has everything we need. We are in the process of updating it."

In the Iranian context, much of the scholarship on Islam and human rights, spanning the traditionalist to modernist approaches to exegesis, extrapolates from Shi'i Islam's rationalist history (Jawadi-Amuli 1998; Mujtahid-Shabistari 2000). My interlocutors often reminded me of the Prophet Ali's treatise *Nahj-al balagheh* (Peaks of Eloquence) as the first Shi'i source for human rights. On December 10, 2003, Nobel Peace Prize winner Shirin Ebadi, an Iranian human rights lawyer, cited the cylinder of the ancient Persian leader Cyrus in her acceptance speech, marking the history of civilization and concern with human rights as one that precedes the advent of Islam to the region.

In addition, in Iran today, there is a proliferation of legal and political infrastructure surrounding Islamic human rights, another articulation of the new discursive spaces of rights emerging within Iran. The faculty at Qom's Mofid University, an Islamic university, organizes bi-annual international meetings that attract scholars from all over the world to discuss many aspects of human rights, including women's rights. This interpretive space of human rights, moreover, is manifested in tangible governmental and nongovernmental organizations emerging within Iran to deal with questions of human rights. So the question remains: why *human rights*?

I return briefly to my meeting with the women's affairs representative at the Ayatollah Khomeini Complex. Dr. Kermani spoke about "Western arrogance," citing international human rights organizations and the press, which wrote about Iran in their papers to make Islam and Iranians look like "barbarians." Dr. Kermani was specifically referring to an event that had taken place in Iran in which a young man was controversially convicted of murder during the holy month of Ramadan and sentenced to death by hanging.[9] A last-minute reprieve by the victim's father, permitted under Iranian criminal law, freed the young man. To make her point, Dr. Kermani showed me a stack of English-language papers that reported on the reprieve. She remarked that the journalists only interview well-established critics of Iran and not people who understood what the Islamic republic is about.

> They are opposed to us, trying to brainwash the Western public into thinking that Islam is severe, wild, and barbarous. They cannot accept that at the core of Islam is mercy and forgiveness. They need to talk about Islam in this way so they can have an easier time colonizing us, but we won't let that happen. Go tell them that in Iran, there are human rights, we have Islamic human rights which conform to our culture and beliefs. We don't need the West to tell us about human rights.

The relationship between human rights and how civilized the state is, and therefore the nation of people, emerged often in my conversations with state officials across the political spectrum, but also with the people in Tehran with whom I discussed the topic. Human rights came up in many contexts while I conducted fieldwork. One important occasion was just a couple of days after the death sentence had been imposed on the young man in this controversial homicide. While having dinner in the home of friends one evening, people discussed the sentence. Maryam, a practicing Muslim, raised the question of whether, according to Islam, the sentence was just. Her husband, Hossein, who also considered himself a Muslim, answered, "We cannot only think about Islam. It's true we are an Islamic country, but we must show that Islam is not against the human rights of the people. Islam provides for human rights because Islam is concerned with justice." Maryam and Hossein called attention to the politics surrounding the post revolutionary state and how Islamic law relates to international human rights. In a more apparent case, as I took a taxi home that evening, the driver asked me if I had heard the good news.

"They didn't execute that boy. We have human rights here; we have thousands of years of civilization."

These conversations show that Iranians have a strong concern about how Iranian state practices reflect in the world community. Many situate their ideas in the reactive stance to what the broader international message about Iran's human rights might be.

When I asked Dr. Kermani about the utility of the very term "human rights," which has its sources in Western liberal political theory,[10] she noted the hegemony of Western liberal theory as she explained,

> We have to respond to these claims that we have no human rights. Since they use "human rights" to talk about our laws and culture, then we need to explain to them in terms that they will understand. We are saying that our Islamic system concurs with Western notions of human rights, but our human rights do not necessarily come from these Western philosophies. They come from our own history, culture, and understandings of what rights are. Our system is foremost a system of justice and the goal is to have a just society. This is what Islam teaches and our human rights emerge from this point.

Nonstate actors have also attempted to produce new nonstatist sites for human rights monitoring of state actors through nongovernmental human rights organizations inside Iran. For instance, Nobel laureate Shirin Ebadi formed the Center for the Defense of Human Rights. She attempted to show that Islam properly interpreted poses no threat to international human rights standards. In the summer of 2006, Ebadi's NGO was ordered closed by hard-line state officials who claimed the organization did not obtain proper licensing. This action, as well as the arrest and imprisonment of political science professor Ramin Jahanbegloo, occurred amid the clampdown on "secular" human rights work in response to overt calls for regime change in Iran by U.S. conservative forces who loudly offered up $75 million for scholars and activists to bring about regime change in Iran from the inside. It should be noted that neither of these examples were recipients of the earmarked U.S. funds.

Others have attempted to deploy human rights discourse with little reference to Islam. For instance, reformist presidential candidate Mostafa Moin ran in the 2005 presidential elections promising to address human rights concerns, but he did not bother to qualify the term within Islamic values. In the 1990s, reform movement platforms self-consciously worked to promote a relationship of conformity if not accommodation between human rights and Islamic values, but increasingly, reformers see little need for the justification of an *Islamic* human rights system, arguing rather that justice, inherent in Islam, is the predominant factor making human rights a central concern to Iranians.

The proliferation of organizations and academic scholarship on human rights notwithstanding, state institutions also work to deploy a discourse on human rights. To observe how one organization operates, I explored the mandate for Iran's Islamic Human Rights Commission. Worthy of note, however, is the way Iran's Islamic human rights apparatus manifests in comparison with contemporary transnational frameworks and institutions, including its Islamic Declaration of Human Rights, complete with preamble and twenty-five articles, just like the Universal Declaration of Human Rights (UDHR). This work of expressing Islamic human rights proves productive of both the meaning of Islamic justice and the application of human rights.

THE ISLAMIC HUMAN RIGHTS COMMISSION

In the early 1990s, the Iranian government came under pressure by international human rights groups to establish a monitoring body within Iran in light of its reluctance to permit outside observers to investigate its human rights practices.[11] As a result, in 1994, seventy-five leaders of the country came together and with the then-head of the judiciary, Ayatollah Mesbah Yazdi, established the IHRC as a national institution in conformity UN guidelines.

The IHRC's general secretary, Mohammad Hossein Ziaeefar, discussed with me concerns that Iran's judiciary had in creating a body that was not quite an independent organization. At its inception, government administrators had hoped to have greater control over the IHRC's activities, since it was not separate from governmental authority but a national institution. The IHRC was founded for dual purposes, however. While one of its aims was to address concerns with the lack of national monitoring institutions, another was to help "Westerners" understand human rights through the perspective of Islam. As Ziaeefar confirmed in a 1997 interview, "It should be an institution to be both independent and at the same time be able to explain Islamic human rights in the modern language. That is because we are really faced with shortcomings in explaining Islamic human rights. The Westerners never express human rights correctly as viewed by Islam."[12]

As he continued, Ziaeefar explained a distinction between the creation of a "national institution" as opposed to a "nongovernmental organization," arguing that the latter had less credibility in some countries. Thus, from the very start, the IHRC was not intended to be a nongovernmental organization. Building on this latter idea, the IHRC's informational brochure notes that "After the victory of the Islamic Revolution in Iran, and the codification and ratification of the country's constitution, a system of governance based on 'Islamism' and 'republicanism,' as two irrevocable axes, was wholeheartedly embraced by the people."

During my 1999 meeting at the IHRC, Ms. Tazeh confirmed the secretary's position on the multiple purposes of the IHRC. She explained that in light of its reluctance to permit outside observers to examine its human rights practices, the judiciary head moved to create the IHRC. "Instead of permitting the international bodies to be the sole arbiters of Iran's human rights record, Ayatollah Yazdi commissioned the creation of Iran's own human rights body, based upon what are deemed to be Islamic foundations."

By mid-1999 the judiciary granted independence to the IHRC in response to critics, both in and outside of the country, who claimed that under the discretion of the judiciary, the IHRC was not an independent body fit to assess Iran's human rights, and that Iran was lacking in sufficient internal human rights monitors to put it in compliance with its international obligations. Since its separation from the judiciary, the IHRC investigates human rights complaints ostensibly without oversight. Since its creation, and even after its disaggregation from the judiciary, the IHRC's efforts to monitor human rights have been under fire from internal groups as well as outside observers. IHRC staffers I met with in September 2005 told me that they receive over ten thousand complaints a year but are equipped to address only a small number.[13]

As Ms. Tazeh elaborated on IHRC's formal structure, pointing out her specific legal expertise, she also continued to highlight the modern technologies at play in making human rights a legible legal script for observers and monitors. The Office of the Legal Division where she worked consisted of four committees: Women and Children's Rights, Science, Domestic Affairs, and International Affairs. Each committee was charged with oversight, review, and follow-up on claims by individuals and groups who alleged that the government or its representatives had somehow transgressed the principles contained in the Declaration of Islamic Human Rights. The IHRC further interfaces with governmental institutions to educate people about their rights. The different committees conduct follow-up studies in order to observe the efforts of state-run programs designed to advise various individuals and groups of their rights.

Ms. Tazeh, who works on the Women and Children's Rights Committee, explained that the IHRC interfaces with governmental institutions to educate women about their rights. The primary aim of the IHRC, it seemed, was one of education, not monitoring, despite the fact that the IHRC was conceived in part to abate international pressures to permit monitoring. The state-run national radio and television station and the universities, Ms. Tazeh explained, offer educational programs for women.

The committee of twelve members meets regularly to discuss and evaluate formal complaints brought before the IHRC. Complaints range from domestic disputes, such as marital grievances, maintenance, and child custody issues, to charges against the city for failing to provide adequate dwellings. When I asked Ms. Tazeh what the committee does with the reports, she responded that the women who use the IHRC really seek it out as a last resort. "First of all, not many people are aware of the existence of the IHRC, and second, the committee writes reports on behalf of a deserving party, if it sees fit, and submits the report to the interested government body." Mostly, however, she continued, "the IHRC writes political reports and communicates with, for instance, the UN representative for the Commission on Human Rights. In this way, the IHRC liaises with international human rights bodies."

As a liaison to international monitors, the IHRC does not act as an independent body, but as a source or advocate for Iran's human rights record, despite its official separation from the government. The advocacy role to which Ms. Tazeh refers points to IHRC's productive role in establishing and evaluating Iran's human rights record. More importantly, IHRC is active in claiming and deploying a particular kind of discourse of human rights in Iran. Human rights in Iran, initially set forth by the government, then decentralized through the deregulation of the IHRC, is presented by the government as a mechanism of an indigenous theory of rights, like the theocratic republic itself. As an advocate for Islamic human rights, the IHRC acts more as defender of Iran's human rights record internationally than as an arbiter of Iran's human rights. As a body, the IHRC becomes one of the institutions of a rational bureaucratic state and one of the markers of legitimacy and how civilized it is insofar as it recognizes and protects the dignity of its citizens, even if in name only.[14]

And, while some of my informants expressed cynicism about the IHRC, the judiciary's creation of this human rights body points to a definitive stance on human rights and advances Iran's place as a leader in the "Muslim world." An interesting feature of this localized expression of Islamic human rights is that it takes shape largely through a rationalized and institutionalized system of law, based on forms and processes strikingly similar to those of the United Nations and of the 'West.' Thus, while Iran perhaps cannot compete with first-world nations in terms of economic development or gross national product, an existing legal infrastructure and human rights standards, in particular, play key roles in its assertion of sovereignty and legitimacy.[15]

One needs also attend to the local politics and difficulties of acting on behalf of a concept, "human rights," which many hard-line officials in the government believe is a wing of Western imperialist politics. The IHRC's works often go unrecognized, if not dismissed altogether. In its promotional brochure, a footnote refers to the IHRC's own vexed position with regard to the political effects of an independent human rights monitoring body within the country:

> It is worthy of mention that ever since he has taken office as Head of the Judiciary in Iran (August 1999), the new Head of the Judiciary has neither personally attended the IHRC's High Council meeting, nor has he had a representative introduced to the Commission. . . .The disapproval stems from the fact that the Head of the Judiciary would very much like to see the Commission affiliated to the Judiciary branch. However, the IHRC, bent on upholding its independence, has adamantly refuted the idea.

In a conversation in the fall of 2005, a staff member at the IHRC expressed his exasperation at the task ahead for Iranian human rights activists. While he had started at the IHRC as a self-proclaimed "moderate" and supporter of the Islamic republic's hard-line factions, his own investigations in human rights, branching out from his inability to perform his job, gave him pause for the case of pursuing human rights violations in Iran. My last correspondence with the IHRC came again in the fall of 2005 in an exchange of e-mails in which I inquired about its impending web site. The response came in the form of an apology that due to the increased tensions in the political climate, hard-line state forces were growing too "sensitive" of human rights, and the IHRC was putting some of its activities, including the web site, on hold indefinitely.

In some ways, in performing and practicing human rights, the Iranian government demonstrates to the world community that it is among the civilized nations that possess human rights and so does not need the so-called civilizing dominance that was once the rationale for Western colonialism or imperialism. Immanuel Wallerstein's understanding of the role of human rights discourse in imperialism helps us understand Iran's insistence on using the language of human rights: "From the beginning, the human rights of 'civilized' nations were predicated on the assumption that they were indeed 'civilized.' The discourse of imperialism was the other side of the coin. The duty of the countries that claimed to respect human rights was therefore to 'civilize' those that did not—those with 'barbarous' customs that made it necessary to take them in tow and teach them, as children might be taught" (1995).

Yet, the apparent willingness on the part of some Iranian state officials to be held accountable to international standards of human rights, by virtue of their ratification of numerous human rights accords, indicates some inclination to participate in the larger international community, but the comments of many state actors I encountered also showed an awareness of the idea of human rights as a possible pretext for imperialism.[16] Inasmuch as international review of a government's actions toward its internal polity is a limit on sovereign rule, the ability of a state to enter into transnational treaties is an act only a sovereign state can perform. By reappropriating terms like "human rights," such Iranian state forces locate their practices at once in the global and in a distinct native or local culture and a history full of complexities. Indeed, this flexible relationship to human rights has also allowed Iranians to voice their own disdain for human rights violations in the very Western countries that criticize them. In doing so, Iranian human rights observers create new arenas of human rights concerns and point, moreover, to the all too obvious contradictions within increasingly diverse societies such as France, whose headscarf ban Iranian critics deeply criticized as a failure of the French government to protect the human rights of France's Muslim minorities.[17]

Islamic Declaration of Human Rights: Similar yet Different

During my conversation with Ms. Tazeh, the attorney from the IHRC, I sought to understand what "Islamic human rights" is and means. She momentarily left the room and returned with a small yellow pamphlet with Persian print. The cover page depicted the title in Persian and English, *Islamic Declaration of Human Rights*. When I asked about the differences between the Islamic declaration and the UN declaration, she explained that they were so negligible, she did not remember what they were. But then the obvious question: what is the point of having a separate document?

Ms. Tazeh explained that what Islamic human rights offers is the certitude that the tenets are based on the foundations of Islam, that it has been so researched and established. She continued, "Sometimes people may mistakenly think that Islamic human rights means human rights for Islamic people are different, but that is not what it means." Her approach was not to distance the Islamic declaration from international human rights standards; rather she suggested that Islamic human rights are so similar that any differences with the Universal Declaration of Human Rights (UDHR) are insignificant. And yet there is a standard of Islamic human rights that serves to distinguish it from the UDHR. The attorney's characterization situates Islamic human rights outside of the purview of Western-based regimes of human rights. But, by acknowledging a system that is so similar that an expert such as herself could not remember the differences, she simultaneously indicated that Iran has comparable valuations of human rights. Not only did she gloss over context-based differences, but she highlighted the similarity of the formal structures of human rights in Iran to those of the UDHR. "Both are declarations, the contents of which are laid out in article form," rendering, in effect, legal entitlements upon citizens, to be guaranteed by appropriate institutions of the state. Despite claims that Islamic human rights are based on Islamic principles, it is also clear from their similarity to "Western" human rights that what we are seeing is a new production of liberal rights, and that Islamic human rights emerge as something recognizable to the Western principles of rights.

In our discussion, Ms. Tazeh clearly side-stepped the substantive issues that separate the UDHR from the Islamic Declaration of Human Rights (IDHR). However, the comments made by Secretary Ziaeefar—"The Westerners never express human rights correctly as viewed by Islam"— clarify the point that there are major differences.

Indeed, the trajectory of the development of Islamic human rights began long before the IDHR was created and even well before the 1979 revolution in Iran. In 1972 representatives from thirty countries came together in Jeddah, Saudi Arabia, to create the Islamic Conference, an organization based on Islamic values. Iran participated in the meeting and joined the conference, its parliament ratifying the Declaration of the Islamic Conference, but on the condition that decisions taken by the Islamic Conference would not supersede those of the United Nations.[18] In the nineteenth session of the Islamic Conference in 1990, held in Cairo, the representatives approved the Islamic Declaration of Human Rights. The declaration draws human rights principles in accordance with the Islamic shari'a. Like the UDHR, the IDHR consists of a preamble, twenty-five articles, and, as a mere declaration, does not have the force of law.

The IHRC offers a text explaining the differences between the UDHR and the IDHR written by an Islamic scholar, Sheikh Muhammad Ali Taskhiri, Iran's representative to the Organization of the Islamic Conference (OIC) during the drafting of the document. He notes that the sources for Islamic human rights are to be found in the Qur'an and the sunna of the Prophet Mohammad as well as the "thesis on human rights" as composed by the fourth Imam Ali ibn Hussain, Sajjad (Tashkiri 1997: 11). Here again, Taskhiri is making a reference to Prophet Ali's treatise, *Nahj-al balagheh*.

The differences between the two declarations fall into roughly two categories: the sources and the protections offered. In the IDHR, the "only" source is Islamic law, as stated in article 25 of the document. Each article therefore relates back to a relationship and attachment to the divine. The IDHR articles are grounded in a belief in the essential precepts of Islam, in the oneness of God, and in the prescriptions for life given in the Qur'an, the sunna, and the accompanying explications. While some believe the UDHR is a secular document, its creators strived to make the declaration accord with the most basic values underlying the principles of any culture, tradition, or religion.

The types of protections outlined in the IDHR are also offered in tandem with Islamic values that take into consideration a person's role in society and family. Article 16 of the UDHR is the right to found a family and states that this is the case without discrimination based on "race, nationality, or religion," but in the Islamic context, women are enjoined to marry a Muslim, so in the IDHR, the discriminatory basis of religion is retained.

The IDHR has also added several types of protections that are absent in the UDHR, for instance, article 3 protects against environmental destruction and article 2, paragraph (d), calls for the proper treatment of corpses.

This discussion is not intended to be an exhaustive account of the similarities and differences between the IDHR and the UDHR, but aims to highlight the underlying bases for distinction and to acknowledge the often too subtle points of connection—that the documents are written as part of the transnational infrastructure of human rights as embodied and articulated in principles espoused in local practices. And however flawed secular-minded advocates of the UDHR may find it, this engagement on the part of the religious leadership—most prominently the hardliners—opens up another new interpretive space for dialogue, innovation, and a legitimate basis for critique, from inside as well as outside of Iran.

Through the production and establishment of a rationalized rule of law, human rights typology, and legal processes that interact with transnational legal technologies, Iran asserts sovereignty both outward, toward the international arena, as well as inward, toward its own populace. As champions of Islamic human rights, powerful voices in the Iranian state demonstrate the wealth of Iran's civilization vis-à-vis other Islamic states. State actors simultaneously resist and accept universal human rights; rejecting, on the one hand, that the "West" is the sole locus of human rights, but accepting the liberal-based rationality that is associated with human rights and the rule of law. The Iranian state reclaims a rational heritage that summons up and produces a discourse of human rights, which state agents, across a spectrum, may claim is native to their own culture and traditions. The move is an important one for the state whose revolution sought to cleanse itself of Western decadence, and most of whose factions now quietly seek international legitimacy through an emphasis on rational modes of law and sovereignty.

One way of obtaining the approval of the international community is for state agents to develop a transparent and accessible system of law. The acceptance of and accession to the nation-state system and a republican polity are also expressions of political rationality so subtle that they are often overlooked by scholars, not to mention politicians and journalists, who argue that Islam is incompatible with democracy. For instance, Samuel Huntington (1996: 174) notes that "among Muslims generally," the "structure of political loyalty has been opposite that of the modern West. For the latter, the nation has been the apex of political loyalty." Huntington further notes that "the idea of sovereign nation states is incompatible with belief in the sovereignty of Allah and the primacy of the *ummah*. As a revolutionary movement, Islamist fundamentalism rejects the nation-state in favor of the unity of Islam" (175).

With regard to Iran, the nation's strength is found precisely in its attempt to shore up a strong central state on the basis of joining Islamic unity and the modern republican nation-state, however fraught this may be in practice. The forthright claim to Islamic human rights is Iran's claim about how civilized (or, on an evolutionary trajectory of progress, developed and modern, and therefore legitimate, independent, and without the need for international intervention) it is. The reflection of Islamic human rights as opposed to Iranian human rights suggests Iran's desire to serve as an example and guide for other Islamic nations.

Iran's human rights program, ostensibly rooted in its ancient culture and traditions, is a step toward independence and legitimacy, but also toward interdependence and inclusion. Thus, realizing a verifiable program of human rights, the state also allows itself to be called to account by the international community. For, if nothing else, participating in an international regime of human rights is every nation's assent to a limitation on its sovereignty. Scholars sometimes fail to recognize these tensions when characterizing the seeming conflicts between relativism and universalism.[19]

Finally, in discussing the political and social role of the IHRC and the IDHR, I have located some of the conditions for their creation and have examined the limits of statist hegemonic claims to cultural difference that lie beneath claims of different human rights practices. Both the Iranian state's framework as a theocratic republic and its discordant and inconsistent institutions make for a fascinating assessment of the resulting human rights program. On the one hand, the theocratic arms separate Iran's state from modern secular states, but the republican framework, with its elected bodies and attendant legal and political institutions, make the Islamic republic as an entity, however dispersed, amenable to critique, both internally and externally.

WOMEN, REPRESENTATION, AND HUMAN RIGHTS

One afternoon in late spring of 1999, I was in a meeting with the principal of a girl's middle school. The principal explained to me the importance women's attire has for society at-large: "You see, girls in our society grow up to be the parents of all the children. They are the ones who teach children how to behave properly. For this reason in our society we place great emphasis on women's character (*shakhseeat*). The hejab sanctifies her modesty and protects her in the society."

In exploring Iran's human rights as a cultural practice situated within the contours of state power, the issue of "women's rights" is central. Since the revolution, the trope of "woman" in Iran's Islamic republic performed symbolic roles necessary in the creation of the "authentic" and "virtuous" in new statist imaginings (Moallem 2005). Numerous government officials and scholars have taken decisive steps toward carving out native meaning in the Iranian human rights context, but symbols of "modest women" still serve as the ideals of what is considered honorable and just. These symbolic deployments of women have also been the grounds for debates between different factions in government. Some of President Khatami's reforms sought to lessen the attention to women's public attire, while the hardliners in government sought to curtail them.

The family is said to be "the fundamental unit of society" (Iranian Constitution 1979, revised 1989), and its ultimate success, and hence that of the nation, is understood to depend on women's moral virtue. For this reason, women's honor is not a private matter, but one of public concern. This is how many hard-line state actors justify the need for surveillance and intervention. By recognizing women's productive powers in nurturing the nation and its citizens, state actors acknowledge women's participatory roles within social and political contexts. In turn, women have avenues through which they make claims on the state institutions asking them to make good on promises of equal protection under the law. Thus if women are emblematic of the nation's virtue, then their claims to human rights, of which the state is the guarantor, reflect back on the nation's virtue and legitimacy as well. And for the world outside of Iran, women's status has been and continues to be a persistent marker with which to measure human rights within Iran. From Ayatollah Taleghani's statement declaring that women in Iran should voluntarily take up the chador to the enduring images of women clad in black chadors, the status and position of women in Muslim societies is still a common starting point for discussing human rights in the "Muslim world."

"Projecting" Women's Human Rights

One of the main agenda items of the reformers in the period when they had power in the executive and legislative branches, especially during Khatami's two-term government, was the issue related to "women's rights," with special attention to discriminatory laws in place. The relationship between human rights in Iran and the state's discourse around women's rights can be explored through an investigation of one group's attempts to convince Iran's leaders to ratify the International Convention on the Elimination of Discrimination Against Women (CEDAW). The Center for Women's Participation (CWP) is among the many organizations in Iran that work on behalf of women's and children's rights, but it is not an NGO. The CWP is an arm of the state's executive branch, and in 1994, as the Bureau of Women's Affairs, it successfully lobbied Iran's legislature to ratify the Convention on the Rights of the Child. Today the CWP works on many different issues pertaining to international law and human rights.

In 1997, as if to return the favor of the millions of women who voted for him, President Khatami upgraded the Bureau of Women's Affairs to the Center for Women's Participation. For the next eight years, the CWP functioned as part of the official President's Office and was "responsible for coordination, planning, providing support services, and policy-making regarding women's affairs."[20]

The CWP's introductory brochure related six primary goals: (1) lobbying various governmental branches for the formal adoption of policies and formulation of legislation and regulation, (2) presenting advisory opinions to the president, (3) studying ways of strengthening women's roles in family and in society, (4) raising awareness of women's issues in the general public, (5) presenting role models for Muslim women, and (6) exploring the breadth of women's issues in society, the family, and the workplace, with the goal of fostering change on formal and informal levels.[21]

With resources coming directly from the President's Office, the CWP drew from the aims of the executive in control at the time. During Khatami's first term, the CWP saw formidable increases in its budget, and more so when the reformist sixth Majlis took control of the legislature.[22] Since the inauguration of President Mahmoud Ahmadinejad in August 2005, the CWP has seen its budget slashed, although it retains its position as an executive branch office. In the fall of 2005 the CWP, like any other executive agency, went through a transition led by the new president. The center's leadership was given over to the hard-line members of government. The name of the center was also changed to the Center for Women and Family, highlighting a shift in emphasis from women's rights and participation in civil and political society to a focus on women's roles in the family.

When I began my fieldwork in 1999, however, the CWP served as a clearing house on women's issues and liaised not just with government, but also with members of the public, the domestic and international media, and researchers from all over the world. Located in downtown

Tehran, not far from the university, the building that houses the CWP includes five floors, the top of which was the office of the CWP's head, Zahra Shojaei. The building also housed CWP's library and a publishing division that produced books, pamphlets, brochures, and CD-ROMs in English for foreign investigators seeking information on women's issues.

While I did not have an opportunity to meet with Zahra Shojaei myself, in an interview with an Iranian daily newspaper, she spoke about the CWP's attempts to mainstream gender issues in the government's planning. Speaking of the government's Third Economic Development Plan, Ms. Shojaei explained that the inclusion of gender concerns was an important step toward broader economic planning and development. She described three kinds of views on gender in government development planning: neutral planning, which does not specifically address gender; planning that has specific attention to women's issues but is distinct from other planning that regards development for the community at large; and planning that is gender-oriented in that it regards the special roles men and women play in society. Interestingly, Ms. Shojaei was careful to distinguish that the basis for gender-oriented planning was based on distinct social roles that men and women have rather than their gender as such:

> By this gender-oriented viewpoint, we mean that women and men, due to their social roles (and not because of their gender) have special plans, tools and needs. Therefore if the needs, features, and demands of men and women (who have different roles in community) are considered in the plans, full-scale justice would be achieved.[23]

Here, Ms. Shojaei departed from the biological essentializing that Mutahhari wrote of and instead heeded what she saw as distinct roles based on the society's needs, and thus plans. In doing so, she suggested that society's values, based not on biology but on social roles, were constructed from present-day concerns. She intimated that differences between sexes are not natural but social, thus rejecting any basis for discrimination against women rooted in arguments that women are naturally or biologically inferior to men.[24]

On a number of occasions during fieldwork and on follow-up trips, I made my way to the offices of the CWP. My visits primarily took place at the Legal Affairs Division where I met with the international coordinator for legal affairs, a woman whose job duties included meeting foreigners who are interested in learning about women's status in Iran. The coordinator has a staff of experts trained in law who research and write about women's legal issues.

My first trip to the CWP was in 1999 when I went to ask specific questions regarding the status of the Iranian government's accession to international treaties and their relationship to human rights. At the downstairs reception, I was asked to show identification and then escorted to the third-floor offices. At the time, the director of the division was absent and I was shown to the large room in which several desks were occupied by female staff members. The mandate of this office of the CWP was to liaise with foreign visitors, like me, who inquired about women's status in Iran. There I met Ms. Mowlaverdi, a legal expert who researched whether the issues presented in CEDAW were in agreement with the principles of Islamic jurisprudence. In her mid-thirties at the time, Mowlaverdi was very impressive in her kind but stately manner. She was gracious in her responses to my questions and elegant in her long black chador, from under which a brightly colored headscarf peeked out.

CEDAW and the Achievement of "Full-Scale Justice"

During the periods that I conducted fieldwork in Iran, the Iranian parliament was considering ratification of CEDAW, which was fully supported by the CWP. Teams of legal experts worked to consider the issues at stake for the Islamic republic in ratification and drew up various proposals with which to lobby the public and the government.

In December 2002 I met with the CWP's legal team, noting that Ms. Mowlaverdi had by then been promoted to division director. Now sporting a bright headscarf and overcoat, she sat down with me in her private office ready to answer my questions about the CWP's work and its efforts regarding the ratification of CEDAW. At the time, the CWP had moved a draft bill through the executive branch, having received the support of the president's cabinet in 2001. The bill was sent to the full parliament, where it was tabled by the Cultural Commission for further investigation. The commission then invited the CWP, among other groups, to discuss the provisions of CEDAW and the possibility of ratification. Having been convinced of CEDAW's conformity with Iran's Islamic values, the commission approved and forwarded the draft legislation for a full vote by March 2001.

In a 2002 meeting, Ms. Mowlaverdi conveyed that the concerns with ratification were easily remedied with two reservations that Iran could take. The first concerned the issue of Islamic values: the CWP offered language for a reservation that would except Iran from following the articles of CEDAW that were found to conflict with Islam. A second reservation dealt with sovereignty: Iran would not accept the jurisdiction of the International Court of Justice on matters dealing with CEDAW. Ms. Mowlaverdi suggested that with these two reservations, the convention would not conflict with the values of the Islamic republic and that other Muslim-majority countries that had ratified the treaty had done the same. She was thus hopeful that CEDAW would be approved by parliament and the Council of Guardians.

In the summer of 2003, CEDAW was approved by the reform-dominated sixth Majlis and was being considered by the Council of Guardians, which would determine whether the convention conformed to Islamic principles. During my fall 2003 visit, it was clear that the CWP's position was that Iran could and should ratify CEDAW. In a number of visits over the years that followed, Mowlaverdi explained that the CWP's position on CEDAW was that it did not conflict with Islamic values, and that it firmly stood by the convention and its concordance with Islamic values, which required equality in rights between men and women. Certainly some reformers, like her, believed that CEDAW, irrespective of reservations, was in conformity with Islam.

In a follow-up visit with Ms. Mowlaverdi in September 2004, I learned that the Council of Guardians had rejected the bill just a month before. Ms. Mowlaverdi, though disappointed, was calm in her demeanor and expressed hope that the issues preventing ratification were political in nature and did not reflect CEDAW's incompatibility with Islamic values. Ms. Mowlaverdi then suggested that while the CWP would continue to work on the passage of the bill, the CWP's work to encourage women's participation was not limited to the ratification of CEDAW, but extended across a range of issues relating to women's greater participation within the society, including literacy, education, public health and welfare, as well as legal affairs (CWP, National Report 2005). Indeed, the head of the CWP, Ms. Shojaei, conveyed a similar viewpoint in a 2003 interview:

> At the moment, we are reviewing the civil, trade, social, and political rules related to women, and we do not consider our work dependent upon acceptance of the convention. Agreeing to the convention helps us to promote Islam and its divine and righteous values, which is against any discrimination. We do not want to unjustifiably be accused of discrimination against women.

In a 2003 interview, Nobel laureate Shirin Ebadi explained the matter of ratifying the convention as a political issue amid partisan factions of the Iranian government and suggested that in fact a more conservative government, which was poised to take over parliament in February 2004, might be better situated to ratify the convention:

> I even anticipate that if the government of President Khatami were not in charge we would have joined this convention without any controversy. The resistance that was observed against joining this convention was mainly politically motivated. Meanwhile we joined the Convention on the Rights of the Child. The

rules violating the Islamic laws were also not allowed in this convention. But there was no resistance that was observed against joining this convention. However, in the Convention on the Rights of the Child, many of the women's rights are obeyed. . . .In fact, if the contents of the children's rights convention would have been implemented, maybe 70 percent of the contents of the Convention on the Elimination of Discrimination Against Women would also be obeyed. . . . The resistance was mainly due to the political viewpoint.[25]

Advocacy attempts notwithstanding, there were many other issues within the country that legal advocates such as Ms. Mowlaverdi were committed to and actively engaging in. The sources of tension among Islamic principles, human rights, and specific discriminatory practices were subjects of constant conversations among these advocates. More often than not, pious Muslim women's rights advocates spoke of the patriarchal misapplications of Islam. These tensions were not inherent in Islam, they conveyed, but in the discriminatory manner in which these ideas were being mobilized. For instance, Dr. Kermani, in a discussion of women's status, raised a number of legal status arguments to illustrate her point that "Westerners" do not understand the cultural values of Iranians and therefore cannot act on or judge them. By way of example, she explained the legal issues underlying the discriminatory inheritance laws that give males members of families twice the portion allotted to females members. It should be noted that this law can be set aside by a written will, but in the absence of such, the law gives two portions to males inheritors over females. Dr. Kermani explained,

> In our law and in our culture, women do not have to work or earn money. Any money that is earned by a woman is hers to keep. On the other hand, by law, males in our society are bound to care for female members of the family, those who have no guardian (*sarparast*). The point is that men are legally responsible for women. So this is why the inheritance system gives more to men. This is the same issue with blood money (*dieh*). Even in the matter of polygamy. The Prophet says only take one wife, but if you take more than one, be sure that you can treat them all equally. Obviously no man can treat four women the same. The problem was that in the years when these words were uttered by the Prophet, the world was in great turmoil and there were many wars. With many men dying, there were many widowed and single women who had no economic means. So to remedy this problem, God said to Mohammad that this was the way.[26]

I had heard the arguments about men's economic obligation frequently when in Iran, but I also heard complaints of the actuality of this issue never coming to pass. In practice, many women complained to me, this never happens. So I persisted, "But many women never actually receive the economic support they are legally entitled to."

"Yes, this is a problem," Dr. Kermani replied, but it is a problem of enforcement. We are trying to get the laws to work the way they are intended to work. We are also adding new laws, working on laws that would change the inheritance for women without male guardians or women with children to be the same as men."

In February 2004 the law to ameliorate the inheritance disparity passed in the reformist parliament, but a year later it was dealt a blow by the Council of Guardians, who determined that it indeed conflicted with Islamic jurisprudence. Dr. Kermani's views differ greatly from those of some of my other informants, who did not believe that religious values should be sole determinants of women's legal rights.

Ms. Mowlaverdi offered yet another point of view: while she is a practicing Muslim, her reformist views manifest a different interpretation of women's rights in Iran. Her take was one that firmly supported redefinitions of Islamic texts and allowed wide latitude for interpretation given the challenges of the times. "Islam allows for reasoning and logic, in fact, requires it. We can see when society is changing and certain issues are no longer good for the society and are no longer healthy. This is how we think about our attempts to ban stoning." In a conversation in the fall of 2004, I raised this issue with her and mentioned that it is a cause of great indignation for many people I have talked to, both in Iran and outside. She agreed and said that the CWP was actively working to prohibit the practice. At the time of this interview, both she and the other women in the room, including my secular, nonstatist companion, felt that the issue was being used by Western media outlets for their own political purposes. Ms. Mowlaverdi explained that there are groups who have researched this law in the texts of the Qur'an and elsewhere and in 2002 were able to convince Majlis to place a ban on stoning, also known as lapidation. Since I was not aware of this, and in fact had been told of stoning still happening in Iran even after that period, I asked Ms. Mowlaverdi to clarify her point. She explained, "Unfortunately we have had some, though very few, still occur. This is no longer the official policy of the state and it is not the state that is handing out this punishment. I know of one that occurred in a rural area. It is not enough for the state to ban it; people must change their customs, too."[27]

Although my research and interviews with women who are legal experts reveal a great deal of advocacy and commitment to the idea that Islam is in conformity with international human rights treaties, other viewpoints also exist. These viewpoints help trace some of the political controversies surrounding human rights discourses in Iran.

REPRESENTING "WOMEN'S AFFAIRS"

While the fixation on the attire of some Muslim women is complex and difficult to understand, within Iran it is just as complex an issue. The dress code is not the sole measure of the state's attitude toward women's human rights, and the chador cannot be seen as only an indicator of women's rights. As many scholars have noted, the issue of women's dress in Iran as well as in other Muslim societies also serves as a social marker of a woman's virtue and is a key signifier of the postrevolutionary state's legitimacy. In my research I found that as women became "virtuous," that is, adopted the regimentation that state institutions required of them in order to participate in those institutions and society more broadly, their actions and attire also reflected virtue back onto the state system. This system in turn endowed the women with credibilty to make claims on those state institutions.

So it is not surprising that conversations I had with state officials about women's rights were emblematic of the state's own virtue as well. Thus the need to rehabilitate women was an essential starting point for state-building at the inception of the Islamic republic. Public statements, prayers, and speeches were replete with discussions about the morality of women and the importance of women's modesty in raising honorable sons and daughters. Since one of the stated aims of the revolution was to restore the moral social order through women, the new leaders encouraged education and even claimed to respect women's rights to work outside of the home, provided that women were still able to perform their primary duty of raising children. This led to some interesting results in government offices, including on-the-job day care, nursing breaks at the workplace, and school vans that bring children to their mother's workplace. In addition, each ministry has a women's affairs representative charged with addressing the particular concerns that women employees might have. At the Ministry of Housing, I met with just such a woman, Ms. Nazari, and asked her about her position, her role, and her views.

At the age of forty, Ms. Nazari had reached the zenith of her career—she was about to be promoted to the head of public relations at the ministry. Ms. Nazari met me in her office on the fourth floor. Despite her numerous duties, she rolled her chair right up next to mine, and appeared genuinely happy to see me.

Ms. Nazari held two posts. She was the parliamentary deputy for women's affairs (*mauven-e dafter-e majlis*) and was also the housing minister's representative for women's affairs (*namayande ye vasir e maskan dar umur e zanan*). In her second post, which she had held for some eleven years, she dealt with all the issues that women at Housing came to her with. In the Ministry of Housing, she told me, "There are 750 women and I deal with whatever problems they may have; they include giving loans, housing, and training." Ms. Nazari expressed her point of view about her role in the government and the status of women in society as part of a broader concern for women that grew out of the revolution:

> Ayatollah Khomeini said that women are mothers and managers of the home. He gave women a lot of consideration that they did not previously have; he said that it is from the skirts of women (*daman-e-zan*) that anyone grows. Because it is from women that men and society grow, it became very important to consider women in society.

Like other government officials whom I sat down with, Ms. Nazari constantly emphasized women's importance to society. Her views on the relevance of women to society justified her own position in the ministry and enabled a discourse about how state institutions needed to accommodate women's important social roles. She emphasized this view when I asked her about the biggest changes in regard to women's status after the revolution.

> With a lot of work, women showed that they can work, be mothers and wives, and they can do it all, as long as men and women both understand each other. It requires a shared understanding. Everything takes time. We planted the seeds for change. In considering women's situation, we must take account of how it was before, how it is now, and what we want.

As a woman whose family supported the overthrow of the previous government and whose own work focused on women's situation, Nazari described some of the improvements that she saw in women's situation in Iran since the revolution:

> After the revolution, there were three women in parliament, then four, then nine, then twelve, and now there are fifteen. They are professors and mothers as well. All of them, like men, work. A woman can really do it all. And then of course they have certain expectations, for instance that the laws will afford them some credit. There are more women going to college now as well.

I then asked how her work supports women status.

> In my post at Majlis, I am working on trying to get housing for single women with children. This is a problem for women. I am also working on changing the law of custody for children in divorce, or in the event of the death or disappearance of the father. The law says that the guardian is either the paternal grandfather or paternal uncle. Also, with regard to dissolution, we are working on a law to divide the wealth of the couple in half.[28] At Housing, we are working on

providing government housing for the poor, young couples, and single parents. But the difficulty is that single parents, who are usually women, have no earning potential. And so we are trying to create community networks for them. We are producing the housing. At Housing we deal more with housing for the people in need. This year [1999], we built ten thousand government units.

In Tehran, the population is very high and there is a shortage of housing. When people come to us, we send them to the newly created sections of town, usually on the outskirts. There are four newly constructed divisions. Inside Tehran, we are building high rises. People want to own their own place to live. When they come to us, we give them a form to fill out. In order to qualify, they must be five years past marriage, at least five-year residents of Tehran, a single person with children, a person who has an account at Maskan Bank, or a family of a war victim.

Additional job duties that I have include helping out the women who work here. For instance, there is a woman here whose husband is in jail. She gets free shuttle service to and from work. In the summer, Housing provides programs for children. They attend swimming and other sports classes. This leaves their mothers' minds free of worry so that they may work with the peace of mind that their children are well provided for and busy. There is also a day-care center here. If a woman wants to work, she must do so with a clear conscience.

In my post at Majlis, I am the intermediary between the ministries and the MPs. I act in support of the laws and plans being executed. I work with the mayor's office, architectural firms, and buildings, like hospitals and colleges that are in need of renovation.

Ms. Nazari stopped to ask me about centers for people with disabilities in the United States. She added that one of her projects is finding suitable living situations for these kinds of people, that is, people with special needs. She said that she was trying to get NGOs to work on housing cooperative projects since the government housing for people with special needs required people to leave after they reached the age of forty. For them to have a place to go afterwards, her staff at Housing was trying to get women to live together, by either sharing or buying houses cooperatively.

Ms. Nazari's position as a government-sector worker and an agent of the state was not lost on me. I knew from conversations I had had with nongovernment officials, as well as the outburst in the IHRC, that many were critical of the actions of government and that housing was a particular problem in the city. I was also aware that Ms. Nazari was interested in showing issues in the best light to me, since she knew I would be writing about Iran for audiences abroad. She was not unique among people I spoke with who wanted a more complex view of Iran and Iranians to be presented abroad. When I asked her about difficulties that women face, she did not hesitate to answer. She described the issues as legal issues, not issues of culture, tradition, or biology:

> There are a series of difficulties women face, and these are due to four possible reasons: (1) the lack of laws; (2) the lack of implementation of the laws; (3) the weakness of law and its inability to resolve the central issue or problem; and (4) problems with interpretation of the laws. There is no consistency with the interpretation of the laws. Also, women themselves must believe in these laws and in themselves. It is in their upbringing their self-confidence. No one offers more self-sacrifice than the Iranian woman. The Iranian woman will give up everything in order to permit her child to be raised with two parents.
>
> In our society, our view toward boys and girls is different. God gave some things to the boys and some to the girls. We don't agree that men and women can do all [the same] things because women must be gentle, in order to be mothers, must have gentle souls. But it is important that equal conditions be available to women. The issue is that now in government offices there is a woman who knows about the women's situation. Like in Housing—women will eventually be living in the housing that is built, so let the women partake in the decisions that will affect them. It is important to have women in the places where decisions are being made.

Ms. Nazari's concern with equal conditions and participation was in line with the reformist ideas to which the administration for which she worked ascribed. Knowing that Ms. Nazari had studied law and lived in Europe, I asked her about her views on human rights: "In Iran, is there a difference between human rights as Islamic human rights and international human rights?" She indicated that she understood my question as being about the insertion of Islam into the text of human rights:

> The difference is not about Islam; the difficulties depend on the people putting the laws into practice. Each country has its own customary laws. And each country has sovereignty. We can get along with international human rights. In Majlis, there is a Commission for Family and Women to deal with the important issues for women and families today. Some people say, "Why is there only a committee for women, why not men?" Or, "If women want to be equal to men, why then have these special committees?" The answer is that to the extent that women have particular difficulties, we must have these committees, because women are not yet equal to men before the law.

Ms. Nazari's explanation about human rights echoed what Ms. Tazeh at the IHRC as well as Ms. Mowlaverdi at CWP had said to me. All were government workers in a reformist administration, and each quietly emphasized a language of entitlement and rights and associating those with Islam or Islamic values. They each also recognized the legitimate claims that women have on state institutions for their claims. Ms. Nazari went one step further and spoke specifically of equality and the status of the law. These women, each working for different sectors of the government, offered statements about human rights that, in the spring of 1999, were in line with a concern by other reformists working in Khatami's government for women's rights, and their attempts, like CWP's work on CEDAW, gave way to a period of great potential and inspiration among the many women and men across a broad spectrum with whom I spoke that summer. Dr. Kermani, who worked in the hard-line branch of government, more than the other women emphasized the broader political concerns that the term "human rights" brings with it to a country like Iran, although the others were no doubt aware of these issues. It is also significant that each viewed me in a particular light, and their answers reflected, perhaps, how they wanted to convey human rights given my position as a researcher from the United States. While I was interested in showing an awareness of and engagement with the term by varied groups, they also saw me as an interlocutor and approached their conversations with me in light of that.

As each of the government personnel I spoke with focused on the relationship between human rights and Islam, it would appear that the binary relationship here is being reinforced even as they try to profess compatibility between the two. This would be far too simplistic a picture, however, of the many ways in which people I spoke with conveyed the values of human rights in Iran. It is for this reason that I noted at the beginning of this chapter the highly politicized context of the discourse of human rights in terms of the state's relationship with it. Once beyond the purview of governmental voices on human rights, I saw a range of views about the subject in Iran.

CONCLUSION

An ethnography of human rights calls for detailed studies of human rights concerns with attention to the actions of the numerous social actors involved, and with regard for the historical context of institutionalized power (Wilson 1997). Further discussions on the topic of human rights reflect how a reading of the Iranian state actors' deployments of human rights also reveals a set of politics associated with the broader meanings conveyed by human rights discourses—that human rights are indicative of how civilized a society is in the view of international groups.

My exploration of Iran's statist human rights discourses reveals actions and intentions aimed at sending a message, not just to Iran's own citizenry, but also to Western proponents of international human rights.[29] This message effectively tells Western human rights workers that the Iranian state has a qualified arbiter to determine the propriety of its treatment of its populace. For some years, Iran refused entry to the special representative of the UN Human Rights Commission.[30] When the report of the commission was published in April 1999, the Iranian Foreign Ministry spokesman, Hamid-Reza Asefi, rejected it, stating, "Iran was relying on its Islamic and cultural values and considers the resolution as illegitimate with no basis for cooperation."[31] A month later, a member of parliament similarly denounced the commission's report pertaining to charges it made about women in Iran. Representative Karrubi remarked that the statements in the report "stem from the lack of proper understanding of Islamic teachings, especially those in connection with women's hejab."[32] She explained, "the realities on the status of women in the Islamic republic and their massive participation in social, cultural and political area are being revealed to other nations. According to Articles 20 and 21 of the constitution, there is no sex discrimination under the Islamic system." Even while asserting a particularized standard of human rights, state forces attempt to locate culturally specific practices through a rational theory of law and the language of human rights, even if they are located, *as well*, within Islamic values of the Islamic republic.

Of course state actors' legitimation of their "cultural" practices through references to local constructions of human rights may be a part of the state's political machinations. Scholarly debates between cultural relativists and universalists often ignore the role of the modern state in defining rights for its people. That is, even while officials in the Islamic republic assert cultural bases for the derivation of human rights, which appear to elude Western-based assessments of Iran's human rights records, they also approach human rights through the prism of the modern republic and the rule of law.

As my interlocutors described, in the Iranian context, human rights emerge from a number of different sources. They conveyed the complex and fluctuating condition of rights. Their notions of rights are not derived entirely from Islamic principles. Instead, what constitutes perceptions of rights is more an amalgamation of many ideologies that come together within the context, in Iran, of Islam and republic. We cannot say whether any or all of these sources exist inside or outside of Islam; indeed, these ideas determine Islam by being somehow related to Islam, and Islam determines the ideas in the context of the Islamic republic by embodying them—even if that relation is one of opposition. Thus these knowledge categories coexist and constitute one another.

As noted, rights exist within the Islamic republic. That is, other sources of rights still fall within and are condoned by the state constructions of Islam, which can be distinguished from other constructions of Islam; this is not a monolithic Islam. My interlocutors notably pointed out that rights are contingent and relational: "Rights depend on who and where we are." In the same breath, this thought was qualified by adding that, as human beings, we have some basic rights. Thus, my informants expressed an appreciation for *both* a basic level of rights, by virtue of being human, and a finite quality to those rights, based on the contexts in which those rights arise. How these speculations play out practically in women's lives through practices that necessarily engage government policies and politics has been one of the aims of this chapter. The interviews show that perceptions of rights may be grounded in numerous categorizations but are also contingent on many factors, including settings and the entitlements being considered. Rights are thus both universal and situational, and individual concerns help situate perceptions of rights amid the broader context of discourses of women's rights and human rights in Iran.

In a globalized world, human rights are expressions of a nation's civility and legitimacy. State forces in Iran serve to advance beliefs in human rights but qualify them by particularizing human rights as native and culturally authentic. By positing this dual notion, these state forces participate in the international community by assenting to a limit on their nation's sovereignty. And yet, by locating an authentic Islamic position on human rights, state forces send a message that only they can arbitrate what constitutes the state's proper treatment of their citizenry. This poses the problem of understanding and evaluating human rights cross-culturally when states make claims that their notions of human rights are culturally authentic and therefore inscrutable to outsiders. Thus scholars should examine the naming and defining of "culture" as an assertion of power. The "debate" between universalism and relativism should also be repositioned to recognize that "human rights" is itself a cultural practice that needs to be explored as a constructed category, wherever it appears, including in Western contexts.

In Iran, some state actors employ human rights as a culturally specific practice, and yet others have attempted to participate in the international human rights context, serving as both critics and advocates of Iranian human rights. The attempt to ratify CEDAW and the attention to women's rights practices more generally are sites upon which Iranian state actors have located their human rights culture-practice. Concerns for women's rights and status have been issues integral to the state's legitimacy. While some state policy makers have advanced chador-clad women as the symbol of change and new-found virtue in Iran, some women are now using the same language of rights, sanctioned by an Islamized republic equipped with human rights, to demand just that equality and those rights that only thirty years ago were unsavory demands imposed by "corrupt Western influences." The tensions mounting in Iran amid these contests reveal the nonnatural, nonessential quality of the meaningful manifestation of rights. While the reflection on common core concepts, such as justice, rights, and mercy, contribute to a shared or global discourse of human rights, those rights are revealed and only find their material form at the axes of ever-changing social, political, and legal trajectories.

"Women's Rights" as Exhibition at the Brink of War

HOW A MODERN LIBERAL THEORY of rights is mapped onto an Islamic Middle Eastern society, specifically through women's articulations of rights, has been the focal point of this book. The Iranian experiment of creating an Islamic republic from France's postwar vision of secular democracy warrants greater attention in understanding the socio-political underpinnings of women's perceptions of rights. An examination of Iranian women's rights provides the perfect point of entry into exploring the secular and religious simultaneously, and for contesting the binaries to which earlier scholars have reverted when exploring Islamic states. How Islam and liberal state impact women's rights, moreover, highlights the contingency of practices of rights. The broader relevance of my work bears on the seemingly contradictory notions of human rights and Islam. How Iranians think about these issues represents a local analysis much needed in understanding human rights cross-culturally.

· · ·

On March 17, 2006, I was asked to participate in a discussion on relations between Iran and the United States for a broadcast on a Seattle public radio station.[1] I spoke at length with the show's producer, who asked me to address women's rights in Iran. As it turned out, the show focused on Iran and nuclear proliferation, with all three of the other guests being experts on nonproliferation. It was unclear to me what role I, as a specialist on women's rights, was intended to play. As my segment came to a close, I had a chance to mention the role of women's affairs representatives in Iran's ministries. I pointed out that each ministry has a female representative charged with overseeing the concerns of female employees. The response from the show's host was one of surprise—not about the existence of women's affairs representatives, but about the fact that Iranian women work outside the home.

The response from the radio show's host signaled the ease and subtle acceptance with which the binaries of Western freedom and Islamic oppression travel through our society. It led me to think about the work that the enduring trope of the "oppressed Muslim woman in Iran" does in the current geopolitical climate and then extrapolate its logic to understand how it affects the work that we as scholars do. In other words, what is the logic behind the relationship between women's rights in Iran and the U.S. policy of regime change there? It seems to be a good thing, perhaps even a natural thing, for us to be concerned with women's rights in Iran, but then what are the hermeneutical limits of our understanding of Iranian women's rights and status in light of the intensified rhetoric against Iran over a thirty-year period?

In *Colonising Egypt,* Timothy Mitchell took up the question of "exhibitions" of the Middle East in and by Europeans. Through non-European eyes, he studied exhibitions as practices that exemplified the nature of the modern European state. He explored what he referred to as "the mischief" of putting Middle Eastern visitors on display under the irrepressible eagerness of Europeans "to stand and stare" (1988: 2). In the world of exhibitions, Mitchell's Egyptian interlocutors revealed, Europeans felt their gaze had no effect. The ability to see without being seen confirmed their separation from the world and corresponded with a position of power over it (26). The "Orient," or in this case Iran, comes to be a place that one already knows, that one only *rediscovers.*

Exploring contemporary exhibitions helps us to locate the logic of what may otherwise be regarded as natural concerns for women in Iran. Mitchell argued that a shift occurred in the culture of representation with the emergence of capitalism and the development of the modern nation-state. This book was published a little more than a decade before September 11, 2001, so perhaps a more specific exploration into contemporary "exhibitions on women's rights" will help us trace a more exacting logic about what we "already feel we know" about women in the Middle East. And so today it would be fruitful to explore exhibitions on "women's rights" in order to locate their variable contexts, meanings, and implications, with regard to the era that we are in. By that era, I am not solely referring to the events of 9/11 nor to the so-called global war on terror, but rather to the stated aims of the Bush administration's power-brokers, the neoconservatives, whose agenda it is to remake the Middle East (also known as "regime change").

Returning, then, to the initial inquiry—what is the relationship between women's rights in Iran and the global war on terror? A clue to the answer may lie in the words of former Bush speechwriter David Frum, author of the phrase "axis of evil," and Richard Perle, formerly of the defense policy board that advises the Pentagon. In 2003, while fellows at the American Enterprise Institute, Frum and Perle published a "manual for victory" in the war on terror, entitled *An End to Evil: How to Win the War on Terror.* In it, they explain why attention to women's issues is important to winning the war on terror. Using freedom as a defining point of cultural difference between American and "Islamic" culture, the authors invoke women as a site of such critical struggles: "Those who mocked President Bush for explaining that the terrorists attacked the United States because they hate American freedom should consider the remark from the point of view of America's—and the world's—women. For the terrorists *do* hate the freedom of Western women, not the least because they fear it is putting ideas into the heads of *their* women" (2003: 149).

In a section entitled "Women's Freedom," they present a series of undifferentiated anecdotes that characterize the "Islamic world" as a monolith engaged in the routine oppression of women. Frum and Perle do not offer any context—historical, political, or otherwise—nor do they differentiate between countries that the United States considers an ally, such as Saudi Arabia and Pakistan, and those considered a foe, such as Iran. Moreover, their consistent reference to "Islamic" society suggests that religion is the single unifying source among extremely varied peoples throughout the world and overstates religion as the sole factor distinguishing "them" from "us."

Highlighting the power of the Internet to reach people the world over, Frum and Perle argue that an inability of Muslim radicals to control the images that enter into Islamic societies and give women, among others, a taste of "freedom" has fueled terrorist vitriol and dogmatism. Initially it seems that Frum and Perle are drawing from a centuries-old argument advanced by British and French imperialists to justify colonialism to their own citizens: the exploitation of hyperbolic anecdotes about women's status to justify military intervention—what is today, in a postcolonial world, illegal. Frum and Perle, however, take the argument one step further, linking women's status with "Islamic terrorism."

Asserting that "women's oppression contributes to terror" (2003: 149), Frum and Perle relate a story from another book, *Nine Parts of Desire*, by Australian journalist Geraldine Brooks (1995). In it, Brooks reports on a visit to an Iranian family where women are making bread. The authors encapsulate the story with telling narrative cues: "A society that treats women like slaves will teach its men all the cruelty and violence of the slaveholder" (Frum and Perle 2003: 149). Having clarified how readers should understand the story, they begin: "On a visit to an Iranian family, journalist Geraldine Brooks was startled to watch a girl as young as six put to work making bread—and then to see the girl's slightly older brother rush into the room and laughingly snatch the fresh-baked bread from her hands and shove it in his mouth. He had already learned the first law of life in his society: He and those like him ruled; his sisters, his mother, even his elderly grandmother, must obey."

Frum and Perle explain that the story is striking because it illustrates how boys learn at such a young age that women toil and that men do not have to. David Frum clarified this argument in a speech at the University of Washington in January 2004, using the same story to extrapolate a larger claim:

> [I]n these societies in the Islamic world which have been struggling with the pains of modernity . . . one of the essential pieces is a reassertion of a new kind of clampdown on women. One of the things that Islamic groups do when they become active is target women as they try to cope with failed modernization in a heavy-handed way. One of the central ideological struggles we have is the role of women. [The] U.S. must encourage the education of women because education of mothers is a predictor of education levels of children. And educated children will not attend the free *maddrassahs* where they train terrorists.[2]

The falseness of Frum's argument is exposed by the simple check of statistics on literacy and education. In Iran, women's' education has been on the rise for the last fifteen years.[3]

But we are not now in the colonial context that Mitchell wrote about, but rather are in a new era in which even colonies have positioned themselves in the Euro-American geoculture. This geoculture, to which Wallerstein (1995) alludes, is the cultural framework within which the world-system operates, and it refers specifically to the uneven, if not contradictory, logic of the modern nation-state on the colonies or "spheres of influence."[4] So what effects do Frum and Perle's assertions have in the contemporary world system?

There are many, but most problematic is that the authors encourage their readers to think in binary terms: modernity versus Islam. They turn the conversation into one of an epic ideological struggle between a Western liberal humanism that espouses freedom and individual expression, and Islamic traditionalism, referred to as radicalism, which is always the opposite of "Western" values. Their argument, moreover, masks the political goal they are advocating. Frum and Perle are making a case for preemptive war, for which there is no legal justification. And women, as reified objects, are the tropes they use to make a case for war. Women's status, they tell us, is what is at stake for freedom-loving people. And if we care about freedom, then we will support them.

In their examples, Frum and Perle argue that radical Islamists force women to submit to their authority, then attempt to illustrate it with the Iranian example. By naturalizing their political goals in what the authors would like us to believe is an episode of everyday village life, the authors also make a case for extralegal intervention. In spite of the existing international apparatus that prohibits preemptive war, which provides a diplomatic path to engagement, the authors use issues regarding women as their basis to argue for intervention. They do so by characterizing women's issues as a problem of "freedom," and thus ideology, as Frum and

Perle put it, as opposed to foreign policy, for which the international legal apparatus would be appropriate.[5]

Some activists may argue that the attention to women's status in these regions that is generated is significant, despite the problems with how it is characterized. My concern is that we have not fully or adequately considered that these portrayals are interventions that also produce the social and political conditions through which we understand women's status. They color our understanding by setting the terms and shaping our perceptions of the realities of women's lives, activities, and concerns. As scholars, we know that "cultures" are productive, ever-changing, and internally inconsistent, but now we can also see how the idea of culture as bounded and static, homogenous and monolithic, is exploited to the point where it appears that no in-between space is possible. By studying the discursive effects of popular politics, we can see how the notion of culture can be isolated, reified, and decontextualized to create the problem that Kuper (1999) warned of, that is, culture goes from something to be described, understood, or explained to being the explanation itself.

Frum and Perle contend that women's status is related to the way daughters are trained to toil. The authors read women's roles through a cultural prism and in doing so strip their argument of its political components. When the authors say they are talking about freedom, they are perfecting the language of liberalism, in its American instantiation, as an abstract universal quality. These are, however, the epistemological assumptions that political commentators subtly draw on when making claims about women in Middle Eastern or so-called Muslim societies to make political points.

Historically, in political debates aimed at justifying imperialism or struggling against colonial domination, women's bodies have served as the grounds of these struggles. Often women needed to be saved, whether from imperial perpetrators or from their male brethren. The political discourse about imperial intervention on the sides of both colonialists and anticolonialists consisted of a dialogic exchange that brought about concerns for woman's status; it actually produced the field of concern for women's status and set the epistemological terrain, denoted as "the woman question." And the woman question was not about the material conditions of women's lives within their social circumstances but rather was borne of the "political encounter between a colonial state and the supposed 'tradition' of a conquered people" (Chatterjee 1993).

When the topic of women's rights emerges as an issue in contemporary international debates, we often see the replication of not only binary terms (i.e., freedom versus oppression), but also the potential discursive elision of women's everyday subjectivities, experiences, needs, and demands, such as those we saw with Frum and Perle and even Brooks. Concern with women's rights, however, cannot preclude an understanding or exploration of the political stakes involved nor the dialogical processes that themselves produce the nation's or the international community's claims to foster and protect women's rights. International politics becomes part of the hermeneutics of understanding women's status.

The material and hermeneutic effects of the cold war, global capitalism, and colonialism on our understandings of women in different Middle Eastern and Muslim majority societies are starting to be explored (Abu-Lughod 2002; Ahmed 2005; Hirschkind and Mahmood 2002). In a similar vein, I have attempted to offer a way to think about the status of women in Iran that does not depend on the depiction of "the rule of radical Islamists," but instead involves a rethinking of the terms of the debate itself and forces us to move beyond the binaries of East and West, premodern and modern.

How do we think about these (mis)characterizations in the Iranian context? That is to say, is there a response by Iranian anti-imperialists to the use of women as put forth by Brooks and later Frum and Perle and others, just as there was among Indian anticolonial nationalists? This work has been an attempt to call attention to the political and ideological components that forge questions around women's rights concerns in Iran. In exploring the contemporary Iranian discourses on women's rights, I have considered the Iranian Revolution—specifically the role that the trope of "women's rights" played in the anti-imperialist discourse of 1979 and in the creation of the postrevolutionary nation-state, an Islamic republic, as the critical moment when women's rights are rearticulated in the renewed hybrid legal space of Islamico-civil law. A core conceptual point in this moment is that women's rights and human rights are emerging through global discourses and initiatives as well as local ones. Human rights issues have consistently plagued Iran's leaders who, both pre- and postrevolution, have been influenced by the desire to appear "civilized" before the world community, as this book's opening quote from Khatami shows. The developments of women's rights and human rights, while sometimes portrayed by Iranian nationalists or religious leaders as somehow "native," are also in dialogue with the wider global discourses of rights.

In the hybrid Iranian framework, I have shown that we are seeing an instance of liberalism and liberal values, but in a very novel context, an Islamic republic. And it is those voices that are forged at the juncture of Islamic liberalism that are obscured and even suppressed in the debates that produce discourses about women's status in binary terms. The 1997 election of a progressive cleric, Mohammad Khatami, to the Iranian presidency led some people to push for social and legal reforms in what has been often characterized as a repressive government. In its early reform period, Khatami's government, however, attempted to make changes through the existing governmental framework, an Islamic republic, which itself emerged not only from Islamic principles but a hundred-year history of constitutional and legal institutions.

I have sought to explore how this theocratic republic, with an unusual mixture of liberal republic and Islamic principles, offers a unique setting in which women are beginning to re-create their place in Iranian society. While the liberal state provides the possibility for women to position themselves as equal partners with men, at least theoretically, Islam legitimizes that agency by authenticating the discourse of equality. I argued that women's notions of rights are born of the complexities of their specific circumstances and incorporate multiple ideologies of rights. Through a study of women's understandings of rights, I exposed the specific relations, be they class, education, geographic, demographic, or a combination thereof, that mediate some Iranian women's conceptions and articulations of rights. I showed that specific groups of women, in specific positions, have specific opinions about rights. These opinions, moreover, are shaped by the discourses of rights available in the contexts in which women find themselves. Such discourses include liberal notions of individual rights, Islamic ideals, and pre-Islamic Iranian ideals. And of course women's experiences in one context shape the range of experiences in other contexts. For instance, the women involved in the courts, dealing with their state-regulated rights, also consult one another about their Islamic rights in bi-weekly Qur'anic meetings; it is with these heterogeneous understandings of rights that women make choices about their lives.

Punditry and geopolitics in part formulate and then depend upon binary conceptualizations, thereby occluding the complex internal and transnational dynamics fashioning women's rights activists' responses to political oppression. In Iran, we are seeing the tensions surrounding contemporary debates about the role of women in a liberal Islamic republic, contradictory as that may sound to some. Indeed, these problems are those connected with the logic of the modern nation-state. If we can be led to believe that certain people are backwards and thus abstract politics from geography, then we can also justify a redrawing of the map of the Middle East without regard for the world of nation-states and the laws that pertain to them. Nation-states are legal entities, laws entail diplomacy and negotiation, but the focus on the treatment of women in Iran leads to a different conclusion (that no law can justify such oppression). Yet, in a world of nation-state sovereignty, how do we also understand our own national missteps—the illegal unilateral invasion of Iraq, Abu-Ghraib, Guantanamo, state-sanctioned and sometimes sponsored torture? This is to say that the violence of law that is referenced in the circulation of images representing oppressed Muslim women is not exceptional, but contained within a modern legal apparatus of the nation-state system.

In Iran, exceptional violence is just that, violence carried out by non-state actors or belligerent state actors. By understanding this, the cause-and-effect relationship between the unmodern and the possibility of these violent acts and events is disrupted. The modern Islamico-civil state and the laws of that state produce the system that we have. The challenge to law's violence has two key dimensions: intranational (domestic) and transnational.

Thus, it is not enough to think about the political nature of the issue as it is being presented, whether by Frum and Perle or by others. There is something more at issue here, and that is that these conditions produce the filter through which we consider women's rights, cordoning off other kinds of inquiries. My call is to focus on critically understanding the relations between the nation-state and this new performance of Islamic modernity, emphasizing the roles that women, both as agents and as reified figures, play. Exploring legal process allows for dynamic illustrations of the ways in which the law can be put to work for women. It also allows us to see how they are participating in reshaping these venues and these institutions in an attempt to rethink, reclaim, and indeed, rearticulate women's status, politically and socially, making claims on state institutions to make good on revolutionary promises to improve conditions for women.

Thus, in this book I have wanted to make two main points. First, the trope of women's rights is deeply politicized, and it is this politics that sets the terms of the discussion and delimits the terrain of inquiry both for the outside analyst and for the inside activist. There is no such thing as a cultural essence (of women's rights) in practice, even though there are material consequences for women's rights given these politics. Second, in Iran, the populist and anti-imperialist tenor of the revolution made an issue of women's rights; recognition of this context is crucial to understanding the way many Iranian women make claims on the institutions of the Islamic republic for their rights today. It also reveals some of the limits of their calls for "rights," especially as the trope of women's rights is used to fulfill certain political conditions in international politics that have little to do with concerns for material conditions of women's lives. As scholars, we need to pay greater attention to the punditry that pervades even our seemingly more enlightened understandings of women's status. The effects of contemporary discourses of regime change that highlight women's rights can actually hurt internal reform movements more than they help them. This is because as the attacks are framed increasingly in "ideological" terms, the response is to further determine and restrict the field of possibility for women's status, one that is also ideological and binary, and thus not only occludes but even critically shifts the on-the-ground possibilities for women.

In the case of women's rights, when we understand process and destabilize the unproblematized notion that rights must be examined through a secular lens, when we pay attention to the particularities of the way religion is working through the law, we can then see the critical moments in which women articulate their rights in the fluid hybridity of multiple ideologies of law, of transnational legalities, as opposed to the outside discourses that set the only acceptable parameters as international and Western law. Looking at the Iranian example, it is important to consider the religio-political, ideological state institutions through which women's rights materialize: Islamic principles and republican state institutions.

The Iranian Marriage Contract

A. At the time of signing the marriage contract, or through a separate binding contract, the bride has made it a condition that in case her husband asks for a divorce and should the court decide that this request does not arise out of the wife's failure in her marital duties or her misconduct or misbehavior, the husband shall be bound to transfer to her half the wealth accumulated during the marriage.

B. The husband gives the wife a permanent power of attorney to obtain a divorce through the court under any of the following conditions:

Signature of the groom   Signature of the bride

The conditions and situations under which the wife has the right to petition the court to issue a Divorce Authorization are as follows:

1. If the husband has not paid maintenance for six months for whatever reason, or has refused or failed to fulfill his other obligations towards her for six months.
2. If there has been maltreatment or disrespectful behavior on the part of the husband towards the wife.
3. If the husband contracts an incurable or difficult to cure disease which renders married life dangerous to the health of the wife.
4. If the husband becomes insane and annulment of the marriage is not possible under any other shari'a law.
5. If the husband continues with an occupation which the court has ruled is detrimental to the social and economic welfare of the family.
6. If the husband is sentenced to five or more years of imprisonment, even if this happens as a result of a monetary fine or financial debt that he has been unable to honor.
7. If the husband has an addiction which in the opinion of the court threatens the foundation of family life and makes the continuation of married life difficult for the wife.
8. If the husband deserts the family without an acceptable reason or is continuously absent for six months. It is up to the court to decide what reasons are acceptable.
9. If the husband is convicted of an offence which damages the wife's reputation or family honor. However, it is for the court to decide whether the wife's reputation and honor have been damaged by his criminal conduct.

10. If the wife has been unable to conceive after five years because of her husband's infertility or other physical inabilities.
11. If the husband has disappeared and still cannot be located six months after the wife has petitioned the court.
12. If the husband takes another wife without the consent of the first wife, or if the court finds that he does not treat his wives fairly.
13. Other conditions:

[Here the bride and groom can also stipulate other conditions to the marriage contract, provided they do not conflict with either spouse's marital responsibilities. The most common conditions stipulated by brides are:

   i. The right to place of residence and mobility. This means that the bride can choose the location of the marital home and does not need her husband's permission to leave her residence, travel, or obtain a passport.
  ii. Many brides include the right to continue their education even though this right is not taken away on marriage.
 iii. Many women now include the right to be employed or to continue in their professions.][1]

Notes

1. The work of Franz Boas is foundational because his methodology challenged previous approaches to understanding cultures. Boas showed that a deep, interpersonal approach to understanding the way others think, exemplified through participant-observation, interviews, and historical research, sheds light on the internal logic of cultural practice. Later, Geertz's interpretive approach to cultures (1973, 1983) added greater depth to the Boasian turn in fieldwork. In the last half century, anthropological methods have been further enhanced with more historical approaches that also take relationships of power into consideration.

2. In this sense, cultural relativism is philosophically distinct from the ethical or moral relativism that leaves us with the inability to judge cultural practices (Renteln 1988). Sahlins offers a clear account of relativism as method: "Relativism in this methodological sense, however, does not mean that any culture or custom is as good as any other, if not better; instead, it is the simple prescription that, in order to be intelligible, other people's practices and ideals must be placed in their own context, understood as positional values in a field of their own cultural relationships, rather than appreciated in terms of intellectual and moral judgments of our making. Relativism is the provisional suspension of one's own judgments in order to situate the practices at issue in the historical and cultural order that made them possible" (2000: 21).

3. Coined by Jalal Al-e Ahmad in 1952, the term referred to the state of being plagued by the "West" and described the spread of Western cultural norms for defining gender relations. Colloquially, it referred to women who dressed in Western attire and adopted so-called Western attitudes by smoking, laughing loudly, wearing excessive makeup, and mingling unself-consciously with men in public (Al-e Ahmad 1982).

4. I am not pointing to the truth-value of such statements, but rather to the way that entitlements are discussed in terms of "rights before law" as opposed to another configuration of rights, such as through appeals to Islamic values alone.

5. For instance in France, with the headscarf debate, by the very presence of Muslims, the French are obliged to rethink what it means to live in a free society, to have rights to expression and religion. Iranian state and nonstate actors deliberately invoke the contradictions embedded in liberalism, which lie at the philosophical base of human rights. All actors must now consider readapting and reimagining human rights, even in France. Indeed in France, the headscarf issue has crystallized the question of cultural difference, the universality of human rights, and the meaning of women's rights.

6. Certainly Iranians made rights-based claims before the postwar era, during the constitutional revolution (1905–11), for instance, and during the struggle for

equal rights for women in the Babi and Baha'i movements in the mid-nineteenth century. This rights talk, however, with special emphasis on the rights-bearing individual, has specific new meaning as part of a global hegemonic discourse since World War II.

7. Chanock (2000) points out that while such rights are not necessarily universal by nature, they have universalizing tendencies, something which he sees as a productive foil to rigid claims of cultural exception by despotic leaders.

8. See also Mehta (1999). On racial and gendered exclusions, see Razack (2000); Stepan (1998); and Stoler (1995).

9. Iranian Muslims by and large (about 89%) are part of the Shi'i branch of Islam, as opposed to the Sunni branch, which is the predominant branch of Islam. Shi'i believe that Ali, the Prophet's son-in-law and cousin, was the Prophet's immediate successor. See Cole and Keddie (1986); Momen (1985).

10. Ninety-three percent of the women I interviewed referred to themselves as middle class or working class; 7 percent referred to themselves as poor or lower class.

11. Iran's rate of population growth had increased dramatically in the decade after the revolution, in which time the population had more than doubled. In the early 1990s, Iran embarked on a population growth policy that has successfully harnessed runaway population growth.

12. Hoodfar (1997) echoes this view.

CHAPTER ONE
A GENEALOGY OF "WOMEN'S RIGHTS" IN IRAN

1. This is not intended as an exhaustive discussion of the literature. For more complete scholarly reviews, see Keddie (2000–1, 2002).

2. The names in this book have been changed to preserve the privacy of the speakers.

3. *Chador* literally means tent but refers to the type of garment some women in Iran wear—a long sheet draped over the head and covering the entire body.

4. Suffrage is universal and extends to all Iranians sixteen years and older.

5. Khomeini's speeches to the mostazafin were couched as a materialist challenge to the corrupt lifestyles of Westerners and the Iranians who tried to imitate them, rather than in purely Islamic terms.

6. Although Al-e Ahmad (1982) called for a return to Islam, he diagnosed the state of gharbzadeghi through a Marxist class analysis. Khomeini latched onto these ideas about the inequalities of income and wealth distribution to condemn some of the shah's economic policies and emerge as the representative of the oppressed.

7. The first Islamic society is that created by Mohammad in 622 CE (the first year of the Muslim calendar), after the *hegira*, or Mohammad's flight from Mecca when he learned of a plot to murder him there. Mohammad fled to Madina, where he is thought to have created the model theocratic state.

8. The Qur'an is the holy book for Muslims, the sacred text of Islam, consisting of the verbatim words of God as revealed to Mohammad during a period of

twenty-three years. The revelations are divided into 114 chapters (*suras*). The *sunna*, the way or example, is a record of collected sayings and anecdotes of Mohammad's daily life, chronicled by companions, and is the example for Muslims to follow.

9. This statement is excerpted from a speech that was given on the day of the formal proclamation of the Islamic Republic of Iran in Qom (Algar 1981).

10. The concept of revolution is itself modern, having emerged in the eighteenth century after the French Revolution. The Iranian Revolution in many ways tried to accomplish what the other revolutions did, such as redistribute wealth, expropriate from the dominant class, develop social services, and export the revolution abroad (Halliday 1999).

11. Khomeini presented the theological framework and justification for Velayat-e Faqih in a series of lectures he gave between January 21 and February 8, 1970, while in exile in Najaf, Iraq. The idea of Velayat-e Faqih requires justification as it contravenes one of Shi'i Islam's core tenets, that all government, in the absence of the Hidden or Twelfth Imam, is profane. The Velayat-e Faqih developed two major concerns of Shi'i Islam that Khomeini had written and spoken on in the early 1960s, while in Qom: (1) the economic, political, and cultural invasion of the "West," and (2) the issue of justice for Iranians.

12. When the Iranian government fell on February 14, 1979, Iran's parliament was immediately dissolved. The leaders of the revolution, who had formed a Revolutionary Council a month earlier, took control and dealt with immediate transitional issues, including the legislative function of the state until a new parliament could be elected. The Provisional Government was the executive branch of the Revolutionary Council and supervised the transformation of all political and legal institutions.

13. The latter included women whose families would previously not have allowed their daughters to go to university or work in offices alongside men.

14. With the withdrawal of British troops from Iran in January 1921, Iranian leaders were already speaking of establishing a republic (Martin 2003: 65). In March 1924, while he was prime minister of the last Qajar government, Reza Khan (later Reza Shah) introduced the idea of a centralized state modeled on a republic. Iran's parliament rejected the proposal. The 'ulama were the main opponents of republican centralization and saw it as enforced secularism (Banani 1961), while Reza Khan's progressive political opponents feared it as a means to establish autocracy (Martin 2003).

CHAPTER TWO
PRODUCING STATES: WOMEN'S PARTICIPATION AND THE DIALOGICS OF RIGHTS

1. *Iran News*, Feb. 27, 1999.

2. In urban areas, 49,991 candidates were men and 3,958 were women; in rural areas, 242,265 were men and 2,257 were women (*Tehran Times*, quoting Election Headquarters of the Interior Ministry, Feb. 27, 1999).

3. *Iran Daily*, Feb. 26, 1999.

4. Ibid.

5. The term *shahanshahi* refers to rule by a shah or king and means, literally, reign of the King of Kings. The term refers expressly to the type of leadership in Iran for twenty-five hundred years, and, for proponents of the new government, right up until 1979.

6. Women's Islamic covering in Iran consists of a minimum of a headscarf and an overcoat. Numerous variations and styles appear throughout the country. In Tehran, the upper-echelon elites of the northern areas liberally interpret the dress code. Women working in the public sector adhere to a stricter code of attire, including darker colors, longer and looser fitting overcoats, and often a hood (*maghne'eh*) instead of a headscarf.

7. Shi'ites, unlike Sunnis, pray three times a day, by combining prayers.

8. Khatami's second-term landslide came as a surprise to analysts, who predicted his reelection but not with even more votes than he had garnered in the previous election. In 1997 Khatami received 70 percent of the votes, whereas in 2001 he received 77 percent. In both elections, however, women's votes were key to Khatami's mandate (*Payam-e Hajjar*, Feb. 13, 1999).

9. The newspapers and magazines that were closed down were charged with violating Iran's Press Law, which was passed by the legislature in 1986 but amended on July 7, 1999. The Press Law created a court to oversee the contents of print media and rein in media that was deemed to contravene Islamic principles or the goals of the revolution. When Khatami tried to introduce a more lenient version of the law, the Council of Guardians deemed it to be a transgression of Islamic principles.

10. By the parliamentary elections of 2000, however, the percentage of reformists had grown to about 73 percent.

11. All figures from *Iran Daily*, May 2, 1999.

12. *Iran Times*, June 9, 2001.

13. The July 7, 1999, amendment to the Press Law included a clause that sought to put an end to this practice.

14. In addition, the members of parliament who sought impeachment noted that Mohajerani revived the Writers Association and gave awards to authors whom they believed should not have received honors from the Islamic republic. Among other allegations, the censure motion claimed that the minister's press activities had harmed national unity, while the circulation of certain books distorted the history of the revolution. The MPs also claimed that the films Mohajerani approved were vulgar and ignored the "values and exalted personality of women from the viewpoint of Islam."

15. *Iran Daily*, May 1, 1999; *Iran News*, May 2, 1999.

16. *Iran News*, May 2, 1999.

17. Of 270 members of parliament, 263 were present that day.

18. The Special Court for Clergy handles cases involving the country's clergy. The editor of *Salaam*, Ayatollah Mohammad Khoeinia, was politically allied with the president and a close advisor to him. The newspaper was closed after the Information Ministry filed a complaint against it for printing portions of a confidential letter written by Saeed Emami, a former employee of the Information Ministry. Emami, who had been jailed for master-minding the killings of Iranian intellectuals in 1998, had written the letter to his superiors suggesting press restrictions

that were very similar to the newly approved amendments to the Press Law. When news of *Salaam*'s imminent closure reached the public, the Information Ministry withdrew its complaint, but that did not stop the closure of *Salaam* (*Iran News*, July 10, 1999).

19. *Iran News*, July 11, 1999.

20. *Iran Daily*, July 11, 1999; *Iran Times*, July 11, 1999.

21. *Iran News*, July 13, 1999. Excerpts from Khatami's speech were printed in all the major newspapers.

22. Schacht is primarily regarded as a Sunni legal scholar.

23. Although *qadi* is often translated as "judge" and today references judges in what are often civil courts (as we will see in the following chapters), what the term references in "qadi-justice" is actually jurisprudential expertise, which Weber did not associate with mere civil law judges.

24. Rosen makes a similar assessment with regard to (Sunni) Moroccan law (1989).

25. The term Twelver refers to the belief in twelve divinely ordained leaders or imams of Shi'ism. The Twelvers constitute the largest branch of the Shi'i sect of Islam. The name of the jurisprudence, Ja'fari, references the name of the sixth Shi'i imam, Ja'far al-Sadiq.

26. The Akhbari school is associated with less openness to independent interpretation, leaving some to assert that the main difference between the Akhbari and Usuli schools is that the Akhbari do not believe in *ijtihad*. Gleave (1997), however, has shown that unlike the Usuli, the Akhbari includes not only the Prophet's hadiths in the sunna, but those of the imams as well.

27. A limited notion of the guardianship of the jurist can be traced back to the tenth century CE (4 AH) when Shi'i scholars introduced the concept of ijtihad.

28. The more absolute version of velayat was introduced in the Shi'i jurisprudence through the well-known text *Javaher-al-Kalam* (Theological Jewels). Later, Ayatollah Molla Mohammad Mahdee Naraqi (1749 CE/1128 AH–1830 CE/1209 AH) encouraged a more modest level of political engagement for the 'ulama, or a limited version of Velayat-e-Faqih.

29. Khomeini's views with respect to the 'ulama-state relations shifted over time. Initially, he called for the 'ulama to have a limited role in governance, but in later writings he called for greater state intervention by the 'ulama, or a more absolute guardianship. See Algar (1981); Abrahamian (1982).

30. It was not immediately clear that the nation's governing body would be that of a theocratic state. Lay reformers such as Mehdi Bazargan, who founded and led Iran's Liberation Movement, had formed a coalition with Khomeini and his supporters to oust the shah and the imperialist threat. Once the U.S. Embassy was seized, however, the Islamic leaders used documents found in the embassy to discredit Bazargan, then the provisional prime minister, and contain power within the 'ulama (Arjomand 1988).

31. Paidar (1995) details the confusion in choices of laws and courts in adjudicating divorce, and Zubaida (2005) discusses the disorder that ensued in drafting penal sanctions.

32. Debates on this issue persist. See Salimi (2003); Soroush (2000).

33. In February 2008 the government ordered the closure of *Zanan* after almost twenty years of publication.

34. Since 1997, in some parts of Tehran, women wear makeup, nail polish, and shorter veils when they venture out of their homes. A seeming relaxation of restraints appeared when several men running for Tehran's first city council race since the revolution posted their likeness around the city bearing neckties. None of the necktied men won, however. Today, it appears, such an action could disqualify them.

35. One example of such meeting groups is the wildly popular Wednesday evening meeting held by the religious scholar and intellectual Dr. Abdolkarim Soroush, who had been an early supporter of Khomeini and even helped in authoring some of the 1979 constitution. Soroush later fell out of favor with the Khomeini establishment because of his reformist views. Not long thereafter, Soroush's talks were met with attacks by vigilante Islamist groups. Such pronouncements do not easily fit within dichotomous reformist and hardliner agendas.

36. This is not to make light of the overwhelming support received by Khatami in his re-election bid of 2001

CHAPTER THREE
QUR'ANIC MEETINGS: "DOING THE CULTURAL WORK"

1. I do not intend to convey that with the emergence of liberal entitlements come natural or automatic expressions of equality, freedom, or liberation.

2. Torab (2002: 143) similarly notes that women's increased religious activities must be regarded as "part of an increasingly politicized religious environment rather than any essential 'Islamic' world-view or so-called fundamentalism."

3. Hossein was the grandson of the Prophet Mohammad and the son of Ali, the Prophet's son-in-law and cousin. He and a group of about seventy others were said to have been besieged by a large Umayyad army at Karbala, in present-day Iraq. The Umayyad leader at that time, Yazid, wanted Hossein and his group to pay allegiance to the caliph and to submit to his authority. When they resisted, Yazid sent his soldiers to find their leader, Hossein. Hossein's death was seen as a martyrdom to all the partisans of Ali (Shi'ite Muslims) and is commemorated as Ashura, every year on the tenth day of Moharram, of the Muslim calendar.

4. My use of the term *habitus* refers, of course, to Bourdieu's (1977) concept, which he defines as "the durable, transposable system of definitions" acquired by very young children in their families' homes and carried on and reproduced throughout their lives. Habitus, moreover, is a generative practice that comes to be embodied as part of a person's natural world. See also Bourdieu (1984).

5. Indeed, much work has revealed the ways in which the control of women has been justified in Muslim and postcolonial societies in which women are depicted as temptresses, vixens, bearers of national and family honor, too emotional, or readily corruptible (Ahmed 1992; Mernissi 1987; Tohidi 1994).

6. See, for instance, Kandiyoti's edited volume, *Women, Islam and the State* (1991).

7. Esfahan is an ancient capital in central Iran. For many, Esfahan is also the country's cultural capital.

8. It is interesting to note that in Persian, "modest" or "modesty" is denoted by the word *ba-hayya*. In common parlance, the term, hejab is used to convey both the actual dress as well as the concept of "modesty." Thus, the speaker pointed out that just because one is dressed modestly, it does not necessarily mean that the person is modest. This distinction was often brought to my attention during fieldwork.

9. This discussion may remind some readers of the debates around abortion in the United States.

10. This is not to imply that there were no means of disciplining women's sexuality prior to the revolution.

11. The commencement of modest dress and prayer for girls is formally ritualized in their schools. Girls at this grade level perform a ceremony to mark their initiation into a spiritual phase of life. The age conforms loosely with the onset of puberty.

12. In 1999 Iranian President Mohammad Khatami made the nation's first state visit to Europe since the revolution when he was received by the French government. In that same year, Iran made an important oil concession deal, the first oil concession granted a European country in many years, with the Italian government, which defied U.S. sanctions against Iran. Finally, the Iranian president gave a speech at the United Nations in New York seeking to advance his own cultural-global initiative, Dialogue among Civilizations.

13. Another example is the earlier-mentioned meetings held by the religious scholar and intellectual Dr. Abdolkarim Soroush. Both men and women attended the meetings.

14. The title is derived from a story from one part of the chapter, where Moses wanted the Children of Israel to sacrifice a cow, or a golden calf, to God alone.

15. The translation of the Qur'an that I chose is that of *The Message of the Qur'an*, translated and explained by Muhammed Asad (1980).

16. A *maghneh'eh is a* hoodlike head covering with extra length to cover the neck and chest area. Most government workers and schoolgirls are required to wear a maghneh'eh at their place or work or school.

17. Kian-Thiébaut notes a similar "autonomization and individualization of women" as an effect of the further institutionalization of Islamic law after the revolution (2002: 127).

18. Questions of individual will and freedom have long occupied scholars of Islam. In exploring the status of the individual in Islam, scholars have given great weight to law and to legal texts but have not examined social praxis. Bulliet (1996: 190) argues that the status of individuals in Islamic societies is extremely diverse, and that "Muslims remake their religion in every generation at both the individual and the community level, and they do so by exercising an uncommon degree of personal choice inherited as part of the template of religious practice that slowly emerged in early centuries of Islam."

19. The biological determinism referenced by Mutahhari's thinking and writing on Islam is not unique to Islam but is evident in many religions as well as some secularist movements. What is clear, however, is that in the postrevolutionary vi-

sion of creating a system of governance that took into account Shi'i Islam, Mutahhari's work, especially on gender, was dominant.

20. See also Mirsepassi (2000)

21. *Mahrieh*, or *mahr*, for short, is the bride's portion or bride price, negotiated upon signing the marriage contract. Women rarely receive their mahr during the course of their marriage. Instead, women increasingly ask to execute the mahr as a consequence of divorce. Some scholars have referred to the mahrieh as a gift because it is referenced as such in the Qur'an. In Iran, however, the mahr has emerged as a legally enforceable sum arising from the marriage contract, to be paid by the husband directly to the wife upon marriage at any time she wishes to have it executed. Generally, mahr becomes enforceable in full upon consummation of the marriage. See also El Alami and Hinchcliffe (1996); Moors (1995); Welchman (2004).

22. Unlike many other countries that have the bride price, in Iran mahr is paid by the groom's family directly to the bride, as opposed to the bride's family. In addition, where the parties' financial conditions would permit, a woman might also bring to the marriage a dowry consisting of household furnishings. In the wealthiest families, the bride's family may even provide a whole house. Negotiations are often conducted between the bride's family and the groom's family. Most often, the parties' mothers discuss and negotiate the terms of the marriage contract with consent of the children. In most courtships the groom's mother calls upon the bride's mother to officially ask for her daughter's hand in marriage.

23. Chapter 4 has a detailed discussion on this topic.

24. Certainly at the time of its founding, there were disagreements as to what the governing political framework of Islamic Iran would be. That the founders ultimately laid plans for what was to become a tripartite federal republic with the added components of Islamic guidance was the result of negotiation and compromise. Now, however, the accession of its many promises, including the entitlements of its citizenry, is proving to invoke just the kinds of debates that fed its original creation: the extent and limits of individual freedoms and the range and diversity of political parties.

25. Qom is the current and traditional capital of Shi'i Islamic training and theorizing.

CHAPTER FOUR
COURTING RIGHTS: RIGHTS TALK IN ISLAMICO-CIVIL FAMILY COURT

1. The term divorce is an imprecise translation for the term talaq. Dissolution of marriage can occur in a variety of ways. Talaq literally means repudiation and is a right which belongs only to husbands. For a discussion of the various kinds of dissolution, see Mir-Hosseini (1993). All the methods to gain dissolution, but one, however, are colloquially referred to as talaq which I have translated as divorce for the purposes simplification here. The other term, *faskh al-nikah*, to which I will refer shortly, is rescission of a marriage contract and can be compared with annulment.

2. Under Iran's civil marriage code, the husband has a legal responsibility to financially provide for his wife's living needs, including housing, food, and clothing. The wife has a reasonable expectation of maintenance in accordance with the economic standards to which she is accustomed.

3. *Hajj agha* is a term literally referring to a person who has made the pilgrimage, or hajj, to Mecca. *Agha* is a polite term of address of a male figure, equivalent to "sir." In colloquial Persian, the term *hajj agha* is an address intended to designate the deepest reverence bestowed on one who has made the holy pilgrimage, whether or not the person has actually made it. It is sometimes used jokingly or even sarcastically.

4. See chapter 3, note 21, for a detailed definition of the mahr, or bride's portion.

5. When employing the terms Islam or Islamic values, I am not referring to religion per se, but to the idea of a holistic system of values that many Muslims believe provides all the answers to greater enlightenment. While the answers may be provided in the Qur'an and associated texts, the means and practices needed to follow through might be found elsewhere.

6. This building is no longer used as a courthouse. During the time I conducted fieldwork for this project, Tehran's municipal government disaggregated the family court. In the fall of 2002 it opened a new courthouse on the outskirts of town and created smaller branch courts in various locations throughout the city.

7. New legislation passed in 2003 raised the legal age for when a father automatically obtains custody of a son from two to seven.

8. The grounds for divorce are much more complicated than expressed here. The stipulated grounds are listed in the marriage contract provided in the appendix.

9. Legal training in the university system contains some instruction in Islamic jurisprudence but is to be distinguished from instruction at the Islamic seminaries that train akhunds. Most, but not all, judges are akhunds with extensive training in Islamic jurisprudence.

10. The *Iran Statistical Yearbook 1381* (Statistical Centre of Iran 2002) shows a steady rise in the number of divorces registered. Scholars have also noted the recent trend in the rise of divorce. Mir-Hosseini (1993: 45) observed that women's divorce petitions outweighed men's. See also Paidar (1995: 292) and Afshar (1998:195).

11. A 1992 law requires men to go to court to attend arbitration and to obtain a letter of noncompatibilty, whereas before that date they were only required to register the divorce at a local notary.

12. Of sixty divorced women I asked, 5 percent were represented in court by legal counsel. A much larger number, 87 percent, had sought the advice of a lawyer, friend, or family member before coming to the court, and just over 8 percent went to the court, like Sahar, to obtain information for the first time. Obviously, class factors into these findings. Women represented by lawyers were often wealthy and upper or upper-middle class, whereas those who went straight to the court were working class.

13. In 1994 the parliament enacted the Law of Formation of General Courts. This law, which had ordered the creation of sixteen judicial complexes throughout Tehran, also resulted in the dissolution of the Special Civil Courts.

14. The Family Protection Law was also an expression of Mohammad Shah's modernization program, called the White Revolution. The 1963 White Revolution was a national reform program that included the enfranchisement of women.

15. The 1967 law was considered an improvement for women because initially they had to have the permission of their husbands to obtain employment outside of the home. The 1967 law shifted the burden to the husband to prove that the gainful employment was detrimental to the family (Vatandoust 1985). The 1975 law equalized this rule for both spouses, although the court could not force a husband to stop working unless the family had ample means.

16. Vatandoust (1985: 118–19) confirms this as well.

17. Special Civil Court Act of 1979.

18. Khomeini coined the term *taghuti*, which refers to idolatry or idol worship, the object of worship being the "West."

19. *Faskh al-nikah* must occur before the wedding (i.e., consummation) and may be compared to an annulment in the Western-Christian context. As a result, the marriage is not on record, and the woman's socio-legal identity is not "marred" as a divorced woman.

20. In fact, obedience to her husband is a wife's stated duty in the marriage contract.

21. I differ in my approach to understanding rights talk by focusing on the conditions that produce rights-bearing subjectivities. In doing so, I distinguish the conditions of possibility from the active "adoption" that Merry finds (2003: 344). As do other studies exploring courts as spaces for maneuver (Hirsch 1994; Lazarus-Black 1994; Merry 1990; Yngvesson 1993), Merry considers her informants' "adoption of a rights consciousness" (2003: 344). In contrast, I examine the courts as ideological spaces that inflect subjectivity where subjectivity is an expression of selfhood—how one perceives the self in a social order. While agentive, its performativity is not necessarily conscious (Butler 1993). Whereas Merry contends that "one of the powerful consequences of bringing gender violence cases to the attention of the legal system is the victim's and perpetrator's encounters with the new subjectivity defined within the discourses and practices of the law" (2003: 346–47), I consider what those discourses and practices of law (in Iran) are and ask what conditions have come together to allow for such new possibilities. The difference in my argument lies in my claim that consciousness of rights and modern liberal subjectivities, although related, are not the same. One may inhabit a subjectivity of rights bearer, but not necessarily be conscious of it in the same way that Merry's informants are conscious of their rights because of their interactions with "police, prosecutors, judges, and probation officers" (2003: 343).

22. There is, of course, an increased use of the legal structures by both men and women, since now both are required to file petitions before the courts and the divorce rate is on the rise. Women's petitions are greater than men's because women, as I have discussed, also file petitions for other reasons, such as to renegotiate the terms of their marriages and divorces, and to execute the mahr. This

greater reliance on the courts and legal apparatuses by women arises from the fact that the wife, unlike the husband, cannot initiate divorce without cause.

23. I do not dispute that they also amount to highly personal rewards.

24. I prefer to use the term "hybrid" as opposed to "plural" because of the frequent characterization of the latter as referring to separate legal spheres. Fitzpatrick (1992) notes that increasingly studies of legal pluralism recognize the blending of legal systems as well.

25. Zubaida adds, "Codification as civil law practiced in civil courts denudes the shari'a of all its institutional religious garb, it is 'dis-embedded' and de-ritualized" (2005: 134).

CHAPTER FIVE
PRACTICE AND EFFECT: WRITING/RIGHTING THE LAW

1. In respect of her privacy, I have changed her name although she is a public figure.

2. This is not to say that one facet of a woman's identity is necessarily to the exclusion of another. A religious woman could easily have shunned the current government and/or consider herself a nationalist as well.

3. Obedience in this context refers specifically to sexual submission. The distinction makes it clear that while the consideration for obedience is the mahr, there is no consideration for other work that a woman does in the home she shares with her husband. Tabrizi argued that upon divorce, a woman can and must be compensated for that other work.

4. Sarat and Kearns draw from Raymond Williams to define moving hegemony, "a complex interlocking of political, social, and cultural forces" (1977).

5. Iran was never colonized, but it came under the sphere of influence of various powers, among them Britain and Russia in the nineteenth and twentieth centuries and the United States until the revolution. For this reason I find "postimperialist" more apt than "postcolonial."

6. Obviously this phenomenon is not limited to women in Iran as Mani (1989) and others have pointed out.

7. New legislation passed in 2003 raised the legal age of a son at which a father automatically obtains custody from two to seven.

CHAPTER SIX
HUMAN RIGHTS: THE POLITICS AND PROSE OF DISCURSIVE SITES

1. The idea of "human rights," as Henkin notes, carries with it values from liberal political theory. When stating that "human rights is the idea of our time," he is also simultaneously suggesting that the world has accepted liberalism as an ontological framework for making sense of the world. This is precisely where the concept encounters confusing aporias.

2. As I discussed in the preface to this book, the idea that universalism and relativism form an oppositional framework has been debunked.

3. Friedman goes on to explain why this is: "Many Arab-Muslim states today share the same rigid political structure. Think of it as two islands: one island is occupied by the secular autocratic governments and the business class around them. On the other island are the mullahs, imams and religious authorities who dominate Islamic practice and education, which is still based largely on traditional Koranic interpretations that are not embracing of modernity, pluralism or the equality of women. The governing bargain is that the governments get to stay in power forever and the mullahs get a monopoly on religious practice and education forever" (*New York Times*, November 16, 2001).

4. Friedman refers only to "Arab-Muslim" states and may not include Iran.

5. The category of "religion" as a sociopolitical term is also a product of modernity (Asad 1993). Religion became a category that reflected anti-modern forms when secular states, that is, no longer divinely ordained, emerged, most notably after the French Revolution. Thus, religious states and societies exist as a foil to those that are deemed to be secular. These categories, we have now come to see as heuristic devices to create clean distinctions when such distinctions are never clear.

6. Keddie (1995: 113) disagrees, noting that human rights played a role in the shah's overthrow, but mostly among intellectual opponents of the shah, not religious.

7. *Tehran Times*, April 25, 1999.

8. During the revolution and for some years afterwards, Iran was the focus of attention for its human rights abuses, but when Iranians complained to the United Nations about Iraq's invasion and use of chemical weapons, the UN turned a blind eye.

9. I have written about this incident in Osanloo (2006b).

10. The *Oxford English Dictionary* notes the first usage of the term "human rights" in Thomas Paine's 1791 work, *The Rights of Man*.

11. Amnesty International's country conditions reports on Iran for the years 2000 and 2001 noted Iran's reluctance to admit outside monitors. Iran's foreign minister, Reza Asefi, was quoted as stating that the 1998 report by the special representative was based on allegations provided by Iranian opposition groups (*Iran Daily*, April 28, 1999). The Human Rights Watch Country Conditions report for Iran in 2000 noted that Iran's leader publicly suggested that one of its monitors was a spy.

12. *Payam-e Emrouz (News of Today)*, April 1997. Ziaeefar confirmed this aim in an interview I had with him in the fall of 2004.

13. The surge in complaints points also to the greater recognition of human rights as a vehicle for obtaining Islamic justice, and increased awareness of the IHRC.

14. This is not to suggest that the IHRC is ineffective. Instead, my concern is with critiques that the IHRC members are apologists for the Iranian government. What I am arguing is that the mere bureaucratic institutionalization of the IHRC, with its Islamic Declaration, gives Iran greater international legitimacy. For example, the January 18, 2000, report of the special representative stated, "The Special Representative has followed the evolution of this commission for some years. Obviously it should be a cornerstone in the establishment of a culture of human

rights. The commission is clearly making progress and now seems to be addressing such difficult issues as the need for society to be able to debate the death penalty and, more generally, other public issues which, for some at least, touch on Islamic verities," despite not having been invited to Iran in more than a year (*UN Report of the Special Representative*, Maurice Danby Copithorne, para. 69, submitted 18 January 2000, E/CN.4/2000/35).

15. Other examples of the expression of sovereignty are found in Iran's participation in the United Nations, diplomatic representation in some countries of the world, and national security and defense forces. Human rights, unlike the other expressions of sovereignty, have become a distinct trope of the flexible nature of sovereignty, in that it is at once an expression of sovereignty and a surrender of it.

16. As a result of its participation in the United Nations, Iran has also agreed to allow monitoring by outside, independent human rights observers. Until April 2002 Iran was on the list of countries to which the UN Human Rights Commission sent a special representative, although Iran had not permitted the special representative to visit the country for the previous several years. On April 22, 2002, the commission voted against continuing the special representative's evaluations of Iran's human rights record, a decision decried by Human Rights Watch (Human Rights Watch Press Release, April 22, 2002). In February 2005 Iran allowed the UN Human Rights Commission's rapporteur on violence against women to visit and write a report.

17. The IHRC also issued a press release during the 1999 headscarf debacle in Turkey when an elected member of parliament was not permitted into the state building for the opening session because of the headscarf prohibition there.

18. For a review of the Declaration of the Islamic Conference, see Ebadi (2000).

19. Since the twentieth century, this system has grown vastly more complex and is now in danger of being dismantled by virtue of U.S. dominance, which allows it to avoid international laws by acting unilaterally.

20. Center for Women's Participation brochure, *At a Glance*, August 2004.

21. Ibid.

22. According to a June 2003 interview with the center's head and presidential advisor, Zahra Shojaei, the center's budget increased fifty-nine times since its inception in 1997. *Yas-e No*, June 25, 2003 (http://www.netiran.com).

23. Ibid.

24. I do not suggest that my more conservative interlocutors, such as Dr. Kermani, claim that women are inferior to men. I was told that women are not naturally or biologically inferior to men, but rather, that they are equal to, but not the same as, men, and because men and women are biologically different, they have separate social roles to fulfill.

25. *Fekr-e Rooz*, May 25, 2003 (http://www.netiran.com). Iran ratified the Convention on the Rights of the Child in 1994.

26. She was referencing a verse from the Qur'an.

27. Despite the governmental ban, there have been several reported stonings. For detailed information on this and other cases, including the debate over the

ban, see Stop Stoning Forever Campaign (http://www.meydaan.org/stoning/default.aspx).

28. This law that provides for the equitable division of the couple's assets upon dissolution was created to benefit women who, in the event of their husband's repudiation, could otherwise be left with only what they brought into the marriage.

29. Although at times belatedly, the Iranian government, through the Ministry of Foreign Affairs' Human Rights Department, complies with treaty regulations that require state parties to submit periodic reports. In its interim report to the General Assembly on the situation of human rights in the Islamic Republic of Iran for the period January 1–August 15, 2000, the special representative of the Commission on Human Rights reported in the section on "torture and other cruel, inhuman or degrading treatment or punishment" that "the head of the judiciary believes that it should avoid acts which could insult and taint the country's image" (Special Representative of the Commission on Human Rights 2000).

30. On July 26, 2002, the Iranian government agreed to allow human rights monitors into the country.

31. *Iran Daily*, April 28, 1999.

32. *Tehran Times*, May 25, 1999.

Conclusion
"Women's Rights" as Exhibition at the Brink of War

1. "Iran and the U.S," *The Conversation*, http://kuow.org/defaultProgram.sp?ID=1039 (March 17, 2006).

2. KUOW, "Speakers' Forum: David Frum," http://www.kuow.org/default Program.asp?ID=7116 (April 14, 2004). This is a speech that Frum gave at the University of Washington on January 22, 2004. It was subsequently broadcast on Seattle's public radio station, KUOW.

3. Shavarini (2006) notes that two-thirds of students entering university are female. See also Population Reference Bureau, Women of Our World (2005).

4. For Wallerstein, the geoculture of liberalism in the modern world system as inherited from the French Revolution is "self-contradictory," in that liberalism's discourse of equality comes into conflict with its charge to bring rights to others. Today this contradictory logic is evident in Iraq and Afghanistan, where international laws aimed at protecting sovereignty and civilians are abrogated to bring human rights and the rule of law to those very places.

5. I am referring to the posturing that goes on in foreign policy debates, like the nuclear issue, as a dialogical process that occurs between centralized state forces. This debate is a legal one about the principle of nonintervention, a foundational concept of international law memorialized in article 2(7) of the UN Charter and that upholds the notion of sovereign nation-states. This principle is the rule, with the exception of intervention possible only when there is a breach to the peace, a threat to the peace, or an overt act of aggression. Chapter 7 of the UN Charter outlines the types of intervention that may be authorized by the Security Council. These include military as well as nonmilitary. Historically the charter

was important because it made into positive law the idea that a country's internal actions are subject to review by outside forces, by an international community. With the genocide convention and other human rights agreements, the treatment of a polity by central state forces, through either action or inaction, became a legitimate concern for the international community, though it is rarely enough to trigger the military intervention needed under chapter 7 of the UN Charter.

APPENDIX
THE IRANIAN MARRIAGE CONTRACT

1. *The State of Women, Islamic Republic of Iran.* Tehran: United Nation's International Children's Education Fund (UNICEF), 1998.

Glossary

Note on Transliteration: I have followed the transliteration system of the *International Journal for Middle East Studies*, but without diacritical marks.

aaramesh — inner sanctity
aghd-i kharji-e lazim — written oath or legally binding contract
aghd-nameh — marriage contract
agha — sir
akhund — member of the religious community
Allah — God
amammeh — turban
andarooni — indoor spaces
anjoman — political councils, including women's societies
ayat — verse; *aya*, plural
ayatollah — mid-ranking religious scholar
ba-hayya — modest or with modesty
ba hejab — modest or with modesty
bad hejab — immodest, or literally refers to a woman whose appearance does not conform with the state-prescribed rule
balleh — yes, polite form of an affirmative response
besouz-o besauz — burn and make do; colloquial phrase refers to living with difficulties
chador — literally, tent; refers to the full-length veil, almost always black, worn by some Iranian women
control — control
dalil al-aql — logical reasoning
daman-e zan — skirts of women; colloquial phrase refers to women's influence in child-rearing
Divan-e Aali-ye Keshvar — highest court of Iran's justice system
dieh — form of criminal sanctioning that requires payment of monies to victims or their families for damages
dokhtar — virgin; colloquially means girl
doosheezeh — maiden
dowreh — circle; denotes "group," sometimes refers to an intellectual gathering, such as a "salon"
ejbar — obligation
enghelab-e Islami — Islamic revolution
ensan — gender-neutral term for human
ettela'at — information
faskh al-nikah — rescission of contract (of marriage)
fatva — legal ruling based on Islamic principles, issued by qualified jurists

fatavi — religious opinions; plural of "fatva"

fiqh — jurisprudence

gharbzadeh — weststruck or to be struck by the "West"

gozasht — give in, pardon

gozinesh — investigation

hadith — recorded practices of the Prophet Mohammad; for Muslims, one of the sources of law

hajj — pilgrimage to Mecca

haqq — rights

hay'at — assembly or council

hegira — Mohammad's flight from Mecca

hejab — literally used to refer to the veil, but refers more broadly to modesty

hokm-e rosht — order of majority issued by court/judge

Hookoomat-e Islami — *Islamic Government*, title of book by Ayatollah Khomeini

hooqooq — civil or legal rights

hooqooq-e bashar — human rights

Hooqooq-e Zan — *Women's Legal Rights*, name of journal

hosseinieh — room adjoining a mosque, which serves as a gathering place for worshippers and for members of the 'ulama to deliver sermons

ijma — community consensus

ijtihad — independent juridical interpretation; refers to interpretive rulings based on Qur'anic principles

istishab — respecting the validity of independent reasoning of learned scholars

istislah — in juridical rulemaking, intervention in the public interest, permitted in the event of an otherwise harsh or unjust ruling or when a question arises for which there is no existing rule

jahaz — dowry

jaleseh — meeting

jaleseh-ye Qur'an — Qur'anic meeting, or, as referencing here, Qur'anic reading group

jame'eh — society

jashn-e mashrutiat — celebration of constitution

Javaher-al-Kalam - *Theological Jewels*, title of influential book

jesmee — physical

jomhuri — republic

jomhuri-e Islami — Islamic republic

khanumha — plural of *khanum*, literally, lady or gentlewoman

kharab kara — trouble-makers

khoms — a type of religious tax, literally, one-fifth

khostegari — courtship

khul — mutual divorce

kian-e khanevadeh — foundation of the family

koocheh-pas-koocheh — alley by alley

m'afqhood al-asr — legal term meaning missing or disappeared

madhab (Arabic); *mazhab* (Persian) — an Islamic school of thought or jurisprudence

maghne'eh — hoodlike head cover with extra cloth to cover the neck and chest area

mahr — bride's portion, abbreviated

mahr al-mesl — bride's portion in-kind; an approximation of bride's portion when none has formally been designated

mahrieh — bride's portion

mahzar — notary public

Majlis — national assembly or parliament

Majlis-e Shura-ye Islami — Islamic Consultative Assembly

manavee — mental/spiritual

manaveeyat — spiritual life

manteau — overcoat

mareez — ill

mareez-e ravanee — insane

marja-ye taqlid — source of emulation, title of highest religious authority in Shi'i hierarchy

masaleyeh-zan — the woman question

mauven — deputy in charge

mazloom — subjugated, oppressed

mesl — like, similar

mohtarram — honorable

mo'men — literally, man of God; colloquially, religious

mostazafin — dispossessed

mozd — compensation

mujtahid — learned scholars of the Qur'an, literally, one who is qualified to perform ijtihad

mullah — member of the religious community

nafagheh — maintenance during marriage

Nahj-al balagheh — Peaks of Eloquence, title of Prophet Ali's influential text

Neshat — name of a former newspaper

ojrat al-mesl — postdivorce maintenance

osr va haraj — literally, poverty and cruelty; legal concept used in divorce when no other grounds exist

pasdaran — revolutionary moral police

picheh — face covers

qadi (Arabic); *qazi* (Persian) — Islamic judge/jurist

qiyas — analogical reasoning

Raf-e Mozahemat — legal restraining order, literally, cease to bother

rahbar — supreme leader

rahhat — comfortable

rashid — mature, competent (legal)

ravanee — mad, insane

roshan-fekr — enlightened

rowzeh — ritual performance associated with the martyrdom of Hossein

rusari — headscarf

Salaam — literally, peace; name of former newspaper

sarparast — guardian

shahanshahi — monarchical government
shakhseeat — character or integrity
shari'a — Islamic law/guidelines
shir- moze — blended banana milk drink
shomal-e shahr — north of the city
showra — consultative council
sokhanran — speaker
sunna — the way or example; a record of collected sayings and anecdotes of Mohammad's daily life, chronicled by companions who lived with him
sura — chapter (of Qur'an)
tafsir — authoritative textual explication
taghuti — perjorative term that literally refers to idolater or idol worshipper, colloquially refers to those who emulate Western values
tahrick — provoke
talaq — dissolution of marriage; technically means "repudiate"
tamkin — wife's legal duty to submit sexually to her husband
tatliq — dissolution of marriage by judicial process
tazahorat — demonstrations
'ulama — religious community
umma — community of believers
velayat — guardian or guardianship
Velayat-e Faqih — Guardianship of the Jurist
Zan — literally, woman, name of first-ever woman's daily newspaper
Zanan — women, plural of woman, title of women's weekly magazine
Zan-e Ruz — *Woman of Today*, name of journal
zanha — women
zarooree — mandatory
zojeeat — couple

Bibliography

Abrahamian, Ervand
  1982 *Iran between Two Revolutions.* Princeton: Princeton University Press.
  1993 *Khomeinism: Essays on the Islamic Republic.* Berkeley: University of California Press.
Abu-Lughod, Lila
  1986 *Veiled Sentiments: Honor and Poetry in a Bedouin Society.* Berkeley: University of California Press.
  1993 *Writing Women's Worlds: Bedouin Stories.* Berkeley: University of California Press.
  1998 "Feminist Longings and Postcolonial Conditions." In *Remaking Women: Feminism and Modernity in the Middle East.* Lila Abu-Lughod, ed. Pp. 3–31. Princeton: Princeton University Press.
  2002 "Do Muslim Women Really Need Saving? Anthropological Reflections on Cultural Relativism and Its Others." *American Anthropologist* 104 (3): 783–90.
Adelkhah, Fariba
  2000 *Being Modern in Iran.* New York: Columbia University Press.
Afary, Janet
  1996 *The Iranian Constitutional Revolution, 1906–1911: Grassroots Democracy, and the Origins of Feminism.* New York: Columbia University Press.
Afkhami, Mahnaz
  1995 "Introduction." In *Faith and Freedom: Women's Human Rights in the Muslim World.* Mahnaz Afkhami, ed. Pp. 1–15. Syracuse: Syracuse University Press.
Afkhami, Mahnaz, and Erika Friedl, eds.
  1994 *In the Eye of the Storm: Women in Post-Revolutionary Iran.* Syracuse: Syracuse University Press.
  1997 *Muslim Women and the Politics of Participation: Implementing the Beijing Platform.* Syracuse: Syracuse University Press.
Afshar, Haleh
  1998 *Islam and Feminisms: An Iranian Case Study.* London: Macmillan.
Afshari, Reza
  1994 "An Essay on Islamic Cultural Relativism in the Discourse of Human Rights." *Human Rights Quarterly* 16 (2): 235–76.
  1995 "An Essay on Scholarship, Human Rights, and State Legitimacy: The Case of the Islamic Republic of Iran." *Human Rights Quarterly* 18 (3): 544–93.
  2001 *Human Rights in Iran: The Abuse of Cultural Relativism.* Philadelphia: University of Pennsylvania Press.

Agamben, Giorgio
   1998   *Homo Sacer: Sovereign Power and Bare Life.* Stanford: Stanford University Press.
   2000   *Means without Ends: Notes on Politics.* Minneapolis: Minnesota University Press.
Aghaie, Kamran Scot
   2004   *The Martyrs of Karbala: Shi'i Symbols and Rituals in Modern Iran.* Seattle: University of Washington Press.
Ahmed, Leila
   1992   *Women and Gender in Islam: Roots of a Modern Debate.* New Haven: Yale University Press.
   2005   "The Veil Debate Again: A View from America in the Early Twenty-First Century." In *On Shifting Ground: Muslim Women in the Global Era.* Fereshteh Nouraie-Simone, ed. Pp. 153–71. New York: Feminist Press at the City University of New York.
Al-e Ahmad, Jalal
   1982   *Gharbzadegi.* John Green and Ahmad Alizadeh, trans. Lexington, MA: Mazd'a Press.
Algar, Hamid
   1973   *Mirzā Malkum Khān: A Study in the History of Iranian Modernism.* Berkeley: University of California Press.
   1981   *Islam and Revolution: Writings and Declarations of Imam Khomeini.* Berkeley: Mizan Press.
Altorki, Soraya
   2000   "The Concept and Practice of Citizenship in Saudi Arabia." In *Gender and Citizenship in the Middle East.* Suad Joseph, ed. Syracuse: Syracuse University Press.
Amin, Camron Michael.
   2002   *The Making of the Modern Iranian Woman: Gender, State Policy, and Popular Culture, 1865–1946.* Gainesville: University Press of Florida.
Amin, Samir
   1996   "The Challenge of Globalization." *Review of International Political Economy* 3 (2): 216–59.
An-Na'im, Abdullahi A.
   1987   "Islamic Law, International Relations, and Human Rights: Challenge and Response." *Cornell International Law Journal* 20: 317–34.
   1990   *Toward an Islamic Reformation: Civil Liberties, Human Rights, and International Law.* Syracuse: Syracuse University Press.
   1995   "The Dichotomy between Religious and Secular Discourse in Islamic Societies." In *Faith and Freedom: Women's Human Rights in the Muslim World.* Mahnaz Afkhami, ed. Pp. 51–60. Syracuse: Syracuse University Press.
Anwar, Zainah
   2005   "Sisters in Islam and the Struggle for Women's Rights." In *On Shifting Ground: Muslim Women in the Global Era.* Fereshteh Nouraie-Simone, ed. Pp. 233–48. New York: Feminist Press at the City University of New York.

Appadurai, Arjun
1996   *Modernity at Large: Cultural Dimensions of Globalization.* Minneapolis: University of Minnesota Press.
Arendt, Hannah
1951   "The Decline of the Nation-State and the End of the Rights of Man." In *The Origins of Totalitarianism.* Pp. 267–302. New York: Harcourt.
Arjomand, Said Amir
1988   *The Turban for the Crown: The Islamic Revolution in Iran.* Studies in Middle Eastern History. New York: Oxford University Press.
1989   "Constitution-Making in Islamic Iran: The Impact of Theocracy on the Legal Order of a Nation-State." In *History and Power in the Study of Law: New Directions in Legal Anthropology.* June Starr and Jane F. Collier, eds. Pp. 113–27. Ithaca: Cornell University Press.
Asad, Muhammed
1980   *The Message of the Qur'an.* Dar Al-Andalus: Gibraltar.
Asad, Talal
1993   *Genealogies of Religion: Discipline and Reasons of Power in Christianity and Islam.* Baltimore: Johns Hopkins University Press.
Ashcraft, Richard
1996   "Religion and Lockean Natural Rights." In *Religious Diversity and Human Rights.* Irene Bloom, J. Paul Martin, and Wayne L. Proudfoot, eds. Pp. 195–212. New York: Columbia University Press.
Azari, Farah, ed.
1983   "Sexuality and Women's Oppression in Iran." In *Women of Iran: The Conflict with Fundamentalist Islam.* Pp. 90–156. London: Ithaca Press.
Bahar, Sima
1983   "A Historical Background to the Women's Movement in Iran." In *Women of Iran: The Conflict with Fundamentalist Islam.* Farah Azari, ed. Pp. 170–89. London: Ithaca Press.
Bakhtiar, Laleh, and Kevin Reinhart
1996   *Encyclopedia of Islamic Law: A Compendium of the Major Schools.* Chicago: Kazi.
Bakhtin, M. M.
1981   *The Dialogic Imagination: Four Essays.* Michael Holquist, ed. Caryl Emerson and Michael Holquist, trans. Austin: University of Texas Press.
Banani, Amin
1961   *The Modernization of Iran, 1921–41.* Stanford: Stanford University Press.
Barlas, Asma
2005   "Globalizing Equality: Muslim Women, Theology, and Feminism." In *On Shifting Ground: Muslim Women in the Global Era.* Fereshteh Nouraie-Simone, ed. Pp. 91–110. New York: Feminist Press at the City University of New York.
Bauer, Janet
1983   "Poor Women and Social Consciousness in Revolutionary Iran." In *Women and Revolution in Iran.* Guity Nashat, ed. Pp. 141–70. Boulder: Westview Press.

Bayat-Philipp, Mangol
   1978   "Women and Revolution in Iran, 1905–1911." In *Women in the Muslim World.* Lois Beck and Nikki Keddie, eds. Pp. 295–308. Cambridge: Harvard University Press.
Beck, Lois, and N. Keddie, eds.
   1978   *Women in the Muslim World.* Cambridge: Harvard University Press.
Beck, Lois, and Guity Nashat, eds.
   2004   *Women in Iran from 1800 to the Islamic Republic.* Urbana: University of Illinois Press.
Benhabib, Seyla
   1992   *Situating the Self: Gender, Community, and Postmodernism in Contemporary Ethics.* New York: Routledge.
Benjamin, Walter
   1978   "On the Critique of Violence." In *Reflections.* Peter Demetz, ed. Edmund Jephcott, trans. Pp. 277–300. New York: Harcourt, Brace and Jovanovich.
Bourdieu, Pierre
   1977   *An Outline for a Theory of Practice.* Richard Nice, trans. Cambridge: Cambridge University Press.
   1984   *Distinction: A Social Critique of the Judgment of Taste.* Richard Nice, trans. London: Routledge.
Brand, Laurie
   1998   "Women and the State in Jordan." In *Islam, Gender, and Social Change.* Yvonne Yazbeck Haddad and John L. Esposito, eds. Pp. 100–23. New York: Oxford University Press.
Brooks, Geraldine
   1995   *Nine Parts of Desire: The Hidden World of Islamic Women.* New York: Anchor Press.
Buck-Morss, Susan
   2000   *Dreamworld and Catastrophe: The Passing of Mass Utopia in East and West.* Cambridge: MIT Press.
Bulliet, Richard W.
   1996   "The Individual in Islamic Society." In *Religious Diversity and Human Rights.* Irene Bloom, J. Paul Martin, and Wayne L. Proudfoot, eds. Pp. 175–91. New York: Columbia University Press.
Butler, Judith
   1993   Bodies That Matter: On the Discursive Limits of "Sex." New York: Routledge.
Center for Women's Participation.
   2004   *At a Glance.* August.
   2005   *Annual National Report.*
Chanock, Martin
   2000   " 'Culture' and Human Rights: Orientalising, Occidentalising and Authenticity." In *Beyond Rights Talk and Culture Talk: Comparative Essays on the Politics of Rights and Culture.* Mahmood Mamdani, ed. Pp. 15–36. New York: St. Martin's Press.

Charrad, Mounira
  2001   *States and Women's Rights: The Making of Postcolonial Tunisia, Algeria, and Morocco*. Berkeley: University of California Press.
Chatterjee, Partha
  1993   *The Nation and Its Fragments: Colonial and Postcolonial Histories*. Princeton: Princeton University Press.
Chehabi, H. E.
  2003   "The Banning of the Veil and Its Consequences." In *The Making of Modern Iran: State and Society under Riza Shah, 1921–1941*. Stephanie Cronin, ed. Pp. 193–210. New York: Routledge.
Cherifati-Merabtine, Doria
  1991   "Algeria at a Crossroads: National Liberation, Islamization and Women." In *Gender and National Identity: Women and Politics in Muslim Societies*. Valentine Moghadam, ed. Pp. 40–62. London: Zed Books.
Cole, Juan R. I., and Nikki R. Keddie, eds.
  1986   *Shi'ism and Social Protest*. New Haven: Yale University Press.
Comaroff, John
  1995   "The Discourse of Rights in Colonial South Africa: Subjectivity, Sovereignty, Modernity." In *Identities, Politics, and Rights*. Austin Sarat and Thomas R. Kearns, eds. Pp. 193–236. Ann Arbor: University of Michigan Press.
Cottam, Richard W.
  1986   "The Iranian Revolution." In *Shi'ism and Social Protest*. New Haven: Yale University Press.
Coulson, N. J.
  1964   *A History of Islamic Law*. Edinburgh: Edinburgh University Press.
  1969   *Conflicts and Tensions in Islamic Jurisprudence*. Chicago: University of Chicago Press.
Cowan, Jane K., Marie-Bénédicte Dembour, and Richard A. Wilson
  2001   "Introduction." In *Cultural and Rights: Anthropological Perspectives*. Jane K. Cowan, Marie-Bénédicte Dembour, and Richard A. Wilson, eds. Pp. 1–26. Cambridge: Cambridge University Press.
Cronin, Stephanie
  2004   *Reformers and Revolutionaries in Modern Iran: New Perspectives on the Iranian Left*. London: RoutledgeCurzon.
Dahlén, Ashk P.
  2003   *Islamic Law, Epistemology and Modernity: Legal Philosophy in Contemporary Iran*. New York: Routledge.
Deeb, Lara
  2006   *An Enchanted Modern: Gender and Public Piety in Shi'i Lebanon*. Princeton: Princeton University Press.
Delaney, Carol L.
  1991   *The Seed and the Soil: Gender and Cosmology in Turkish Village Society*. Berkeley: University of California Press.
Donnelly, Jack
  1984   "Cultural Relativism and Human Rights." *Human Rights Quarterly* 6 (4): 400–19.

Ebadi, Shirin
    2000   *History and Documentation of Human Rights in Iran*. Nazila Fathi,
            trans. New York: Bibliotheca Persica Press.
El Alami, Dawoud, and Doreen Hinchcliffe
    1996   *Islamic Marriage and Divorce Laws of the Arab World*. London:
            Kluwer Law International.
Elyachar, Julia
    2005   *Markets of Dispossession: NGOs, Economic Development, and the
            State in Cairo*. Durham: Duke University Press.
Engel, David M., and Frank W. Munger
    2003   *Rights of Inclusion Law and Identity in the Life Stories of Americans
            with Disabilities*. Chicago: University of Chicago Press.
Esfandiari, Haleh
    1994   *Reconstructed Lives: Women and Iran's Islamic Revolution*. Washing-
            ton, DC: Woodrow Wilson Center Press; Baltimore: Johns Hopkins Uni-
            versity Press.
Esposito, John L.
    1998   *Islam and Politics*. Syracuse: Syracuse University Press.
Esposito, John L., and John O. Voll
    1996   *Islam and Democracy*. New York: Oxford University Press.
    2001   *The Makers of Contemporary Islam*. New York: Oxford University
            Press.
Ferdows, Adele K.
    1985   "The Status and Rights of Women in Ithna Ashari Shi'i Islam."
            In *Women and the Family in Iran*. Asghar Fathi, ed. Pp. 12–36. Leiden:
            E. J. Brill.
Ferdows, Adele K., and Amir Ferdows
    1983   "Women in Shi'i Fiqh: Image through the Hadith." In *Women and Revo-
            lution in Iran*. Guity Nashat, ed. Pp. 54–68. Boulder: Westview Press.
Ferguson, James
    1994   *The Anti-Politics Machine: "Development," Depoliticization, and
            Bureaucratic Power in Lesotho*. Minneapolis: University of Minnesota
            Press.
Ferguson, Kennan
    2007   "The Gift of Freedom." *Social Text 91* 25 (2): 39–52.
Fernea, Elizabeth Warnock
    1965   *Guests of the Sheikh: An Ethnography of an Iraqi Village*. New York:
            Doubleday.
Fischer, Michael M. J.
    1980   *Iran: From Religious Dispute to Revolution*. Madison: University of
            Wisconsin Press.
    1990   "Legal Postulates in Flux: Justice, Wit, and Hierarchy in Iran." In *Law
            and Islam in the Middle East*. Daisy Hilse Dwyer, ed. Pp. 115–42. New
            York: Bergen and Garvey.
Fischer, Michael, and Mehdi Abedi
    1990   *Debating Muslims: Cultural Dialogues in Postmodernity and Tradition*.
            Madison: University of Wisconsin Press.

Fitzpatrick, Peter
1992   *The Mythology of Modern Law.* London: Routledge.
Foucault, Michel
1977   *Discipline and Punish: The Birth of the Prison.* Alan Sheridan, trans. New York: Random House.
1978   *The History of Sexuality,* Vol. 1: *An Introduction.* Robert Hurley, trans. New York: Pantheon Books.
2003   *"Society Must Be Defended": Lectures at the College de France, 1975–1976.* David Macey, trans. New York: Picador.
Fraser, Nancy
1992   "Rethinking the Public Sphere: A Contribution to the Critique of Actually Existing Democracy." In *Habermas and the Public Sphere.* Craig C. Calhoun, ed. Pp. 109–42. Cambridge: MIT Press.
Friedl, Erika
1985   "Parents and Children in an Iranian Village." In *Women and the Family in Iran.* Asghar Fathi, ed. Pp. 195–211. Leiden: E. J. Brill.
1989   *Women of Deh Koh: Lives in an Iranian Village.* Washington, DC: Smithsonian Institution Press.
1991   "The Dynamics of Women's Spheres of Action in Rural Iran." In *Women in Middle Eastern History: Shifting Boundaries in Sex and Gender.* Nikki R. Keddie and Beth Baron, eds. Pp. 195–214. New Haven: Yale University Press.
Frum, David, and Richard Perle
2003   *An End to Evil: How to Win the War on Terror.* New York: Random House.
Geertz, Clifford
1973   *Interpretation of Cultures: Selected Essays.* New York: Basic Books.
1983   *Local Knowledge: Further Essays in Interpretive Anthropology.* New York: Basic Books.
Ghamari-Tabrizi, Behrooz
2000   "Globalization, Islam, and Human Rights: The Case of Iran." *Political and Legal Anthropology Review* 23 (1): 33–48.
Ghani, Cyrus
2000   *Iran and the Rise of the Reza Shah: From Qajar Collapse to Pahlavi Power.* New York: I. B. Tauris
2001   "Iran and the Rise of Reza Shah: From Qajar Collapse to Pahlavi Rule." *Peace Research Abstracts* 38 (4): 451–600.
Gilliom, John
2001   *Overseers of the Poor: Surveillance, Resistance, and the Limits of Privacy.* Chicago: University of Chicago Press.
Gleave, Robert
1997   "Akhbārī Shīʿī *usūl al-fiqh* and the Juristic Theory of Yūsuf al-Bahrānī." In *Islamic Law: Theory and Practice.* Robert Gleave and Eugenia Kermeli, eds. Pp. 24–27. London: I. B. Tauris.
Glendon, Mary Ann
1991   *Rights Talk: The Impoverishment of Political Discourse.* New York: Free Press.

2000 "John P. Humphrey and the Drafting of the Universal Declaration of Human Rights." *Journal of the History of International Law* 2 (2): 250–60.

2001 *A World Made New: Eleanor Roosevelt and the Declaration of Human Rights.* New York: Random House.

Göcek, Fatma Müge, and Shiva Balaghi, eds.

1995 *Reconstructing Gender in the Middle East: Tradition, Identity, and Power.* New York: Columbia University Press.

Gramsci, Antonio

1971 *Selections from the Prison Notebooks.* Quintin Hoare and Geoffrey Nowell Smith, trans. New York: International Publishers.

Habermas, Jürgen

1989 *The Structural Transformation of the Public Sphere.* Cambridge: MIT Press.

1992 "Further Reflections on the Public Sphere." In *Habermas and the Public Sphere.* Craig C. Calhoun, ed. Pp. 421–61. Cambridge: MIT Press.

Haddad, Yvonne Yazbeck, and John L. Esposito, eds.

1998 *Islam, Gender, and Social Change.* Oxford: Oxford University Press.

Hallaq, Wael B.

2005 *The Origins and Evolution of Islamic Law.* Cambridge: Cambridge University Press.

Hallaq, Wael B., ed.

2004 *The Formation of Islamic Law.* Aldershot, Hants: Ashgate.

Halliday, Fred

1999 *Revolution and World Politics: The Rise and Fall of the Sixth Great Power.* Durham: Duke University Press.

Hatem, Mervat

1998 "Secular and Islamist Discourses on Modernity in Egypt and Evolution of the Postcolonial Nation-State." In *Islam, Gender, and Social Change.* Yvonne Yazbeck Haddad and John L. Esposito, eds. Pp. 85–99. New York: Oxford University Press.

2006 "In the Eye of the Storm: Islamic Societies and Muslim Women in Globalization Discourses." *Comparative Studies of South Asia, Africa and the Middle East* 26 (1): 22–35.

Hegland, Mary Elaine

1983 "Aliabad Women: Revolution as Religious Activity." In *Women and Revolution in Iran.* Guity Nashat, ed. Pp. 171–94. Boulder: Westview Press.

1991 "Political Roles of Aliabad Women: The Public Private Dichotomy Transcended." In *Women in Middle Eastern History: Shifting Boundaries in Sex and Gender.* Nikki R. Keddie and Beth Baron, eds. Pp. 215–30. New Haven: Yale University Press.

Henkin, Louis

1990 *The Age of Rights.* New York: Columbia University Press.

Higgins, Patricia J.

1985 "Women in the Islamic Republic of Iran: Legal, Social, and Ideological Changes." *Signs* 10 (31): 477–94.

Hirsch, Susan F.
  1994 "Kadhi's Courts as Complex Sites of Resistance: The State, Islam, and
        Gender in Postcolonial Kenya." In *Contested States: Law, Hegemony,
        and Resistance*. Mindie Lazarus-Black and Susan F. Hirsch, eds. Pp.
        207–30. New York: Routledge.
  1998 *Pronouncing and Persevering: Gender and the Discourses of Disputing
        in an African Islamic Court*. Chicago: University of Chicago Press.
Hirschkind, Charles, and Saba Mahmood
  2002 "Feminism, the Taliban, and Politics of Counter-Insurgency." *Anthro-
        pological Quarterly* 75 (2): 339–54.
Hobsbawm, E. J., and T. O. Ranger
  1983 *The Invention of Tradition*. Cambridge: Cambridge University Press.
Hoodfar, Homa
  1994 "Devices and Desires: Population Policy and Gender Roles in the Islamic
        Republic." *Middle East Report* 109: 11–17.
  1997 "The Veil in Their Minds and on Our Heads: Veiling Practices and
        Muslim Women." In *The Politics of Culture in the Shadow of Capital*.
        Lisa Lowe and David Lloyd, eds. Pp. 248–79. Durham: Duke University
        Press.
  2000 "Iranian Women at the Intersection of Citizenship and the Family Code:
        The Perils of Islamic Criteria." In *Women and Citizenship in the Middle
        East*. Suad Joseph, ed. Syracuse: Syracuse University Press.
Hunt, K., and K. Rygiel
  2006 *(En)gendering the War on Terror War Stories and Camouflaged Politics:
        Gender in a Global/Local World*. Aldershot, Hants: Ashgate.
Huntington, Samuel
  1996 *The Clash of Civilizations and the Remaking of World Order*. New
        York: Simon and Schuster.
Ignatieff, Michael
  2000 *The Rights Revolution*. Toronto: Anansi Press.
Jalal, Ayesha
  1991 "The Convenience of Subservience: Women and the State of Pakistan."
        In *Women, Islam and the State*. Deniz Kandiyoti, ed. Pp. 77–114. Phila-
        delphia: Temple University Press.
Jawadi-Amuli, Ayatollah Abdullah
  1998 *Shari'at dar a'inah-yi ma'rifat* [Islamic Law in the Mirror of Knowl-
        edge]. Qom: al-Zahr'a.
Joseph, Suad, ed.
  2000 *Gender and Citizenship in the Middle East*. Syracuse: Syracuse Univer-
        sity Press.
Joseph, Suad, and Susan Slyomovics, eds.
  2001 *Women and Power in the Middle East*. Philadelphia: University of Penn-
        sylvania Press.
Kandiyoti, Deniz
  1991a "End of Empire in Turkey: Islam, Nationalism and Women in Turkey."
        In *Women, Islam and the State*. Deniz Kandiyoti, ed. Pp. 22–47. Phila-
        delphia: Temple University Press.

Kandiyoti, Deniz, ed.
  1991b   *Women, Islam and the State.* Philadelphia: Temple University Press.
Kaplan, Caren, N. Alarcón, and M. Moallem, eds.
  1999   *Between Woman and Nation: Nationalisms, Transnational Feminisms, and the State.* Durham: Duke University Press.
Keck, Margaret E., and Kathryn Sikkink
  1998   *Activists beyond Borders: Advocacy Networks in International Politics.* Ithaca: Cornell University Press.
Keddie, Nikki R.
  1966   *Religion and Rebellion in Iran: The Tobacco Protest of 1891–1892.* London: Cass.
  1995   *Iran and the Muslim World: Resistance and Revolution.* New York: New York University Press.
  2000–   "The Study of Muslim Women in the Middle East: Achievements and
  2001   Remaining Problems." *Harvard Middle Eastern and Islamic Review* 6: 26–52.
  2002   "Women in the Limelight: Some Recent Books on Middle Eastern Women's History." *International Journal of Middle East Studies* 34: 553–73.
Keddie, Nikki R., ed.
  1983   *Religion and Politics in Iran: Shi'ism from Quietism to Revolution.* New Haven: Yale University Press.
Keddie, Nikki R., and Beth Baron, eds.
  1991   *Women in Middle Eastern history: Shifting Boundaries in Sex and Gender.* New Haven: Yale University Press.
Khatib-Chahidi, Jane
  1993   "Sexual Prohibitions, Shared Space and Fictive Marriages in Shi'ite Iran." In *Women and Space: Ground Rules and Social Maps.* Shirley Ardener, ed. Pp. 112–35. Oxford: Berg.
Khomeini, Ayatollah Ruhollah
  1981   *Islam and Revolution: Writings and Declarations of Imam Khomeini.* Hamid Algar, trans. Berkeley: Mizan Press.
Kian-Thiébaut, Azadeh
  2002   "From Islamization to the Individualization of Women in Post-Revolutionary Iran." In *Women, Religion and Culture in Iran.* Sarah Ansari and Vanessa Martin, eds. Pp. 127–42. Richmond, Surrey: Curzon Press.
Kuper, Adam
  1999   *Culture: An Anthropologist's Account.* Cambridge: Harvard University Press.
Kurzman, Charles
  2004   *The Unthinkable Revolution in Iran.* Cambridge: Harvard University Press.
Landes, Joan B.
  1988   *Women and the Public Sphere in the Age of the French Revolution.* Ithaca: Cornell University Press.
Lazarus-Black, Mindie
  1994   "Slaves, Masters, and Magistrates: Law and the Politics of Resistance in the British Caribbean, 1736–1834." In *Contested States: Law, He-*

gemony, and Resistance. Mindie Lazarus-Black and Susan F. Hirsch, eds. Pp. 252–81. New York: Routledge.

2001   "Law and the Pragmatics of Inclusion: Governing Domestic Violence in Trinidad and Tobago." *American Ethnologist* 28 (2): 388–416.

Lazarus-Black, Mindie, and Susan F. Hirsch, eds.

1994   "Introduction/Performance and Paradox: Exploring Law's Role in Hegemony and Resistance." In *Contested States: Law, Hegemony, and Resistance.* Mindie Lazarus-Black and Susan F. Hirsch, eds. Pp. 1–34. New York: Routledge.

Lefèbvre, Henri

1991   *The Production of Space.* Oxford: Blackwell.

Lillich, Richard B.

1991   *International Human Rights: Problems in Law, Policy, and Practice.* Boston: Little, Brown.

McCann, Michael W.

1994   *Rights at Work: Pay Equity Reform and the Politics of Legal Mobilization.* Chicago: University of Chicago Press.

Macpherson, C. B.

1962   *The Political Theory of Possessive Individualism: Hobbes to Locke.* New York: Oxford University Press.

McRobbie, Angela

1996   "Looking Back at New Times and Its Critics." In *Stuart Hall: Critical Dialogues in Cultural Studies.* David Morley and Kuan-Hsing Chen, eds. Pp. 238–61. London: Routledge.

Mahdavi, Shireen

2003   Reza Shah Pahlavi and Women: A Re-evaluation. In *The Making of Modern Iran:State and Society under Riza Shah, 1921–1941.* Stephanie Cronin, ed. Pp. 181–92. New York: Routledge.

Mahmood, Saba

2001   "Feminist Theory, Embodiment, and the Docile Agent: Some Reflections on the Egyptian Islamic Revival." *Cultural Anthropology* 16 (2): 202–36.

2005   *Politics of Piety: The Islamic Revival and the Feminist Subject.* Princeton: Princeton University Press.

Mani, Lata

1989   "Contentious Traditions: The Debate on Sati in Colonial India." In *Recasting Women: Essays in Colonial History.* Kumkum Sangari and Sudesh Vaid, eds. Pp. 27–87. New Delhi: Kali for Women.

Martin, Vanessa

2003   "Muddarris, Republicanism and the Rise to Power of Riza Khan, Sardar-i Sipah." In *The Making of Modern Iran: State and Society under Riza Shah, 1921–1941.* Stephanie Cronin, ed. Pp. 65–77. New York: Routledge.

Mathee, Rudi

2003   "Transforming Dangerous Nomads into Useful Artisans, Technicians, Agriculturalists: Education in the Reza Shah Period." In *The Making of*

    Modern Iran: State and Society under Riza Shah, 1921–1941. Stephanie Cronin, ed. Pp. 123–45. New York: Routledge.

Mayer, Ann Elizabeth
  1991 *Islam and Human Rights: Traditions and Politics*. Boulder: Westview Press.

Mehta, Uday Singh
  1999 *Liberalism and Empire: A Study in Nineteenth-Century British Liberal Thought*. Chicago: University of Chicago Press.

Mernissi, Fatima
  1987 *Beyond the Veil, Male-Female Dynamics in Modern Muslim Society*. Bloomington: Indiana University Press.
  1991 *The Veil and the Male Elite: A Feminist Interpretation of Women's Rights in Islam*. Mary Jo Lakeland, trans. New York: Addison-Wesley.

Merry, Sally Engle
  1988 "Legal Pluralism." *Law and Society Review* 22 (5): 869–96.
  1990 *Getting Justice and Getting Even*. Chicago: University of Chicago Press.
  1992 "Anthropology, Law, and Transnational Processes." *Annual Review of Anthropology* 21: 357–79.
  1994 "Courts as Performances: Domestic Violence Hearings in Hawai'i Family Court." In *Contested States: Law, Hegemony, and Resistance*. Mindie Lazarus-Black and Susan F. Hirsch, eds. Pp. 35–58. New York: Routledge.
  2000 *Colonizing Hawaii: The Cultural Power of Law*. Princeton: Princeton University Press.
  2001 "Changing Culture, Changing Rights." In *Culture and Rights: Anthropological Perspectives*. Jane K. Cowan, Marie-Bénédicté Dembour, and Richard A. Wilson, eds. Pp. 31–56. Cambridge: Cambridge University Press.
  2003 "Rights Talk and the Experience of Law: Implementing Women's Human Rights to Protection from Violence." *Human Rights Quarterly* 25: 343–81.
  2006 *Human Rights and Gender Violence: Translating International Law into Local Justice*. Chicago: University of Chicago Press.

Messick, Brinkley
  1993 *The Calligraphic State: Textual Domination and History in a Muslim Society*. Berkeley: University of California Press.

Mir-Hosseini, Ziba
  1993 *Marriage on Trial: A Study of Islamic Family Law*. London: I. B. Tauris.
  1999 *Islam and Gender: The Religious Debate in Contemporary Iran*. Princeton: Princeton University Press.
  2000 *Marriage on Trial: A Study of Islamic Family Law*. 2nd ed. London: I. B. Tauris.
  2003 "The Construction of Gender in Islamic Legal Thought and Strategies for Reform." *HAWWA* 1: 1–28.

Mirsepassi, Ali
  2000 *Intellectual Discourse and the Politics of Modernization: Negotiating Modernity in Iran*. Cambridge: Cambridge University Press.

Mitchell, Timothy
1988   *Colonising Egypt*. Cambridge: Cambridge University Press.
Mitchell, Timothy, ed.
2000   *Questions of Modernity*. Minneapolis: University of Minnesota Press.
Moallem, Minoo
1999   "Transnationalism, Feminism, and Fundamentalism." In *Between Women and Nation: Nationalisms, Transnational Feminisms, and the State*. Caren Kaplan, Norma Alarcón, and Minoo Moallem, eds. Pp. 320–48. Durham: Duke University Press.
2005   *Between Warrior Brother and Veiled Sister: Islamic Fundamentalism and the Politics of Patriarchy in Iran*. Berkeley: University of California Press.
Moghadam, Valentine M.
1993   *Modernizing Women: Gender and Social Change in the Middle East*. Boulder: Lynne Rienner.
2005   *Globalizing Women: Transnational Feminist Networks*. Baltimore: Johns Hopkins University Press.
Moghadam, Valentine M., ed.
1994a   *Identity Politics and Women: Cultural Reassertions and Feminisms in International Perspective*. Boulder: Westview Press.
1994b   *Gender and National Identity: Women and Politics in Muslim Societies*. London: Zed Books.
Moghissi, Haideh
1993   "Women in the Resistance Movement in Iran." In *Women in the Middle East: Perceptions, Realities and Struggles for Liberation*. Haleh Afshar, ed. Pp. 158–71. New York: Macmillan.
Mokhtari, Shadi
2004   "The Search for Human Rights within an Islamic Framework in Iran." *The Muslim World* 94: 469–79.
Momen, Moojan
1985   *An Introduction to Shi'i Islam: The History and Doctrines of Twelver Shi'ism*. New Haven: Yale University Press.
Moors, Annelies
1995   *Women, Property and Islam: Palestinian Experiences, 1920–1990*. Cambridge: Cambridge University Press.
Mottahedeh, Roy
1985   *The Mantle of the Prophet: Religion and Politics in Iran*. New York: Simon and Schuster.
Mozaffari, Mehdi
1987   *Authority in Islam: from Muhammad to Khomeini*. Armonk, NY: M. E. Sharpe.
Muhaqqiq-Damad, Hojjatoleslam Dr. Sayyid Mustafa
2003   "International Humanitarian Law in Islam and Contemporary International Law." In *Islamic Views on Human Rights: Viewpoints of Iranian Scholars*. Husayn Salimi, ed. Pp. 253–93. Organization for Islamic Culture and Communications, Directorate of Research and Education, Centre for Cultural-International Studies. New Delhi: Kanishka.

Mujtahid-Shabistari, Muhammad
   2000   *Naqdi bar qara'at-i rasmi as din: buhranha, chalishha, rah-i halha* [Critique of the Official Reading of Religion: Crises, Challenges, and Solutions]. Tehran: Tarh-i Naw.
Munson, Henry
   1988   *Islam and Revolution in the Middle East.* New Haven: Yale University Press.
Mutahhari, Ayatollah Morteza
   1981   *The System of Women's Rights in Islam.* Qom: Entesharat Sadra.
Najmabadi, Afsaneh
   1991   "Hazards of Modernity and Morality: Women, State and Ideology in Contemporary Iran." In *Women, Islam and the State.* Deniz Kandiyoti, ed. Pp. 48–76. Philadelphia: Temple University Press.
   1998a "Feminism in an Islamic Republic: Years of Hardship, Years of Growth." In *Islam, Gender, and Social Change.* Yvonne Yazbeck Haddad and John L. Esposito, eds. Pp. 50–84. New York: Oxford University Press.
   1998b "Crafting the Educated Housewife in Iran." In *Remaking Women: Feminism and Modernity in the Middle East.* Lila Abu-Lughod, ed. Pp. 91–125. Princeton: Princeton University Press.
   2005   *Women with Mustaches and Men without Beards: Gender and Sexual Anxieties of Iranian Modernity.* Berkeley: University of California Press.
Narayan, Kirin
   1995   "Participant Observation." In *Women Writing Culture.* Ruth Behar and Deborah A. Gordon, eds. Pp. 33–48. Berkeley: University of California Press.
Nashat, Guity
   1983a "Women in Pre-revolutionary Iran: A Historical Overview." In *Women and Revolution in Iran.* Guity Nashat, ed. Pp. 5–35. Boulder: Westview Press.
   2004   "Introduction." In *Women in Iran from the Rise of Islam to 1800.* Guity Nashat and Lois Beck, eds. Pp. 1–10. Urbana: University of Illinois Press.
Nashat, Guity, ed.
   1983b *Women and Revolution in Iran.* Boulder: Westview Press.
Nashat, Guity, and Lois Beck, eds.
   2004   *Women in Iran from the Rise of Islam to 1800.* Urbana: University of Illinois Press.
Nashat, Guity, and Judith E. Tucker, eds.
   1999   *Women in the Middle East and North Africa: Restoring Women to History.* Bloomington: Indiana University Press.
Norton, Augustus Richard
   2007   *Hezbollah: A Short History.* Princeton: Princeton University Press.
Nouraie-Simone, Fereshteh, ed.
   2005   *On Shifting Ground: Muslim Women in the Global Era.* New York: Feminist Press at the City University of New York.

Ong, Aihwa
    1995   "Women Out of China: Traveling Tales and Traveling Theories in Postcolonial Feminism." In *Women Writing Culture*. Ruth Behar and Deborah A. Gordon, eds. Pp. 350–72. Berkeley: University of California Press.

Osanloo, Arzoo
    2004   "Doing the 'Rights' Thing: Methods and Challenges of Fieldwork in Iran." *Iranian Studies* 37 (4): 675–84.
    2006a   "Islamico-Civil Rights Talk: Women, Subjectivity and Law in Iranian Family Court." *American Ethnologist* 33 (2): 191–209.
    2006b   "The Measure of Mercy: Islamic Justice, Sovereign Power, and Human Rights in Iran." *Cultural Anthropology* 21 (4): 570–602.

Paidar, Parvin
    1995   *Women and the Political Process in Twentieth-Century Iran*. Cambridge: Cambridge University Press.

Papanek, Hanna
    1994   "The Ideal Woman and the Ideal Society: Control and Autonomy in the Construction of Identity." In *Identity Politics and Women: Cultural Reassertions and Feminisms in International Perspective*. Valentine M. Moghadam, ed. Pp. 42–75. Boulder: Westview Press.

Peirce, Leslie P.
    2003   *Morality Tales: Law and Gender in the Ottoman Court of Aintab*. Berkeley: University of California Press.

Peteet, Julie
    1991   Gender in Crisis: Women and the Palestinian Resistance Movement. New York: Columbia University Press.

Pinault, David.
    1992   *The Shiites: Ritual and Popular Piety in a Muslim Community*. New York: St. Martin's Press.

Piscatori, James P.
    1986   *Islam in a World of Nation-States*. Cambridge: Cambridge University Press.

Pollis, Adamantia
    1996   "Cultural Relativism Revisited: Through a State Prism." *Human Rights Quarterly* 18 (2): 316.

Population Reference Bureau
    2005   Women of Our World. http://www.prb.org/Source/ACF199B.pdf.

Powers, David S.
    1994   "Kadijustiz or Qadi-Justice—A Paternity Dispute from Fourteenth-Century Morocco." *Islamic Law and Society* 1: 332–66.

Poya, Maryam
    1999   *Women, Work and Islamism: Ideology and Resistance in Iran*. New York: Zed Books.

Preis, Ann-Belinda S.
    1996   "Human Rights as Cultural Practice: An Anthropological Critique." *Human Rights Quarterly* 18 (2): 286–315.

Rahman, Fazlur
  1983 "The Status of Women in the Qur'an." In *Women and Revolution in Iran*. Guity Nashat, ed. Pp. 37–54. Boulder: Westview Press.
Ramazani, Nesta
  1993 "Women in Iran: The Revolutionary Ebb and Flow." *Middle East Journal* 47 (3): 409–22.
Razack, Sherene
  2000 "Gendered Racial Violence and Spatialized Justice: The Murder of Pamela George." *Journal of Law and Society / Revue canadienne droit et societé* 15: 91–130.
Renteln, Alison Dundes
  1988 "Relativism and the Search for Human Rights." *American Anthropologist* 90: 56–72.
Report of the Special Representative, Maurice Danby Copithorne, to the United Nations Commission on Human Rights, para. 69, 18 January 2000, E/CN.4/2000/35.
Risse, Thomas, Stephen C. Ropp, and Kathryn Sikkink
  1999 *The Power of Human Rights: International Norms and Domestic Change*. Cambridge: Cambridge University Press.
Rofel, Lisa
  1999 *Other Modernities: Gendered Yearnings in China after Socialism*. Berkeley: University of California Press.
Rosen, Lawrence
  1980– "Equity and Discretion in a Modern Islamic Legal System." *Law and*
  81   *Society Review* 15 (2): 217–46.
  1989 *The Anthropology of Justice: Law as Culture in Islam*. Cambridge: Cambridge University Press.
  2000 *The Justice of Islam: Comparative Perspectives on Islamic Law and Society*. Oxford: Oxford University Press.
Rostam-Kolayi, Jasamin
  2003 "Expanding Agendas for the 'New' Iranian Woman: Family Law, Work and Unveiling." In *The Making of Modern Iran: State and Society under Riza Shah, 1921–1941*. Stephanie Cronin, ed. Pp. 157–80. New York: Routledge.
Runciman, W. G., ed.
  1978 *Weber: Selections in Translation*. E. Matthews, trans. Cambridge: Cambridge University Press.
Sahlins, Marshall
  2000 *Culture in Practice: Selected Essays*. New York: Zed Books.
Salime, Zakia
  2007 "The War on Terrorism: Appropriation and Subversion by Moroccan Women." *Signs: Journal of Women in Culture and Society* 33 (1): 1–24.
Salimi, Husayn, ed.
  2003 *Islamic Views on Human Rights: Viewpoints of Iranian Scholars*. Organization for Islamic Culture and Communications, Directorate of Research and Education, Centre for Cultural-International Studies. New Delhi: Kanishka Publishers.

Sanasarian, Elizabeth
  1982   *The Women's Rights Movement in Iran: Mutiny, Appeasement and Repression from 1900 to Khomeini.* New York: Praeger.
  1985   "Characteristics of the Women's Movement in Iran." In *Women and the Family in Iran.* Asghar Fathi, ed. Pp. 86–106. Leiden: E. J. Brill.
Sarat, Austin, and Thomas R. Kearns
  1993   "Across the Great Divide: Forms of Legal Scholarship and Everyday Life." In *Law in Everyday Life.* Austin Sarat and Thomas R. Kearns, eds. Pp. 1–20. Ann Arbor: University of Michigan Press.
  1995   Editorial Introduction. In *Identities, Politics, and Rights.* Austin Sarat and Thomas R. Kearns, eds. Pp. 1–15. Ann Arbor: University of Michigan Press.
  1998   "The Cultural Lives of Law." In *Law in the Domains of Culture.* Austin Sarat and Thomas R. Kearns, eds. Pp. 1–20. Ann Arbor: University of Michigan Press.
Sassen, Saskia
  1996   *Losing Control? Sovereignty in an Age of Globalization.* New York: Columbia University Press.
Schacht, Joseph
  1950   *The Origins of Muhammadan Jurisprudence.* Oxford: Clarendon Press.
  1964   *An Introduction to Islamic Law.* Oxford: Clarendon Press.
Schirazi, Asghar
  1997   *The Constitution of Iran: Politics and the State in the Islamic Republic.* John O'Kane, trans. New York: I. B. Taurus.
Shaheed, Farida
  1995   "Networking for Change: The Role of Women's Groups in Initiating Dialogue on Women's Issues." In *Faith and Freedom: Women's Human Rights in the Muslim World.* Mahnaz Afkhami, ed. Pp. 78–103. Syracuse: Syracuse University Press.
Shavarini, Mitra K.
  2006   "Wearing the Veil to College: The Paradox of Higher Education in the Lives of Iranian Women." *International Journal of Middle East Studies* 38: 189–211.
Silbey, Susan
  1992   "Making a Place for a Cultural Analysis of Law." *Law and Social Inquiry* 17 (1): 39–48.
Sonbol, Amira
  2003   *Women of Jordan: Islam, Labor, and the Law.* Syracuse: Syracuse University Press.
  2004   "Women in Shari'a Courts: A Historical and Methodological Discussion." *Kelam Arastirmalari* 2 (2): 25–56.
Sonbol, Amira El Azhary, ed.
  1996   *Women, the Family, and Divorce Laws in Islamic History.* Syracuse: Syracuse University Press.
Soroush, Abdolkarim
  2000   *Reason, Freedom, and Democracy in Islam: Essential Writings of Abdolkarim Soroush.* Mahmoud Sadri and Ahmad Sadri, trans. and eds. Oxford: Oxford University Press.

Special Representative of the Commission on Human Rights
   2000   *Interim Report.* UN a-55-363. September 8.
Spellberg, Denise A.
   1994   *Politics, Gender, and the Islamic Past: The Legacy of 'A'isha bint Abu Bakr.* New York: Columbia University Press.
Spivak, Gayatri
   1987   *In Other Worlds: Essays in Cultural Politics.* New York: Methuen.
   1988   "Can the Subaltern Speak?" In *Marxism and the Interpretation of Culture.* C. Nelson and L. Grossberg, eds. Pp. 271–313. Urbana: University of Illinois Press.
Starr, June
   1978   *Dispute and Settlement in Rural Turkey: An Ethnography of Law.* Leiden: E. J. Brill.
   1992   *Law as Metaphor: From Islamic Courts to the Palace of Justice.* Albany: SUNY Press.
Starr, June, and Jane Collier, eds.
   1989   *History and Power in the Study of Law: New Directions in Legal Anthropology.* Ithaca: Cornell University Press.
Statistical Centre of Iran
   2000   *Iran Statistical Yearbook* (1379).
   2002   *Iran Statistical Yearbook* (1381).
Stepan, Nancy Leys
   1998   "Race, Gender, Science and Citizenship." *Gender & History* 10 (1): 26.
Stoler, Laura Ann
   1995   *Race and the Education of Desire: Foucault's History of Sexuality and the Colonial Order of Things.* Durham: Duke University Press.
Stop Stoning Forever Campaign. http://www.meydaan.org/stoning/default.aspx.
Stowasser, Barbara
   1994   *Women in the Qur'an: Traditions and Interpretation.* New York: Oxford University Press.
Tabari, Azar, and Nahid Yeganeh, eds.
   1982   *In the Shadow of Islam: The Women's Movement in Iran.* London: Zed Books.
Tabataba'i, Hossein Modarressi
   1984   *An Introduction to Shi'i Law: A Bibliographical Study.* London: Ithaca Press.
Tajbakhsh, Kian
   2000   "Political Decentralization and the Creation of Local Government in Iran: Consolidation or Transformation of the Theocratic State?" *Social Research* 67 (2): 377–404.
Taleghani, Ayatullah Sayyid Mahmud
   1982   *Society and Economics in Islam: The Writings and Declarations of Ayatullah Sayyid Mahmud Taleghani.* R. Campbell, trans. Berkeley: Mizan Press.
Taskhiri, Sheikh Muhammad Ali
   1997   *Human Rights: A Study of the Universal and the Islamic Declarations of Human Rights.* Tehran: Islamic Culture and Relations Organization.

Thompson, Elizabeth
  2000 *Colonial Citizens: Republican Rights, Paternal Privilege, and Gender in French Syria and Lebanon.* New York: Columbia University Press.
Tohidi, Nayereh
  1991 "Gender and Islamic Fundamentalism: Feminist Politics in Iran." In *Third World Politics and the Politics of Feminism.* Chandra Talpade Mohanty et al., eds. Pp. 251–67. Bloomington: Indiana University Press.
  1994 "Modernity, Islamization and Women in Iran." In *Gender and National Identity: Women and Politics in Muslim Societies.* Valentine M. Moghadam, ed. Pp. 110–47. London: Zed Books.
Torab, Azam
  2002 "The Politicization of Women's Religious Circles in Post-revolutionary Iran." In *Women, Religion and Culture in Iran.* Sarah Ansari and Vanessa Martin, eds. Pp. 143–68. Richmond, Surrey: Curzon Press.
Tsing, Anna Lowenhaupt
  1993 *In the Realm of the Diamond Queen: Marginality in an Out-of-the-Way Place.* Princeton: Princeton University Press.
Tucker, Judith E.
  1998 *In the House of the Law: Gender and Islamic Law in Ottoman Syria and Palestine.* Berkeley: University of California Press.
United Nation's International Children's Education Fund
  1998 *The State of Women in the Islamic Republic of Iran.* Tehran: UNICEF.
Vatandoust, Gholam-Reza
  1985 "The Status of Iranian Women During the Pahlavi Regime." In *Women and the Family in Iran.* Asghar Fathi, ed. Pp. 107–30. Leiden: E. J. Brill.
Wallerstein, Immanuel
  1995 "The Insurmountable Contradictions of Liberalism: Human Rights and the Rights of Peoples in the Geoculture of the Modern World-System." *South Atlantic Quarterly* 94 (4): 1161–78.
  2005 *World-Systems Analysis: An Introduction.* Durham: Duke University Press.
Weber, Max
  1970 *From Max Weber: Essays in Sociology.* H. Gerth and C. W. Mills, eds. and trans. London: Routledge and Kegan Paul.
  1971 *The Protestant Ethic and the Spirit of Capitalism.* T. Parsons, trans. London: Unwin University Books.
  1978 *Max Weber: Selections in Translation*, W. G. Runciman, ed., E. Matthews, trans. New York: Cambridge University Press.
Welchman, Lynn.
  2000 *Beyond the Code: Muslim Family Law and the Shari'a Judiciary in the Palestinian West Bank.* Boston: Kluwer Law International.
Welchman, Lynn, ed.
  2004 *Women's Rights and Islamic Family Law: Perspectives on Reform.* London: Zed Books.
Williams, Raymond
  1977 *Marxism and Literature.* Oxford: Oxford University Press.
Wilson, Richard J., ed.

1997   *Human Rights, Culture and Context: Anthropological Perspectives.* Chicago: Pluto Press.

Yanagisako, Sylvia, and Carol L. Delaney, eds.
1995   *Naturalizing Power.* New York: Routledge.

Yeganeh, Nahid
1982   "Women's Struggles in the Islamic Republic of Iran." In *In the Shadow of Islam: The Women's Movement in Iran.* Azar Tabari and Nahid Yega-neh, eds. Pp. 26–74. London: Zed Books.

Yeganeh, Nahid, and Nikki R. Keddie
1986   "Sexuality and Shi'i Social Protest in Iran." In *Shi'ism and Social Pro-test.* Juan R. I. Cole and Nikki R. Keddie, eds. Pp. 108–36. New Haven: Yale University Press.

Yngvesson, Barbara
1993   *Virtuous Citizens, Disruptive Subjects.* New York: Routledge.

Zubaida, Sami
1989   *Islam, the People and the State: Essays on Political Ideas and Move-ments in the Middle East.* New York: Routledge.
2005   *Law and Power in the Islamic World.* London: I. B. Tauris.

Index